Y0-BRM-335

HECTOR BERLIOZ

GARLAND COMPOSER
RESOURCE MANUALS
(VOL. 22)

GARLAND REFERENCE LIBARY
OF THE HUMANITIES
(VOL. 1025)

GARLAND COMPOSER RESOURCE MANUALS

General Editor: Guy A. Marco

HECTOR BERLIOZ
A Guide to Research

Jeffrey Langford
Jane Denker Graves

Garland Publishing, Inc. • New York & London
1989

Library of Congress Cataloging-in-Publication Data

Langford, Jeffrey Alan.
    Hector Berlioz : a guide to research / Jeffrey A. Langford, Jane
Denker Graves.
        p. cm. — (Garland composer resource manuals; vol. 22)
(Garland reference library of the humanities; vol. 1025)
    Includes indexes.
    ISBN 0-8240-4635-8 (alk. paper)
    1. Berlioz, Hector, 1803-1869—Bibliography. I. Graves, Jane
Denker. II. Title. III. Series. IV. Series: Garland composer
resource manuals; v. 22.
ML134.B5L3   1989
016.78'092—dc20   89-139(
                                                                CI｜
                                                                M｜

Printed on acid-free, 250-year-life paper
Manufactured in the United States of America

Garland Composer
Resource Manuals

In response to the growing need for bibliographic guidance to the vast literature on significant composers, Garland is publishing an extensive series of research guides. The series, which will most likely appear over a five-year period, encompasses almost 50 composers; they represent Western musical tradition from the Renaissance to the present century.

Each research guide offers a selective, annotated list of writings, in all European languages, about one or more composers. There are also lists of works by the composers, unless these are available elsewhere. Biographical sketches and guides to library resources, organization, and specialists are presented. As appropriate to the individual composer, there are maps, photographs, or other illustrative matters, and glossaries and indexes.

Contents

Preface

This is an annotated bibliography of writings by and about Hector Berlioz (1803-1869). It includes a list of his musical compositions, his prose writings, and books and articles about the man and his music. We hope that it will serve the user, both student and professional, as a point of departure for research about this composer.

Our goal has been to assemble a selective bibliography of approximately 900 of the most significant pieces of Berlioz research and criticism that have appeared over the years. In order to maintain this limited scope, certain categories of materials have been eliminated from consideration automatically. These include discographies, program notes, short articles in daily newspapers, reviews of sound recordings, and reviews of performances (for exceptions, see introduction to Chapter XIII). Materials in several European languages are included although works in English, French, and German predominate. They represent a thorough search of the Berlioz literature from 1832 through 1988.

In compiling the bibliography we made use of the following databases: OCLC, Lockheed Dialog REMARC (files 421-426), *MLA Bibliography*, *Philosophers' Index*, *Dissertation Abstracts*, and *RILM*. In addition, the following print indexes and abstracts were examined for their complete runs: *RILM*, *Music Index*, *British Humanities Index*, *Readers' Guide to Periodical Literature* (pre-1949), *Social Sciences and Humanities Index*, *Biography Index*, and *Essay and General Literature Index*. Finally, the bibliographies and footnotes in all the books and articles that we annotated were themselves examined for relevant citations.

Since a bibliography is only as valuable as it is convenient to use, we have arranged our citations according to subject: biography, criticism, analysis, genres, individual works, etc. Further access to materials on specific topics can be gained by consulting the author and proper name and subject indexes at the end of the book.

Each bibliographic citation provides the following information (if available): author name, title and pages of article or chapter, book or periodical title, publication information, ISBN or ISSN number, Library of Congress call number, OCLC number (especially useful for interlibrary loan), and a brief annotation summarizing the contents of the item. These annotations are intended to give users enough information to enable them to determine whether to pursue specific items further. With few exceptions they are based on first-hand examination of the items themselves. Annotations for dissertations were usually derived from abstracts, and are so noted in brackets following the annotation. A few items could not be examined directly, but were thought to be significant enough to warrant inclusion without an annotation. These have been indicated with an asterisk following the bibliographical data. In general, references to Berlioz's works within any annotation are given in full title. An exception to this rule was made for the following:

1. *Lélio, ou le retour à la vie*, abbreviated to *Lélio*;
2. *Grande messe des morts*, abbreviated to *Requiem:*
3. *Grande traité d'instrumentation et d'orchestration modernes*, abbreviated to *Traité d'instrumentation;*
4. overtures are abbreviated to their significant words followed by a lower-case "overture."

One of the most important pieces of Berlioz scholarship to have appeared since the composer's death is the pioneering source studies by Julien Tiersot, published serially in *Le ménestrel* between 1904-1906 and 1910-1912 under the collective title "Berlioziana." This entire series appears here divided into separate subjects and fully annotated for the first time. Because no complete English translation of Tiersot's works is available, we have annotated these essays in greater than usual detail.

It is with special gratitude that we acknowedge the contributions of many people who assisted in the preparation of this bibliography. The staff of the Skidmore College interlibrary loan department, including Rosemary Del Vecchio, Marilyn Scheffer, and Shirley Webb, have been especially helpful in procuring books and periodicals not in the New York Public Library, Columbia University Library, or the New York University Library. We also extend our thanks to Irene Block, Gary Ronkin, and Valentin Schiedemeyer, who assisted with the translation of languages with which we were unfamiliar, and to Professor Peter Bloom of Smith College who generously read a draft of this bibliography. Lastly, we invite users of this volume to bring errors and omissions to our attention for inclusion in a future revised and updated edition. Communications may be addressed to Jeffrey Langford at the Manhattan School of Music, 120 Claremont Avenue, New York, N.Y. 10027.

Introduction

Many great composers have excited controversy in their own lifetimes as audiences struggled to understand the newness and individuality of their work. This is no less true of Hector Berlioz than it is of such divergent geniuses as Beethoven and Stravinsky. The difference is that with most such composers the ultimate value of their new music is usually quickly established, if not in their lifetimes, then shortly therafter. Berlioz alone among the great composers of the last century suffered a lack of comprehension lasting far beyond his death in 1869. If this prejudicial opposition seems to have receded in recent years, it is most happily due to the increased exposure Berlioz's compositions have received on recordings and to the commencement in 1969 of a new critical edition of his complete works, both musical and literary. At last a fair and accurate appraisal of his musical style, one of the most idiosyncratic of the entire nineteenth century, is possible.

Born to a doctor in rural France, Berlioz was different from the very beginning. While his musical talent was discovered early, it was nurtured in a most unorthodox manner. Fearing that the ability to play the piano might provide him with an easy route to a worthless career as a virtuoso, Berlioz's father offered his son lessons only on the guitar and flute. What Berlioz learned of the elements of music was therefore necessarily somewhat circumscribed. Instead of the sonatas of Beethoven, he heard the quartets of Pleyel. Rather than copying the scores of the great masters and working through rigorous counterpoint exercises from Fux's *Gradus ad Parnassum* as someone like Haydn had done, he wrote simple guitar accompaniments for popular romances of the day. Just how this early lack of a traditional musical education affected the mature Berlioz, composer of the *Symphonie fantastique* and other shockingly original works, is not clear. One common, but unsubstantiated, theory is that those apsects of his musical style that are most idiosyncratic and untraditional are the direct result of this unorthodox childhood training, his inability to use the keyboard as a compositional tool, and even his possible reliance on the guitar to work out the sounds he wanted to create. Other analyses of the Berlioz style--and there have been many since the 1969 centennial of his death--have looked elsewhere for an explanation of these same untraditional characteristics. Some claim that much of what strikes us as strange about Berlioz's music is actually only part of a common French musical tradition of the late-eighteenth and early-nineteenth centuries, now lost and forgotton. Others suggest that Berlioz's style is simply the product of a revolutionary mind and a unique set of compositional principles. In the final analysis, no single solution provides an adequate answer to this puzzle.

Regardless of how the world has come to view his musical style, the popular image of Berlioz, the man, has long been that of the lone eccentric artist struggling against the complete incomprehension of his audiences. Indeed, this seems to have been the image that the composer himself wanted to promote. His *Mémoires*, one of the most colorful and entertaining musical autobiographies, strain to depict their hero as the Messiah of truth in art, sacrificing his career on the altar of bourgeois Parisian taste and Philistinism. Like most popular images, this one has much truth to it, but some Berlioz scholars have suggested that both Berlioz, in his own lifetime, and some of his Romantically inclined biographers thereafter, have perhaps overplayed the immensity of his struggle without admitting the extent to which official governmental support affected his career.

The shaping forces of his career were all at work during Berlioz's earliest years. Among the most important of these was his father, who introduced him to the great literaure of Classic authors such as Homer and Virgil. From his own accounts, it appears that the painfully sensitive boy was deeply moved by these tales of heroism, suffering, and nobility--so much so that he actually broke down in tears one day while reading aloud from Virgil's *Aeneid*. The protagonists of these dramas became his constant companions, and through his exposure to their lives, he developed a sympathy for all that was noble, serious, and grand, in art as well as in life. In a sense, Berlioz lived the lives of his literary heros. He adopted their ideals; he bore their sufferings as his own.

Following these early years spent with the giants of antiquity, Berlioz found himself at the age of eighteen studying medicine in Paris. But he was soon to find the atmosphere of the dissecting room less stimulating that that of the Conservatory library, where he discovered and eagerly poured over the score of Gluck's operas. Like the Classic literature of his boyhood, these dramas led Berlioz into a world of grandeur and nobility, of high seriousness and moral purpose. They appealed to him because they were populated by the same heroic characters that had so powerfully captured his boyhood imagination. It was during these informative student years that Berlioz began building his musical pantheon, the first god of which was Gluck. The rest of Paris, however, did not share Berlioz's enthusiasm for Gluck, heavy and morbidly serious as he seemed to them. The city was ablaze with excitement over a new star from the south: Gioachino Rossini. Opera audiences were quickly seduced by the graceful tunefulness of this composer's *bel canto* style. As a result, the musical sobriety and asceticism of the old French school was soon forgotten. Forgotten, that is, by everyone but Berlioz, who alone sternly refused to capitulate to the easy attractiveness of this new Italian music. Consequently, he set himself at odds with popular Parisian taste right from the beginning of his career, and was, in a sense, never able to make the reputation for himself as a composer of opera that he so desparately desired. In this way, and others, Berlioz proved to be his own worst enemy, and writers on this subject have generally agreed that the failure of his operatic career can be traced to those basic predispositions instilled in him at an early age.

Today, of course, Berlioz is much better known as a composer of symphonic music. Here too he was controversial, but his success at finding publishers, planning concerts of his own music, and attracting a small but devoted following for the new poetically-inspired instrumental music of the avant-garde partly belies the old image of his failed musical career. Nonetheless, Paris supported no independent audience for concert music, and no composer made a living writing symphonies, overtures, or concertos in Paris circa 1830. This fact alone determined the major events of the remainder of Berlioz's career.

The composer therefore became, out of necessity, a critic. Contributing an occasional essay to various journals as early as 1823, Berlioz eventually secured a permanent position at the *Journal des débats* in 1835. There he was put to work reviewing opera. The irony of a failed opera composer being asked to evaluate the popular but often insipid repertoire of lesser composers did not, of course, escape the notice of the young Berlioz. In a letter to his friend Humbert Ferrand dated April 15, 1835, he complained: "In spite of Mr. Bertin's request, I didn't want to review *Puritani* or that miserable *Juive*. I would have had too much bad to say about them and everyone would have accused me of jealousy" (*Corréspondence general*, vol. 2). Time and again he bewailed the necessity of squandering valuable composing time inventing platitudes about works too inconsequential to dignify with ink and paper. In the *Mémoires* he lamented that the "most horrible humiliation" was having to "give tepid approval to insufferable insipidities" (Cairns translation, p. 356-57). But the biting, sarcastic wit spawned by these circumstances today makes for some of the most incisive and entertaining reading to be found among nineteenth-century music criticism. Much of the recent research into this important aspect of Berlioz's career gives one the sense that despite his constant complaints, Berlioz really enjoyed the opportunity his writing career gave him to proselytize for the virtues of Truth, Honesty, and Nobility in art, while simultaneously mocking and unmasking all that was trivial and banal in the Parisian musical world.

Besides his work as a writer, other facets of Berlioz's career can be traced to his lack of acceptance by Parisian audiences of the time. One result of his inability to make headway in the usual professional music channels was that he was forced to produce concerts of his own music just to get his work heard. In so doing, Berlioz soon discovered that he himself was the only person who could safely be entrusted with the rehearsal and direction of his music. For most of his mature musical life, then, Berlioz became the principal interpreter of his own works, both in France and abroad. With a growing reputation as a precise and meticulous conductor, he soon found himself being invited to appear at the head of various foreign orchestras. Such were his innovations on the podium that some writers have called Berlioz the father of modern conducting.

If Berlioz can be said to have achieved any real success as a composer during his lifetime, it is with his concert appearances abroad. Often ignored or misunderstood by audiences at home, he set off on foreign tours with the hope of finding a warmer reception elsewhere. His first concerts in Germany, again directed by the composer himself, included a mixture of Berlioz's own works with those of his old idols: Gluck, Beethoven, and Weber. At first audiences were confused by this new music. Eventually, however, the native German admiration for "high art," along with Berlioz's close association with Liszt, Wagner, and the "music of the future," combined to bring him a measure of success and popularity abroad that he could never have achieved at home.

Like the mood of the century in which he lived, Berlioz's career began with a buoyant optimism fired by revolutionary ideals, only to burn itself out in despair and loneliness. Although his reputation continued to grow in Germany, England, and Russia, his foreign tours became ever more taxing because of a chronic intestinal neuralgia with which he suffered for years. At home in Paris Berlioz felt isolated and abandoned, partly because the greatest work of his maturity, *Les Troyens*, had fallen on uncomprehending ears in a butchered production mounted at a theater for which it was totally unsuited. Compounding his sense of betrayal and isolation over this defeat was the fact that by that time his only son and his second wife had died. The loneliness of his last years was oppressive, relieved only by the success of a final trip to Russia in 1868.

Today Berlioz's position as a composer of the first rank seems secure. But exactly what that means in terms of his relationship to historical trends in nineteenth-century music is not entirely clear. Frequently Berlioz scholars have granted their subject the distinction of being the only French musician to have actively participated in the Romantic movement. But beyond the common devotion to music inspired by a "poetic idea," Berlioz's brand of Romanticism really shared few points of congruence with the "music of the future" of Liszt and Wagner. Indeed, as the voluminous writing about the contentious Berlioz-Wagner relationship makes quite clear, Berlioz never did understand or appreciate the musical style (especially the chromatic harmony) of his German rival.

Despite his avowed intention early in his career to "ravage the musical world" like an Attila, the inescapable fact remains that the underpinning of Berlioz's style is the Classicism of Gluck blended with the grandeur of Revolutionary composers such as Méhul and Le Sueur. From this point of view, the legend of Berlioz as a wildly undisciplined Romantic genius is at least partially a myth perpetuated through generations of miunderstanding. His Romanticism, such as it was, really grew out of his passionate devotion to the principle of dramatic truthfulness in music. Even his interest in such typically Romantic subjects as Nature and the *mal de l'isolement* (pain of loneliness) was subsumed under this broad general principle. For Berlioz, then, the trappings of Romanticism--detailed programs, new orchestrational effects, unorthodox harmonic progressions, freer forms--were never more than means to achieve the goal of dramatic music (*"le genre instrumental expressif"*), a goal which he felt he had inherited from the greatest of his Classical predecessors.

HECTOR BERLIOZ

I. Works List

The following list, arranged alphabetically by title, is intended to provide easy access to basic information about Berlioz's works, including date of composition, performing forces, date and place of publication, and authors of texts. In parentheses following each title there appears a Holoman number (e.g. H100). This refers to the chronological order of the work as established by D. Kern Holoman in his *Catalogue of the Works of Berlioz* (#194). Information given under the heading "publication" also requires explanation. The notation "OBE" (Old Berlioz Edition) and/or NBE (New Berlioz Edition) followed by a number indicates the volume number in one of the two critical editions of the complete works of Berlioz in which a particular composition can be located. These editions are:

Hector Berlioz Werke, edited by Charles Malherbe and Felix Weingartner. Leipzig: Breitkopf & Härtel, 1900-1907. 20 vols. Reprint. Kalmus, n.d. Commonly known as the Old Berlioz Edition (OBE), this work was neither complete or correct. Its most conspicuous omissions were the operas *Benvenuto Cellini* and *Les Troyens*. Major editorial error and emendations occur throughout. See "Supplement V," (336-59) in Barzun's biography (#210) for details. The Kalmus reprint included both of the missing operas and Berlioz's recitatives for Weber's *Der Freischütz*.

Hector Berlioz. New Edition of the Complete Works, edited by Hugh Macdonald. Kassel: Bärenreiter, 1969-. Commonly known as the New Berlioz Edition (NBE), this work is planned for twenty-five volumes. When complete it will present authoritative texts of all of Berlioz's known compositions.

4 Hector Berlioz

Absence. See *Les nuits d' été*

Adieu Bessy. See *Neuf mélodies*

1. Title: Accompaniment to *Fleuve du Tage* by Pollet
   (H5)
   Genre/medium: song for voice and gtr.
   Text: Joseph Hélitas de Meun
   Date of comp. c. 1819
   Publication: --; OBE--; NBE 22
   Remarks: arrangement of accompaniment of
   composition by Benoît Pollet

2. Title: *Albumleaf* (H96)
   Genre/medium: pf.
   Date of comp: 1844
   Publication: --; OBE--; NBE 23

3. Title: *Amitié, reprends ton empire. Romance*
   (H10)
   Genre/medium: song for 2 sops., bass, and pf.
   Text: Jean-Pierre-Claris de Florian
   Date of comp: 1819-21
   Publication: Paris: Boieldieu jeune, 1823; OBE 16; NBE
   15
   Remarks: original pre-pub. version entitled
   "Invocation à l'amitié"

4. Title: *Apothéose* (H80C)
   Genre/medium: chor. (SSTTBB), mezzo-sop. or ten., and pf.
   Text: Antoni Deschamps
   Date of comp: 1848
   Publication: London: Cramer & Beale, 1848; OBE 16;
   NBE 14
   Remarks: arr. from 3rd movt. of *Grande symphonie
   funèbre et triomphale*

Au cimitière. See *Les nuits d' été*

5. Title: *Aubade* (H78)
   Genre/medium: song for low voice and 2 hns.
   Text: Alfred de Musset
   Date of comp: 1839
   Publication: --; OBE--; NBE 15
   Remarks: revised c. 1852 for voice, 2 cornets, and 4
   hns.; NBE 13

6. Title: *Le ballet des ombres. Ronde nocturne* (H37)
    Genre/medium: chor. (STTBB) and pf.
    Text: Albert Du Boys, after Johann Gottfried von
                     Herder
    Date of comp: 1829
    Publication: Paris: Schlesinger, 1829, as op. 2; OBE 16;
                     NBE 14
    Remarks: work withdrawn by Berlioz; autograph MS
                     lost

7. Title: *Béatrice et Bénédict. Opéra en deux actes
                     imitée de Shakespeare* (H138)
    Genre/medium: *opéra comique* in 2 acts
    Text: Berlioz, after Shakespeare
    Date of comp: 1860-62
    Publication: piano-vocal score (arr. Richard Pohl) Paris:
                     Brandus & Dufour, 1863; overture in full
                     score Berlin: Bote & Bock, 1892; OBE 5
                     (overture) and 19-20 (full score); NBE 3

8. Title: *La belle Isabeau. Conte pendant l' orage*
                     (H94)
    Genre/medium: song for mezzo-sop., chor. (SSTBB), and pf.
    Text: Alexandre Dumas, *père*
    Date of comp: 1843
    Publication: Paris: Bernard Latte, 1844; OBE 17; NBE
                     15
    Remarks: possibly planned as no. 5 of expanded
                     version of op. 19, *Feuillets d' album*, 1852

La belle voyageuse. See *Neuf mélodies*

9. Title: *Benvenuto Cellini* (H76)
    Genre/medium: *opéra semiseria* in 2 acts and 4 tableaux
    Text: Léon de Wailly and Auguste Barbier
    Date of comp: 1834-38, revised 1852-56
    Publication: overture Paris: Schlesinger, 1839; piano-
                     vocal score of 3-act Weimar version (arr.
                     Hans von Bülow) Brunswick: Litolff, 1856;
                     full orch. score of 3-act Weimar version
                     Paris: Choudens, 1886; OBE 5 (overture);
                     NBE 1

10. Title: *Beverley, ou le joueur* (H19)
    Genre/medium: dramatic scene for bass voice and orch.
    Text: Bernard-Joseph Saurin, after Edward Moore

	Date of comp:	1823-24
	Remarks:	lost

11.	Title:	*Canon à trois voix* (H13)
	Date of comp:	1822
	Remarks:	lost

12.	Title:	*Canon libre à la quinte* (H14)
	Genre/medium:	song for alto, bar., and pf.
	Text:	Bourgerie, after Augustin de Pons
	Date of comp:	c. 1822
	Publication:	Paris: Boieldieu jeune, 1823; OBE 16; NBE 15

13.	Title:	*La captive. Orientale* (H60)
	Genre/medium:	song for mezzo-sop. and pf.
	Text:	Victor Hugo, from *Les orientales*
	Date of comp:	1832
	Publication:	--; OBE 17; NBE 15
	Remarks:	several versions: mezzo-sop., vc., and pf. 1832 pub. Paris: Schlesinger, 1833; OBE 17; NBE 15; mezzo-sop. and orch. 1848 pub. Paris: Richault, 1849; OBE 15; NBE 13; pf. arr. by Stephen Heller, pub. Richault, 1849; OBE 17

14.	Title:	*Le carnaval romain. Ouverture caractéristique* (H95)
	Genre/medium:	concert overture for orch.
	Date of comp:	1843-44
	Publication:	Paris: Schlesinger, 1844, as op. 9; OBE 5; NBE 20
	Remarks:	based on themes from *Benvenuto Cellini*

Les champs. See *Feuillets d'album*

Chanson à boire. See *Neuf mélodies*

Chanson de brigands. See *Lélio*

Chanson de Méphistophélès. See *Huit scènes de Faust*

15.	Title:	*Chanson des pirates* (H34)
	Genre/medium:	song for voice and orch.
	Text:	Victor Hugo
	Date of comp:	1829

	Publication:	--
	Remarks:	lost; revised to new text by Berlioz as "Chanson de brigands" in *Lélio*
16.	Title:	*Chansonette de M. Léon de Wailly* (H73)
	Genre/medium:	song for sop. or ten. and pf.
	Text:	Léon de Wailly
	Date of comp:	1835
	Publication:	--; OBE --; NBE 15
	Remarks:	revised as "Choeur de masques" in Act I, scene 1 of *Benvenuto Cellini*

Chant de bonheur. See *Lélio*

Le chant des bretons. Choeur. See *Fleurs des landes*

Le chant des chemins de fer. See *Feuillets d' album*

17.	Title:	*Le chant des chérubins* (H122)
	Genre/medium:	chor. (SSTB)
	Text:	Berlioz
	Date:	1850 or before
	Publication:	Paris: Richault, 1851; OBE 18; NBE 22
	Remarks:	arranged from work by Dmitry Stepanovich Bortnyansky

18.	Title:	*Chant du neuf Thermidor* (H51bis)
	Genre/medium:	ten., chor., and orch.
	Text:	Claude-Joseph Rouget de Lisle
	Date:	c. 1830
	Publication:	--; OBE --; NBE 22
	Remarks:	arranged from *Hymne dithyrambique sur la conjuration de Robespierre et la revolution du 9. Thermidor* by Rouget de Lisle

Chant guerrier. See *Neuf mélodies*

Chant sacré. See *Neuf mélodies*

Chants de la fête de pâques. See *Huit scènes de Faust*

19.	Title:	*La chasse de Lützow. Marche favorite des hussards de la mort* (H63)
	Genre/medium:	4-part male chor., string quintet, and pf.
	Text:	Karl Theodor Körner, tr. Emile Deschamps, later Humbert Ferrand
	Date:	before 1833

Remarks: lost; arranged from work by Carl Maria von
                    Weber

Le chasseur des chamois. See *Sur les Alpes, quel délice!*

20.   Title: *Le chasseur danois* (H104)
      Genre/medium: song for bass and pf.
      Text: Adolphe de Leuven
      Date of comp: 1844
      Publication: Paris: Bernard Latte, 1844; OBE 17; NBE
                       15
      Remarks: possibly planned as no. 6 of expanded
                       version of op. 19, *Feuillets d'album*, 1852;
                       orchestrated 1845 and pub. OBE 15; NBE
                       13

21.   Title: *Le cheval arabe. Cantate* (H12)
      Genre/medium: low voice and orch.
      Text: Charles-Hubert Millevoye
      Date of comp: 1822
      Remarks: lost

22.   Title: *Choeur* (H57)
      Text: Berlioz
      Date of comp: 1831
      Remarks: lost

23.   Title: *Choeur d'anges* (H58)
      Text: anon.
      Date of comp: 1831
      Remarks: lost

Choeur des ombres irritées. See *Lélio*

Choeur de soldats. See *Huit scènes de Faust*

24.   Title: *Le cinq mai. Chant sur la mort de
                       l'Empereur Napoléon* (H74)
      Genre/medium: patriotic cantata for bass, chor. (SSTTBB),
                       and orch.
      Text: Pierre-Jean de Béranger
      Date of comp: 1831-35
      Publication: Paris: Richault, 1844, as op. 6; OBE 13;
                       NBE 12
      Remarks: piano-vocal score, arr. Auguste Morel, pub.
                       Paris: Catelin, 1840

25. Title: *Cléopatre. Scène lyrique* (H36)
     Genre/medium: cantata for sop. and orch.
     Text: Pierre-Ange Vieillard
     Date of comp: 1829
     Publication: --; OBE 15; NBE 6
     Remarks: composed for *Prix de Rome* competition

Collection de 32 mélodies (H139) (compiled 1863). See *Les
nuits d'été*; *Neuf mélodies*; *Vox populi*; *La captive*; *Sara la
baigneuse*; *Tristia* (1st version); *Fleurs des landes*; *Zaïde*; *Les
champs*; *Chant des chemins de fer*; *Choeur d'enfants*; *Le
chasseur danois*; *La belle Isabeau*

Concert de sylphes. See *Huit scènes de Faust*

Le corsaire. See *Ouverture du corsaire*

Le coucher du soleil. Rêverie. See *Neuf mélodies*

26. Title: *Le cri de guerre du Brisgaw* (H23C)
     Genre/medium: one-act intermezzo based on *Les francs-
                       juges*
     Text: Humbert Ferrand
     Date of comp: 1833-34
     Remarks: never completed; only libretto extant (bound
                       with music for *Les francs-juges*); NBE 4

27. Title: *La damnation de Faust. Légende
                       dramatique en 4 parties* (H111)
     Genre/medium: mezzo-sop., ten., bar., bass, chor.
                       (SSTTBB), children's chor. (SS), and orch.
     Text: Almire Gandonnière, Gérard de Nerval, and
                       Berlioz, after Goethe
     Date of comp: 1845-46
     Publication: Paris: Richault, 1854, as op. 24; OBE 11-12;
                       NBE 8a-b.
     Remarks: expanded from *Huit scènes de Faust*

28. Title: *Le dépit de la bergère. Romance* (H7)
     Genre/medium: song for low voice and pf.
     Text: anon.
     Date of comp: c. 1819
     Publication: Paris: Auguste Le Duc, c. 1819; OBE 17;
                       NBE 15
     Remarks: Berlioz's first published composition

29.   Title: *Le dernier jour du monde* (H61)
        Genre/medium: oratorio
        Text: never written; scenario by Berlioz
        Date of comp: 1831-33
        Remarks: never completed

Les derniers soupirs de la harpe. See *Lélio*

Ecot de joyeux compagnons, histoire d'un rat. See *Huit scènes de Faust*

Elégie en prose. See *Neuf mélodies*

30.   Title: *L'enfance du Christ. Trilogie sacrée* (H130)
        Genre/medium: oratorio for sop., 2 ten., bar., 3 basses, chor.
                            (SSAATTBB), and orch.
        Text: Berlioz
        Date of comp: 1854
        Publication: Paris: Richault, 1855, as op. 25; OBE 9;
                            NBE 11
        Remarks: Part I--*Le songe d'Hérode*, comp. 1854
                            Part II--*La fuite en Egypte*, comp. 1850 and
                            pub. separately by Richault, 1852 (H128)
                            Part III--*L'arrivée à Saïs*, comp. 1853-54

Episode de la vie d'un artiste. See *Symphonie fantastique*

31.   Title: *Erigone. Intermède antique* (H77)
        Genre/medium: solo voices, chor., and orch.
        Text: Berlioz, after Pierre-Simon Ballanche
        Date of comp: 1835-39?
        Publication: --; OBE--; NBE 23
        Remarks: incomplete

32.   Title: *Estelle et Némorin* (H17)
        Genre/medium: opera
        Text: Hyancinthe-Christophe Gerono, after Jean-
                            Pierre Claris de Florian
        Date of comp: 1823
        Remarks: lost

Fantaisie dramatique sur La Tempête, drame de Shakespeare.
See *Lélio*

33.   Title: *Fête musicale funèbre* (H72)
        Genre/medium: symphony

	Date of comp:	1835
	Remarks:	never completed; lost

34. Title: *Feuillets d'album* (H121)
    Genre/medium: collection of songs for various voices and pf.
    Publication: Paris: Richault, 1850, as op. 19

    1. *Zaïde. Boléro* (H108)
       sop. and pf.
       Remarks: text by Roger de Beauvoir; comp. 1845; OBE 17; NBE 15; 2nd version with castanets pub. Paris: Bernard Latte, 1845; OBE 17; orchestrated 1845; OBE 15; NBE 13
    2. *Les champs. Romance* (H67)
       ten. and pf.
       Remarks: text by Pierre-Jean de Béranger; comp. 1834; orig. pub. in the journal, *La Romance*, 1834; OBE 17; NBE 15; revised 1850
    3. *Le chant des chemins de fer* (H110)
       ten., chor. (SSTTBB), and pf. (arr. by Stephen Heller)
       Remarks: text by Gabriel-Jules Janin; comp. 1846; orig. version for ten., chor. (SSTTBB), and orch. OBE 14 (full orch. score); NBE 12 (full orch. score)

35. Title: *Fleurs des landes* (H124)
    Genre/medium: collection of songs for various combinations of voices and pf.
    Publication: Paris: Richault, 1850, as op. 13

    1. *Le matin. Romance* (H125)
       mezzo-sop. or ten. and pf.
       Remarks: text by Adolphe de Bouclon; comp. 1850; OBE 17; NBE 15
    2. *Petit oiseau. Chanson de paysan* (H126)
       ten., bar., mezzo-sop., and pf.
       Remarks: text by Adolphe de Bouclon; comp. c. 1849; OBE 17; NBE 15; text same as that for *Le matin*
    3. *Le trébuchet. Scherzo à deux voix* (H113)
       2 sops. (or ten. and bass) and pf.
       Remarks: text by Emile Deschamps and Antoine de Bertin; comp. c. 1846; OBE 16; NBE 15

4.   *Le jeune pâtre breton* (H65)
                        mezzo-sop. or ten. and pf.
Remarks: text by Auguste Brizeux; comp. 1833; pub.
                        Paris: Schlesinger, 1835, with addition of
                        hn. obbligato; OBE 17; NBE 15; arr. for
                        mezzo-sop. or ten. and orch. in 1835 and
                        pub. by Catelin, 1839; OBE 15; NBE 13
5.   *Le chant des bretons. Choeur* (H71)
                        male chor. or ten. and pf.
Remarks: text by Auguste Brizeux; comp. 1835; orig.
                        version partsong for male chor. (TTBB) or
                        ten. and pf. pub. Paris: Schlesinger, 1835;
                        OBE 16 (chor.) and 17 (solo); NBE 14;
                        revised 1849; OBE 16 (chor.) and 17 (solo);
                        NBE 14

36.   Title: *Les francs-juges* (H23A)
      Genre/medium: opera in 3 acts
      Text: Humbert Ferrand
      Date of comp: c. 1825-26, rev. 1829
      Publication: overture only, Paris: Richault, 1836, as op.
                        3; OBE 4 (overture); NBE 4 (overture plus
                        extant fragments)
      Remarks: libretto, 5 musical numbers and some
                        fragments extant; rev. as *Le cri de guerre de
                        Brisgaw*

      Francs-juges Overture. See *Grande ouverture des francs-
      juges*

37.   Title: *Le Freyschütz* (H89)
      Genre/medium: spoken dialogue set as recitatives
      Date: 1841
      Publication: piano-vocal score, Paris: Schlesinger, 1842;
                        OBE --; NBE 22
      Remarks: arranged from opera by Carl Maria von
                        Weber

38.   Title: *Fugue* (H22)
      Genre/medium: academic exercise (*concours d'essai*) for
                        Prix de Rome competition
      Date of comp: 1826
      Publication: --; OBE --; NBE 6

39.   Title: *Fugue* (H24)
      Genre/medium: academic exercise (*concours d'essai*) for
                        Prix de Rome competition

Date of comp:	1827
Remarks:	lost

40. Title: *Fugue* (H28)
     Genre/medium: academic exercise *(concours d'essai)* for
                     Prix de Rome competition
     Date of comp: 1828
     Remarks: lost

41. Title: *Fugue* (H49)
     Genre/medium: academic exercise *(concours d'essai)* for
                     Prix de Rome competition
     Date of comp: 1830
     Remarks: lost

42. Title: *Fugue à trois sujets* (H35)
     Genre/medium: academic exercise *(concours d'essai)* for
                     Prix de Rome competition
     Date of comp: 1829
     Publication: --; OBE 6; NBE 6

Funeral and Triumphal Symphony. See *Grande symphonie
funèbre et triomphale*

43. Title: *Grande messe des morts (Requiem)* (H75)
     Genre/medium: requiem Mass for ten., chor. (SSTTBB), and
                     orch.
     Text: Latin liturgy
     Date of comp: 1837
     Publication: Paris: Schlesinger, 1838, as op. 5; OBE 7;
                     NBE 9
     Remarks: revised 1853 and 1867 (2nd ed. Milan:
                     Ricordi, 1853; 3rd ed. Ricordi, 1867), piano-
                     vocal score, Paris: Brandus, 1882

44. Title: *Grande ouverture des francs-juges* (H23D)
     Genre/medium: opera overture for orch.
     Date of comp: 1826
     Publication: Paris: Richault, 1836, as op. 3; OBE 4; NBE
                     4
     Remarks: 4-hand arrangement by Berlioz pub. Paris:
                     Richault, 1836

45. Title: *Grande ouverture du roi Lear* (H53)
     Genre/medium: concert overture for orch.
     Date of comp: 1831

        Publication: Paris: Catelin, 1840, as op. 4; OBE 4; NBE 20

46.   Title: *Grande ouverture de Waverley* (H26)
       Genre/medium: concert overture for orch.
       Date of comp: 1826-28
       Publication: Paris: Richault, 1839, as op. 1 bis; OBE 4; NBE 20

47.   Title: *Grande symphonie funèbre et triomphale* (H80)
       Genre/medium: symphony for band, strings, and chor. (SSTTBB)
       Text: Antoni Deschamps
       Date of comp: 1842
       Publication: Paris: Schlesinger, 1843, as op. 15; OBE 1; NBE 19
       Remarks: original version of 1840 for band alone; 3rd movt. arr. for voice, chor., and pf. in 1848 as *Apothéose*

      Hamlet. See *Tristia*

48.   Title: *Harold en Italie. Symphonie en 4 parties avec un alto principal* (H68)
       Genre/medium: symphony in 4 movts. for orch. and vla. solo
       Date of comp: 1834
       Publication: Paris: Brandus, 1848, as op. 16; OBE 2; NBE 17

      La harpe éolienne. See *Lélio*

      Hélène. See *Neuf mélodies*

49.   Title: *Herminie. Scène lyrique* (H29)
       Genre/medium: cantata for sop. and orch.
       Text: Pierre-Ange Vieillard
       Date of comp: 1828
       Publication: --; OBE 15; NBE 6
       Remarks: written for 1828 *Prix de Rome* competition

50.   Title: *Huit scènes de Faust* (H33)
       Genre/medium: dramatic scenes for the following:
       1.   *Chants de la fête de Pâques*-- 3 chors. (SA, SA, TTBB) & orch.
       2.   *Paysans sous les tilleuls. Danse et chant*-- chor. (SSATBB) and orch.

3. *Concert de sylphes. Sextuor*--chor.
    (SSATBB) and orch.
4. *Ecot de joyeux compagnons (histoire d'un
    rat)*--bass chor. (TB) and orch.
5. *Chanson de Méphistophélès*--ten., chor.
    (TTB), and orch.
6. *Le roi de Thulé. Chanson gothique*--sop.,
    chor. (TTB), and orch.
7. *Romance de Marguerite*--sop, chor. (TTB),
    and orch.; *Choeur de soldats*--chor. (TTB),
    4 hns., 2 tpts., 2 timp.
8. *Sérénade de Méphistophélès*--ten. and gtr.

Text: Johann Wolfgang von Goethe, tr. Gérard de
                Nerval
Date of comp: 1828-29
Publication: Paris: Schlesinger, 1829, as op. 1; OBE 10;
                NBE 5
Remarks: withdrawn by Berlioz shortly after pub.;
                later expanded into *La damnation de Faust*

Hymne à la France. See *Vox populi*

51. Title: *Hymne des Marseillais* (H51)
     Genre/medium: 2 chors. (TBB, SSTB) and orch.
     Text: Claude-Joseph Rouget de Lisle
     Date: 1830
     Publication: Paris: Schlesinger, 1830; OBE 18; NBE 22
     Remarks: arranged from *Chant de guerre* by Rouget
                     de Lisle; 2nd version, 1848, for ten., chor.
                     (SSTTBB), and pf.; NBE 22

52. Title: *Hymne pour la consécration du nouveau
                     tabernacle* (H135)
     Genre/medium: chor. (SSATTBB) and pf. or organ
     Text: J.-H. Vries
     Date of comp: 1859
     Publication: Paris: privately printed, 1859; reissued,
                     Paris: Bureaux de l'Alliance-Nouvelle,
                     1863; OBE 16; NBE 14

Hymne pour l'élévation. See *Quatre morceaux pour orgue
mélodium*

Hymne pour six instruments à vent. See *Neuf mélodies*

L'île inconnue. See *Les nuits d'été*

53.   Title: *L'impériale. Cantate à deux choeurs* (H129)
       Genre/medium: 2 chors. (SATB) and orch.
       Text: Captain Lafont
       Date of comp: 1854
       Publication: Paris: Brandus, Dufour & Cie., 1856, as op.
                           26; OBE 13; NBE 12

54.   Title: *Intrata di Rob-Roy MacGregor* (H54)
       Genre/medium: concert overture for orch.
       Date of comp: 1831
       Publication: --; OBE 4; NBE 20

55.   Title: *L'invitation à la valse* (H90)
       Genre/medium: orch.
       Date: 1841
       Publication: Paris: Schlesinger, 1842; BE 18; NBE 22
       Remarks: arranged from work by Carl Maria von
                           Weber

       Invitation à louer Dieu. See *Le livre choral*

56.   Title: *Je crois en vous. Romance* (H70)
       Genre/medium: song for ten. and pf.
       Text: Léon Guérin
       Date of comp: 1834
       Publication: Paris: supplement to the journal, *Le Protée*,
                           1834; OBE 17; NBE 15
       Remarks: reused in *Benvenuto Cellini* without text

57.   Title: *Je vais donc quitter pour jamais* (H6)
       Genre/medium: song for voice and gtr. or pf.
       Text: Jean-Pierre-Claris de Florian, from *Estelle et
                           Némorin*
       Date of comp: c. 1819
       Remarks: lost; melody reused in intro. to 1st mvt. of
                           the *Symphonie fantastique*

       Le jeune pâtre breton. See *Fleurs des landes*

       Le jugement dernier. See *Resurrexit*

       King Lear Overture. See *Grande ouverture du roi Lear*

58.   Title: *Là ci darem la mano* (H30)
       Genre/medium: variations for guitar on Mozart's *Don
                           Giovanni*
       Date of comp: c. 1828

	Publication:	Paris: Aulagnier ?
	Remarks:	lost
59.	Title:	*Lélio, ou le retour à la vie. Monodrame lyrique*. op. 14bis (H55)
	Genre/medium:	"mélologue" for various forces
	Text:	Berlioz (except no. 1)
	Date of comp:	1831-32, as *Le retour à la vie, Mélologue en six parties*
	Publication:	Paris: Richault, 1855, as *Lélio, ou le retour à la vie. Monodrame lyrique* . OBE 13; NBE 7
	Remarks:	sequel of *Symphonie fantastique*; contains both music and spoken narrative
	1.	*Le pêcheur. Ballade imitée de Goethe* ten. and pf.
	Remarks:	text by Goethe, tr. Albert Du Boys; comp. c. 1827; orig. pub. Paris: Schlesinger, 1833; OBE 17; NBE 15
	2.	*Choeur d'ombres* chor. (STB) and orch.
	Remarks:	adapted from *Cléopâtre*; original title, *Choeur d'ombres irritées*
	3.	*Chanson de brigands* song for bar., chor. (TTBB), and orch.
	Remarks:	adapted from lost *Chanson de pirates* of 1829; original title, *Scène de brigands*
	4.	*Chant de bonheur* song for ten. and orch.
	Remarks:	adapted from *La mort d'Orphée*; arr. for ten. and pf., pub. Paris: Schlesinger, 1834; OBE 17; NBE 15
	5.	*La harpe éolienne, souvenirs* orch.
	Remarks:	adapted from *La mort d'Orphée*; original title, *Les derniers soupirs de la harpe*
	6.	*Fantaisie dramatique sur La Tempête, drame de Shakespeare* (H52) choral fantasy for chor. (SSATT), pf. 4-hands, and orch.
	Remarks:	originally composed as independent work, *Ouverture de La Tempête* (H52)
60.	Title:	*Le livre choral*
	Genre/medium:	collection of sacred vocal works by various composers including Berlioz

	Date of comp:	1860-68?
	Publication:	Paris: Société générale de libraire catholique, 1885

	1.	Part III, no. 2. *Veni creator. Motet à 3 parties sans accompagnement* (H141) 2 sops, alto, chor. (SSA), and organ ad lib.
	Remarks:	text from Latin hymn; OBE 7; NBE 14
	2.	Part III, no. 17. *Tantum ergo. Solo et choeur pour voix de soprano et contralto* (H142) motet for 2 sops, alto, chor. (SSA), and organ ad lib.
	Remarks:	text from Latin hymn; OBE 7; NBE 14
	3.	Part IV, no. 5. *Invitation à louer Dieu. Air de Couperin mis à 3 voix égales avec accompagnement* (H143) chor. (SSA) and organ (or pf.?)
	Remarks:	arranged from work by François Couperin; OBE 18; NBE 22

61.

	Title:	*Marche de Rakoczy* (H109)
	Genre/medium:	orch.
	Date:	1846
	Publication:	Paris: Richault, 1854; OBE 11; NBE 8b
	Remarks:	arranged from traditional song; used in *La damnation de Faust*

62.

	Title:	*Marche d'Isly* (H108)
	Genre/medium:	orch.
	Date of comp:	1845
	Publication:	OBE--; NBE 22
	Remarks:	arranged from work by Léopold de Meyer

Marche funèbre pour la dernière scène d'Hamlet. See *Tristia*

63.

	Title:	*Marche marocaine* (H105)
	Genre/medium:	orch.
	Date:	1845
	Publication:	Vienna: A. Diabelli, 1846; OBE --; NBE 22
	Remarks:	arranged from work by Léopold de Meyer

64.

	Title:	*Marche religieuse des mages* (H27)
	Date of comp:	c. 1827-28
	Remarks:	lost; assumed to be revised as *Quartetto e coro dei maggi* in 1832 (H59)

65. Title: *Marche troyenne* (H133B)
    Genre/medium: orch.
    Date of comp: 1864
    Publication: Paris: Choudens, 1865; OBE 6; NBE 21
    Remarks: arr. from Act I of *Les Troyens*

Le matin. See *Fleurs des landes*

66. Title: *Le maure jaloux. Romance* (H9)
    Genre/medium: song for ten. and pf.
    Text: Jean-Pierre-Claris de Florian
    Date of comp: 1819-21
    Publication: Paris: Mme. Cuchet, 1822; OBE 17; NBE 15
    Remarks: original pre-pub. version entitled *L'arabe jaloux*

Méditation religieuse. See *Tristia*

La menace des Francs. See *Vox populi*

67. Title: *Messe solennelle* (H20A)
    Genre/medium: Mass for chor. (SATB?) and orch.
    Text: Latin liturgy
    Date of comp: 1824
    Remarks: all but *Resurrexit* lost

68. Title: *Le montagnard exilé. Chant élégiaque* (H15)
    Genre/medium: song for 2 sops. and pf. or harp
    Text: Albert Du Boys
    Date of comp: c. 1822-23
    Publication: Paris: Boieldieu jeune, 1823; OBE 16; NBE 15

La mort d'Ophélie. See *Tristia*

69. Title: *La mort d'Orphée* (H25)
    Genre/medium: cantata for ten., chor. (SS), and orch.
    Text: prob. Henri-Montan Berton
    Date of comp: 1827
    Publication: in facsimile, Paris: Réunion des bibliothèques nationales, 1930; OBE --; NBE 6
    Remarks: composed for *Prix de Rome* competition

70.   Title: *Nessun maggior piacere* (H114)
        Genre/medium: song for sop. or ten. and pf.
        Text: Berlioz, after Dante
        Date of comp: 1847
        Publication: --; OBE 17; NBE 15

71.   Title: *Neuf mélodies* (H38)
        Genre/medium: collection of songs for various voices and
                            pf.
        Date of comp: 1829
        Text: Thomas Moore, no. 1-8 tr. Thomas Gounet,
                            no. 9 tr. Louise Swanton Belloc
        Publication: Paris: Schlesinger, 1830, as op. 2
        Remarks: later called *Irlande*

        1.   *Le coucher du soleil. Rêverie* (H39)
                ten. and pf. OBE 17; NBE 15
        2.   *Hélène. Ballade à 2 voix* (40)
                sop. and alto, or ten. and bass, and pf. OBE
                16; NBE 15
        Remarks: 2nd version rev. 1844 for 2 tens. and 2
                    basses or chor. (TTBB) and orch. OBE 14;
                    NBE 12
        3.   *Chant guerrier* (H41)
                ten. or bass, chor. (TBB), and pf. OBE 16;
                NBE 14
        4.   *La belle voyageuse. Ballade* (H42)
                mezzo-sop. and pf. OBE 17; NBE 15
        Remarks: several different versions: male quartet &
                    orch. (lost); mezzo-sop. and orch., 1842,
                    pub. Paris: Richault, 1844; OBE 15; NBE
                    13; women's chor. and orch. 1851; NBE 13
        5.   *Chanson à boire* (H43)
                ten., chor. (TTBB), and pf. OBE 16; NBE
                14
        6.   *Chant sacré* (H44)
                ten. or sop., chor. (SSTTBB), and pf. OBE
                16; NBE 12
        Remarks: orchestrated version pub. Paris: Richault,
                    1843; OBE 14; NBE 14; arr. 1844 for
                    various wind instruments of Adolphe Sax as
                    Hymne pour six instruments à vent (lost)
        7.   *L'origine de la harpe. Ballade* (H45)
                sop. or ten. and pf. OBE 17; NBE 15
        8.   *Adieu Bessy. Romance anglaise et française*
                (H46)
                ten. and pf. OBE 17; NBE 15

	Remarks:	2nd version in G major pub. Paris: Richault, 1849; OBE 17
	9.	*Elégie en prose* (H47)
		ten. and pf. OBE 17; NBE 15

72.

Title:	*Nocturne à deux voix* (H31)
Genre/medium:	song for 2 sops. and gtr.
Text:	anon.
Date of comp:	1825-30?
Publication:	--; OBE --; NBE 15

73.

Title:	*Nocturne. Mélodie pastorale* (H23B)
Genre/medium:	2 sops., ten., chor. (SSTTBB), and pf.
Text:	Humbert Ferrand
Date of comp:	1828
Publication:	--; OBE --; NBE 4
Remarks:	reduced from the "pastoral trio" of *Les francs-juges*

74.

Title:	*La nonne sanglante* (H91)
Genre/medium:	opera in 3 acts
Text:	Eugène Scribe, after Matthew Gregory Lewis
Date of comp:	1841-47
Publication:	--; OBE --; NBE 4
Remarks:	never completed; libretto later set by Gounod

75.

Title:	*Les nuits d' été* (H81)
Genre/medium:	collection of songs for mezzo-sop. or ten. and pf.
Text:	Théophile Gautier
Date of comp:	1840
Publication:	Paris: Catelin, 1841, as op. 7; OBE 17; NBE 15
Remarks:	orchestrated 1844, 1855-56; pub. Paris: Richault; OBE 15; NBE 13

	1.	*Villanelle* (H82)
	2.	*Le spectre de la rose* (H83)
	3.	*Sur les lagunes. Lamento* (H84)
	4.	*Absence* (H85)
	5.	*Au cimitière. Claire de lune* (H86)
	6.	*L' île inconnue. Barcarolle* (H87)

Ophelia. See *Tristia*

Orfeo. See *La mort d'Orphée*

L'origine de la harpe. See *Neuf mélodies*

76. Title: *Ouverture du corsaire* (H101)
     Genre/medium: concert overture for orch.
     Date of comp: 1846-51
     Publication: Paris: Richault, 1852, as op. 21; OBE 5;
                      NBE 20
     Remarks: original version, 1844, called *La tour de
                      Nice*

77. Title: *Le passage de la mer rouge* (H18)
     Genre/medium: Latin oratorio
     Text: Vulgate Bible?
     Date of comp: 1823-24
     Remarks: lost

78. Title: *Pater noster* (H123)
     Genre/medium: SATB chorus
     Text: Berlioz
     Date: 1850 or before
     Publication: Paris: Richault, 1851; OBE 18; NBE 22
     Remarks: arranged from work by Dmitri Stepanovich
                      Bortnyansky

Paysans sous les tilleuls. See *Huit scènes de Faust*

Le pêcheur. See *Lélio*

Petit oiseau. Chanson de paysan. See *Fleurs des landes*

79. Title: *Plaisir d'amour* (H134)
     Genre/medium: bar. and orch.
     Text: Jean-Pierre-Claris de Florian
     Date: 1859
     Publication: Paris: Richault, 1859; OBE 18; NBE 22
     Remarks: arranged from work by Jean-Paul-Egide
                      Martini

80. Title: *Pleure, pauvre Colette. Romance à deux
                      voix égales* (H11)
     Genre/medium: song for 2 sops. and pf.
     Text: Jean-Marc Bourgerie
     Date of comp: c. 1822
     Publication: Paris: Mme. Cuchet, 1822; OBE 16; NBE
                      15

81.   Title: *Potpourri concertant sur des thèmes italiens*
                          (H1)
      Genre/medium: instrumental sextet
      Date of comp: 1817-18
      Remarks: lost

82.   Title: *Prière du matin. Choeur d'enfants* (H112)
      Genre/medium: children's chor. (SS) and pf.
      Text: Alphonse de Lamartine
      Date of comp: 1846
      Publication: Paris: La France musicale (Escudier), 1848;
                          OBE 16; NBE 14
      Remarks: possibly planned as no. 4 of expanded
                          version of op. 19, *Feuillets d'album*, 1852

83.   Title: *Quartetto e coro dei maggi* (H59)
      Genre/medium: chor. (SATB) and orch.
      Text: anon.
      Date of comp: 1832
      Publication: --; OBE 7; NBE 12
      Remarks: possibly adapted from lost *Marche*
                          religieuse des mages, 1828

84.   Title: *Quatre morceaux pour l'orgue mélodium*
      Genre/medium: orgue mélodium
      Date of comp: 1844
      Publication: Paris: Alexandre, 1844; OBE 6; NBE 21
      Remarks: First piece in collection is by Meyerbeer

      2.   *Sérénade agreste à la madone sur le thème*
                          des pifferari romains (H98)
      3.   *Toccata* (H99)
      4.   *Hymne pour l'élévation* (H100)

85.   Title: *Recueil de romances avec accompagnement*
                          de guitare (H8)
      Genre/medium: voice and gtr.
      Text: various
      Date: 1819-22
      Publication: --; OBE--; NBE 22
      Remarks: arranged from romances of various
                          composers

      Requiem.   See *Grande messe des morts*

86.   Title: *Resurrexit* (H20B)
       Genre/medium: Mass movement for chorus (SATB) and
                           orch.
       Date of comp: 1824 (orig. version burned); revised 1828
       Publication: --; OBE 7; NBE 12
       Remarks: only extant portion of *Messe solennelle*; also
                           known as *Le jugement dernier* (1829); parts
                           reused in *Benvenuto Cellini*, the *Requiem*,
                           and the *Te Deum*

       Le retour à la vie. See *Lélio*

87.   Title: *Rêverie et caprice. Romance* (H88)
       Genre/medium: violin and orch.
       Date of comp: 1841
       Publication: Paris: Richault, 1841, as op. 8; OBE 6; NBE
                           21
       Remarks: also pub. in arr. for vln. and pf., Richault,
                           1841

       La révolution grecque. See *Scène héroïque*

       Rob-Roy Overture. See *Intrata di Rob-Roy MacGregor*

       Le roi de Thulé. See *Huit scènes de Faust*

88.   Title: *Le roi des aulnes* (H136)
       Genre/medium: song for ten. and orch.
       Text: Goethe, trans. Edouard Bouscatel
       Date: 1860
       Publication: Paris: O. Legouix, 1860; OBE 18; NBE 22
       Remarks: arranged from work by Franz Schubert

       Le Roi Lear . See *Grande ouverture du roi Lear*

       Roman Carnival Overture. See *Le carnaval romain*

89.   Title: *Romance de Marie Tudor* (H66)
       Genre/medium: song for male voice and pf. (or orch.)
       Text: Victor Hugo
       Date of comp: 1833
       Remarks: lost

       Romance de Marguerite. See *Huit scènes de Faust*

90.   Title: *Roméo et Juliette. Symphonie dramatique*
                           (H79)

	Genre/medium:	dramatic symphony for alto, ten., bass, 3 chors. (ATB, STB, STB), and orch.
	Text:	Emile Deschamps, after Shakespeare
	Date of comp:	1839
	Publication:	Paris: Brandus, 1847, as op. 17; OBE 3; NBE 18
	Remarks:	2nd edition, Paris: Brandus, 1858; piano-vocal score by Théodore Ritter, pub. Winterthur: Rieter-Biedermann, 1858
91.	Title:	*Salutaris* (H32)
	Genre/medium:	oratorio for 3 voices and pf. or organ
	Date of comp:	1828-29
	Remarks:	lost
92.	Title:	*Sara la baigneuse, Ballade* (H69)
	Genre/medium:	for 3 chors. (STBB, SA, TTBB) and orch.
	Text:	Victor Hugo, from *Les orientales*
	Date of comp:	1834 (orig. version lost); rev. 1849
	Publication:	Paris: Richault, 1851, as op. 11; OBE 14; NBE 12
	Remarks:	orig. version for TTBB quartet and orch. or vocal quartet, chor., orch. (1838)--lost; arr. for sop. and alto (or ten. and bass) and orch. by Auguste Morel pub. Richault, 1850
93.	Title:	*Sardanapale. Cantate* (H50)
	Genre/medium:	ten., chor. (TTBB), and orch.
	Text:	Jean-François Gail
	Date of comp:	1830
	Publication:	--; OBE --; NBE 6
	Remarks:	composed for *Prix de Rome* competition; only a fragment of MS score extant; unpublished performing edition of fragment by Jeffrey Langford and Peter Bloom

Scène de brigands. See *Lélio*

94.	Title:	*Scène héroïque (La révolution grecque).* (H21)
	Genre/medium:	cantata for 2 basses, chor. (SSATTBB), and orch.
	Text:	Humbert Ferrand
	Date of comp:	1825-26
	Publication:	--; OBE 10; NBE 12

Remarks: 2-mvt. version for chor. and military band,
                      1833, variously titled *La triomphe de
                      Napoléon* or *Chant heroïque*

*Sérénade agreste à la madone sur le thème des pifferari
romains* (H98). *See Quatre morceaux pour orgue mélodium*

Sérénade de Méphistophélès. See *Huit scènes de Faust*

95.   Title: *Sketchbook of 1832-36* (H62)
       Date of comp.   c. 1832-36
       Publication: NBE 23
       Remarks: facsimile published to accompany *19th-
                          Century Music* 7 (no. 3 1984). Berkeley:
                          University of California Press, 1984. 79 p.
                          OCLC 13991711.

Le spectre de la rose. See *Les nuits d'été*

96.   Title: *Sur les alpes, quel délice! (Le chasseur des
                          chamois). Chant suisse* (H64)
       Genre/medium: 3-part male chor. (TTB) (and strings and
                          pf.?)
       Text: anon.
       Date: 1833
       Publication: --; OBE --; NBE 22
       Remarks: arranged from Swiss song by Ferdinand
                          Huber; also arr. for voice and gtr.

Sur les lagunes. See *Les nuits d'été*

97.   Title: *Symphonie fantastique en cinq parties.
                          Episode de la vie d'un artiste* (H48)
       Genre/medium: dramatic symphony in 5 movements
       Date of comp: 1830
       Publication: Paris: Schlesinger, 1845 as op. 14; OBE 1;
                          NBE 16
       Remarks: piano reduction by Liszt pub. Schlesinger,
                          1834

Symphonie funèbre et triomphale. See *Grande symphonie
                      funèbre et triomphale*

Tantum ergo. See *Le livre choral*

98. Title: *Te Deum* (H118)
    Genre/medium: 3 chors. (STB, STB, SA--children), ten.,
                             organ, and orch.
    Text: Latin hymn
    Date of comp: 1848-49
    Publication: Paris: Brandus, Dufour, 1855, as op. 22;
                             OBE 8; NBE 10

The Tempest. See *Lélio*

99. Title: *Le temple universel* (H137)
    Genre/medium: 2 chors. (TTBB) and organ
    Text: Jean-François Vaudin
    Date of comp: 1861
    Publication: Paris: L'Orphéon, 1861; OBE 16; NBE 14
    Remarks: orig. version written for choral festival in
                  England; never performed; later version for
                  unacc. chor. (TTBB) (for Paris Exposition
                  of 1867?); not performed; pub. Paris: H.
                  Rohdé, 1868; OBE 16; NBE 14

Toccata. See *Quatre morceaux pour orgue mélodium*

100. Title: *Toi qui l'aimas, verse des pleurs. Romance*
                  (H16)
    Genre/medium: song for ten. and pf.
    Text: Albert Du Boys
    Date of comp: c. 1822-23
    Publication: Paris: Boieldieu jeune, 1823; OBE 17; NBE
                  15

Le tour de Nice. See *Ouverture du corsaire*

Le trébuchet. See *Fleurs des landes*

La triomphe de Napoléon. See *La révolution grecque*

101. Title: *Tristia* (H119)
    Genre/medium: collection of works for chor.and orch.
    Publication: Paris: Richault, 1849, as op. 18 (nos. 1 and 2
                  only); version 2, Paris: Richault, 1852 (all
                  three works); OBE --; NBE 12

     1.   *Méditation religieuse* (H56)
                  chor. (SSTTBB) and orch.

Remarks: text by Thomas Moore, tr. Louise Swanton
                  Belloc; comp. 1831; original version for
                  chor. and 7 wind instruments lost;
                  orchestrated circa 1848; pub. as part of
                  version 1 in reduction for chor., vln., vc.,
                  and pf; piano-vocal score by Mlle.
                  Matteman no. 20 of *32 Mélodies*

2.   *La mort d'Ophélie. Ballade* (H92)
                  chor. (SA) and orch.

Remarks: text by Ernest Legouvé, after Shakespeare;
                  comp. 1848; first version for sop. or ten and
                  pf. comp. 1842; pub. Paris: Revue et gazette
                  musicale and Brandus, 1848; OBE 17; NBE
                  15 ; arr. for chor. (SA) and pf. and pub.
                  Paris: Richault, 1863, as no. 21 of *32
                  Mélodies*, OBE 16 (arr. by Malherbe and
                  Weingartner); NBE 14.

3.   *Marche funèbre pour la dernière scène
                  d'Hamlet* (H103)
                  wordless chor. (SATB) and orch.

Remarks: comp. 1844; OBE 6; NBE 12

102.   Title: *Les Troyens. Opéra en cinq actes* (H133)
       Genre/medium: opera
       Text: Berlioz, after Virgil
       Date of comp: 1856-58
       Publication: piano-vocal score privately printed, 1862;
                        reissued in 2 parts: *La prise de Troie* and
                        Les Troyens à Carthage, Paris: Choudens,
                        1863; full score of Part I, Choudens, 1899;
                        full score of Part II, Choudens, 1885; OBE -
                        -; NBE 2

103.   Title: *Two Quintets for Flute and String Quartet*
                        (H2 & 3)
       Date of comp: c. 1818-19
       Remarks: lost; one theme reused in the *Grande
                        ouverture des francs-juges*

Veni creator. See *Le livre choral*

Villanelle. See *Les nuits d'été*

104.   Title: *Vox populi* (H120)
       Genre/medium: compilation

Publication:	Paris: Richault, 1851, as op. 20; OBE 14; NBE 12
1.	*La menace des Francs. Marche et choeur* (H117)
	2 tens., 2 basses, chor. (SSTTBB), and orch.
Remarks:	text anon.; comp. before 1848; piano-vocal score pub. Richault, 1850; OBE 16
2.	*Hymne à la France* (H97)
	chor. (SSTTBB) and orch.
Remarks:	text by Auguste Barbier; comp. 1844

Waverley Overture. See *Grande ouverture de Waverley*

Zaïde. See *Feuillets d'album*

II. Literary Works and Correspondence

1. PROSE WORKS

This section lists those writings of Berlioz which appeared in book form. It does not include individual feuilletons that were published in musical periodicals, except where reprinted and/or translated as part of one of Berlioz's own collections (e.g., *A travers chants*) or as part of another author's selection of Berlioz's critical writings.

105.   *A travers chants: études musicales, adorations, boutades et critiques.* Collected Literary Works. Vol. 5. Paris: Michel Lévy, 1862. 336 p. ML410 B5A. Facsimile reprint. Farnborough: Gregg International, 1970. 336 p. ISBN 0-576-28422-X   ML410 B5 A56 1970   OCLC 193177.

     a. Critical edition. Texte établi avec notes et choix de variantes par Léon Guichard. Préface de Jacques Chailley (part of Hector Berlioz. Oeuvres littéraires, édition du centenaire). Paris: Grund, 1971. 471 p. ML410 B5 A56 1971 OCLC 782822.

     b. Translated by Edwin Evans in 3 volumes:
       1. *A Critical Study of Beethoven's Nine Symphonies, With "A Few Words on His Trios and Sonatas," a Criticism of "Fidelio," and an Introductory Essay on Music.* London: William Reeves, New York: Charles Scribner's Sons, 1914. Reprint. St. Clair Shores, Michigan: Scholarly Press, 1958, 1977. 165 p. ISBN 0-403-01508-1   ML410 B5 A543 1977 OCLC 284854.

       2. *Gluck and His Operas: With an Account of Their Relation to Musical Art.* London: William Reeves, 1914.

OCLC 8903327. Reprint. London: William Reeves, 1972.
OCLC 1410016. Reprint. Westport: Greenwood Press, 1973.
xiv, 167 p. ISBN 0-837-16938-0 ML410 B5 A543 1973
OCLC 650600.

3. *Mozart, Weber, and Wagner, With Various Essays on
Musical Subjects.* New York: Charles Scribner's Sons, 1917.
London: William Reeves, 1918. Reprint. New York: Somerset
Publishers., 1986. ML410 B5 A543 1986 OCLC 12664400.
London: William Reeves, 1969. xiv, 173 p. ISBN 0-721-
10001-5 ML410 B5 A543 1969 OCLC 103522.

c. *Beethoven*; foreword by J.-G. Prod'homme. 2nd ed. Paris:
Editions Correa, 1941. 181 p. ML410 B4 B85 OCLC
8255360. Paris: Buchet-Chastel, 1979. 181 p. ML410 B4 B35
1979 OCLC 10398982.

d. Translated and compiled by Ralph De Sola as *Beethoven: a
Critical Appreciation of Beethoven's Nine Symphonies and
His Only Opera, "Fidelio," With Its Four Overtures.* Boston:
Crescendo Publishing Co., 1975. 62 p. ISBN 0-875-97094-X
ML410 B5 A543 1975 OCLC 1445883.

Berlioz's final collection of critical essays and reviews
partially reprinted and expanded from *Voyage musical en
Allemagne et en Italie* (#111).

106.   *Le chef d'orchestre, théorie de son art. Extrait du Grand
         traité d'instrumentation et d'orchestration moderne.* Paris:
         Schonenberger, 1856. 47 p.

         a. Translated by Gustav Saenger as *The Orchestral
         Conductor; Theory of His Art.* New York: Carl Fischer, 1902.
         21 p. MT70 K652. 8th ed. New York: Carl Fischer, 1929.

         b. Translated by John Broadhouse as *The Conductor: the
         Theory of His Art.* London: William Reeves, 190?. OCLC
         396512. Reprint. St. Clair Shores, Michigan: Scholarly Press,
         1976. 63 p. ISBN 0-403-00247-8 MT85 B5 C74 1976 OCLC
         4032573.

         An essay on the art and technique of conducting (one of the
         earliest of its kind). For an additional English translation see
         Treatise on Instrumentation (#107c).

107.   *Grande traité d'instrumentation et d'orchestration modernes.*
         Paris: Schonenberger, 1844? 312 p. OCLC 3411672. Nouvelle

édition, revue corrigée, augmentée de plusieurs chapitres sur les instruments récemment inventés et suivie de l'Art du chef d'orchestre. Paris: Lemoine, 1870. 312 p. MT70 B48 1870 OCLC 2914663. Facsimile reprint. Collected Literary Works. Vol. 1. Farnborough: Gregg International, 1970. ii, 312 p. ISBN 0-576-28417-1 OCLC 16200810.

a. Translated by Mary Cowden Clarke as *A Treatise upon Modern Instrumentation and Orchestration; to Which Is Appended the Chef d'orchestre*. London: Novello; New York: Gray, 1850. MT70 B4813 1850a OCLC 5503787. New edition, rev. and ed. by Joseph Bennett. London and New York: Novello, Ewer, 1882. 257 p. MT70 B4813 1882 OCLC 2867940.

b. Translated as *Instrumentationslehre*, expanded and revised by Richard Strauss. Leipzig: C.F. Peters, 1905, 1955. 2 vols. MT70 B484 1955 OCLC 14008702.

c. Translated by Theodore Front as *Treatise on Instrumentation, Enlarged and Revised by Richard Strauss, Including Berlioz' Essay on Conducting*. New York: Kalmus, 1948. iii, 424 p. MT70 B482 1948 OCLC 615294.

d. Translated as *An Abridged Treatise on Modern Instrumentation and Orchestration...Also the Art of Conducting Explained. From Hector Berlioz* (supplement to *Logier's System of Harmony*). Boston: J. White, 1888, 253-316.

Discusses techniques of writing for the orchestral instruments of Berlioz's day, providing many insights into Berlioz's understanding of the aesthetics of orchestration. The expanded version by Richard Strauss augments Berlioz's musical examples with excerpts drawn mostly from the works of Wagner.

108. *Les grotesques de la musique*. Paris: A. Bourdilliat, 1859. 320 p. ML410 B5A OCLC 9629748. Facsimile reprint. Collected Literary Works. Vol. 4. Farnborough: Gregg International, 1969. iv, 308 p. ISBN 0-576-28421-1 OCLC 16190610.

a. Texte établi avec introduction, notes et choix de variantes par Léon Guichard (part of Hector Berlioz. Oeuvres littéraires, edition du centenaire). Paris: Grund, 1969. 415 p. ML410 B5 A495 1969 OCLC 478548.

c. Translated by Francis Harling-Comyns as "Curiosities of
Music." *The Musical Times* 78 (July 1937): 599-601;
(August): 693-95; (September): 791-94. ISSN 0027-4666
OCLC 5472115. Contains "Prologue"; "The Right of Playing
in F"; "A Crowned Virtuoso"; "The Regiment of Colonels";
"Is This an Irony?"; "Appreciators of Beethoven"; "The
Sontag Version"; "One Cannot Dance in E"; "A Kiss From
Rossini"; "Musical Instruments of the Universal Exposition";
"A Rival of Erard."

c. Translated as "Musical Freaks." *The Monthly Musical
Record* 71 (June 1941): 108-9; (July/August): 124-27. OCLC
1605021. Contains "The Evangelist of the Drum"; "The
Apostle of the Flageolet"; "The Prophet of the Trombone"; "A
Concerto for Clarinet"; "Prudence and Sagacity of a
Provincial-- Alexandre's Melodium-Organ."

d. See also Apthorp (#112) for the most complete English
translation. Includes most of the items in b. and c. above, plus:
"A New Musical Instrument"; "A Cantata"; "Orchestra
Conductors"; "Prudent Matches"; "Great News"; "Barley-
Candy--Severe Music"; "The Dilettanti in Blouses and Serious
Music"; "Lamentations of Jeremiah"; "Success of a Miserere";
"Little Miseries of Big Concerts"; "Death to Flats"; "Flight
into Egypt"; "A First Appearance--Despotism of the Director
of the Opera"; "A Saying of M. Auger's"; "Sensibility and
Laconicism--A Funeral Oration in Three Syllables."

A volume of satirical anecdotes, many extracted from
feuilletons of the previous eleven years.

109.   *Mémoires de Hector Berlioz: comprenant ses voyages en
        Italie, en Allemagne, en Russie et en Angleterre, 1803-1865.*
        Paris: Michel Lévy, 1870. iii, 509 p. ML410 B5 A11 OCLC
        2592698. Facsimile reprint. Collected Literary Works. Vol 6.
        Farnborough: Gregg International, 1969. 512 p. ISBN 0-576-
        28423-8 OCLC 16190615.

        a. Chronologie et introduction par Pierre Citron. Paris:
        Garnier-Flammarion, 1969. 2 vols. ML410 B5 A4 1969
        OCLC 1012082.

        b. Translated by Rachel (Scott Russell) Holmes and Eleanor
        Holmes as *Autobiography of Hector Berlioz, Member of the
        Institute of France, from 1803 to 1865.* London: Macmillan,
        1884. 2 vols. ML410 B5 B53. Annotated, and the translation
        revised by Ernest Newman, as *Memoirs...* New York: Tudor

Publishing Co., 1932. OCLC 3639435. New York: Alfred A. Knopf, 1932. ML410 B5 A113 OCLC 401200. Reprint, New York: Dover Publications, 1960, 1966. xxi, 533 p. ML410 B5 A243 1966 OCLC 316620.

c. Translated and edited by David Cairns as *The Memoirs of Hector Berlioz, Member of the French Institute: Including His Travels in Italy, Germany, Russia, and England, 1803-1865.* London: Gollancz, New York: Alfred A. Knopf, 1969. OCLC 100085. Rev. ed. New York: W.W. Norton, 1975. 636 p. ISBN 0-393-00698-0 OCLC 1485224. London: Gollancz, 1977. OCLC 6928557. London and New York: Granada Publishing, 1981 (1981 printing of 1970 Panther edition). 792 p. ML410 B5 A243 1970b ISBN 0-586-03408-0 OCLC 13563966.

Autobiography assembled in part from feuilletons and the *Voyage musical en Allemagne et en Italie* .

110.   *Les soirées de l'orchestre*. Paris: Michel Lévy, 1852. OCLC 5194863. Facsimile reprint (of 1853 edition). Collected Literary Works. vol. 3. Farnborough: Gregg International, 1969. 429 p. ISBN 5-762-84203 ML410 B5 A58 1853a OCLC 1088372. 2nd ed. Paris: Michel Lévy, 1854. Reprint. Paris: Stock Plus Musique, 1980. 473 p. ISBN 2-234-01331-3 OCLC 16113699.

a. Texte établi, avec introduction, notes et choix de variantes par Léon Guichard (part of Hector Berlioz. Oeuvres littéraires, edition du centenaire). Paris: Grund, 1968. 653 p. ML410 B5 A58 1968 OCLC 396525.

b. Translated by Charles E. Roche as *Evenings in the Orchestra*. Introduction by Ernest Newman. New York and London: Alfred A. Knopf, 1929. xxii, 366 p. ML410 B5 A102 1929 OCLC 861462.

c. Translated and edited by Jacques Barzun as *Evenings with the Orchestra*. New York: Alfred A. Knopf, 1956. ML410 B5 A245 1956 OCLC 423947. Chicago: University of Chicago Press, 1973. xviii, 381 p. ML410 B5 A583 1970z OCLC 870867.

d. Translated by C.R. Fortescue as *Evenings in the Orchestra*. London and Baltimore: Penguin Books, 1963. 342 p. ML410 B5 A583 1963 OCLC 861674.

e. See also Apthorp (#112) for a partial translation.

A collection of feuilletons that take the form of satirical anecdotes told by the "musicians of an unnamed orchestra during the performances of bad operas" (Berlioz to Joseph d'Ortigue).

111.   *Voyage musical en Allemagne et en Italie. Etudes sur Beethoven, Gluck et Weber. Mélanges et nouvelles.* Paris: J. Labitte, 1844. 2 vols. OCLC 12123783. Facsimile reprint. Collected Literary Works. Vol. 2. Farnborough: Gregg International, 1970. 2 vols. ISBN 0-576-284173 ML410 B5 A49 1970 OCLC 1013545.

See Apthorp (#112) for a translation of *Voyage en Allemagne et en Italie.*

Letters and memoirs from trips to Germany and Italy (reprinted in the *Mémoires*, #109) with collections of analytical essays on Beethoven's nine symphonies, Weber's *Der Freischütz*, Gluck's *Alceste* (all revised and reprinted in *A travers chants*, #105), recollections of Berlioz's early experiences at the *Opéra* (revised and reprinted in the *Mémoires*), and other short articles which originally appeared in the *Journal des débats*.

2. SELECTIONS

112.   *Hector Berlioz--Selections from his Letters, and Aesthetic, Humorous, and Satirical Writings.* Translated and preceded by a biographical sketch of the author by William F. Apthorp. New York: Holt, 1879. OCLC 747685. Reprint. Portland: Longwood Press, 1976. ix, 427 p. ISBN 0-893-41018-7 ML410 B5 A33 1976 OCLC 3004050.

Includes excerpts from *Voyage musical en Allemagne et en Italie*, *Les soirées de l'orchestre*, *A travers chants*, and the most complete translation of *Les grotesques de la musique.*

113.   *Les musiciens et la musique.* Introduction by André Hallays. Paris: Calmann-Lévy, 1903. OCLC 9623344. Facsimile reprint. Collected Literary Works. Vol. 7. Farnborough: Gregg

International, 1969. 348 p. ISBN 0-576-28424-6 ML410 B5 A54 1969 OCLC 170559.

Review: Jullien, Adolphe. "Feuilletons choisis de Berlioz." In *Musiciens d'hier et d'aujourd'hui*, 147-57. Paris: Fischbacher, 1910. 371 p. ML390 J95 OCLC 4795075.

A selection of feuilletons from the *Journal des débats*, 1835 through 1863.

114. *The Life of Hector Berlioz as Written by Himself, in His Letters and Memoirs.* Translated with introduction by Katharine F. Boult. London: J.M. Dent; New York: E.P. Dutton, 1903. OCLC 399306. Reprint. London: J.M. Dent; New York: E.P. Dutton, 1937. xvi, 303 p. ML410 B5 B511 1937 OCLC 12527938.

Uses a selection of Berlioz's letters to enlarge on autobiographical excerpts taken from the *Mémoires.*

115. Prod'homme, J.-G. "Unpublished Berlioziana." Part 1 translated by Theodore Baker. Part 2 translated by Marguerite Barton. *The Musical Quarterly* 5 (no. 3 1919): 398-412. ISSN 0027-4631 OCLC 1642493.

Includes a translation of the original draft of the autobiographical sketch which Berlioz wrote for d'Ortigue, who used it as the basis for his article published in the *Revue de Paris*, December 23, 1832 (#272).

116. "Hector Berlioz." In *Lettres de musiciens écrites en français du XVe au XXe siècle (de 1831 à 1885)*, edited by Julien Tiersot. Deuxième série, 172-78. Turin: Bocca frères, 1924-36. 2 vols. ML90 T5 vol. 2 OCLC 1630681. Translated as "Berlioz; Biographical Sketch Written by the Composer." In *The Literary Clef; an Anthology of Letters and Writings by French Composers*, compiled by Edward Lockspeiser, 7-13. London: John Calder, 1958. 186 p. ML90 L8 OCLC 957959.

Contains Berlioz's autobiographical manuscript notes that d'Ortigue used as the basis of his biographical sketch of the composer in the *Revue de Paris*, December 23, 1832 (#272).

117. "Rossini's *William Tell.*" In *Source Readings in Music History*, edited by Oliver Strunk, 809-26. New York: W.W. Norton, 1950. xxi, 919 p. ML160 S89 OCLC 385286. New

York: W.W. Norton, 1965. 5 vols. ML160 S89 1965 OCLC 177721.

A translation of "*Guillaume Tell* de Rossini," which originally appeared in the *Gazette musicale de Paris* October 12, 19, 26, and November 2, 1834.

118.   "Hector Berlioz: 'On Imitation in Music.'" In *Fantastic Symphony*, edited by Edward T. Cone, 36-46. Norton Critical Scores. New York: W.W. Norton, 1971. viii, 305 p. ISBN 0-393-02160-2 M1001 B53 op. 14 1971 OCLC 273785.

A translation of "De l'imitation musicale," which originally appeared in the January 1 and 8, 1837, issues of the *Revue et gazette musicale de Paris*. An important statement on Berlioz's theory of program music. Reprinted in *Cauchemars et passions* (#120).

119.   Deans, Kenneth Norwood. "A Comprehensive Performance Project in Saxophone Literature With an Essay Consisting of Translated Source Readings in the Life and Work of Adolphe Sax." D.M.A. dissertation, University of Iowa, 1980. vii, 201 p. bibliography, 191-201. OCLC 9034073.

Contains a translation of "Instruments de musique--M. Ad. Sax," which originally appeared in the *Journal des débats*, June 12, 1842 [from abstract].

120.   *Cauchemars et passions*. Edited by Gérard Condé. Paris: J.C. Lattes, 1981. 376 p. ML60 B4689 OCLC 7977487.

A collection of Berlioz's critical writing on music spanning the years from 1823, when he wrote his first open letters to *Le corsaire*, to 1863, when he retired from the *Journal des débats*. These essays fall into three principal categories: opera reviews, biographical sketches of other composers, and articles on the aesthetics of music. Also included are letters of Berlioz in which he makes reference to his writing career.

Literary Works and Correspondence 39

3. CORRESPONDENCE

Before the publication of the new critical edition of Berlioz's letters as part of the _Oeuvres littéraires_, there was no single collection to which one could refer. The following list, arranged chronologically, includes some of the more important collections published prior to the _Correspondance générale_. Many of these are readily available in libraries, and until the critical edition is completed, they will remain an important source for correspondence from Berlioz's later years. For a more comprehensive list of the earlier collections, see the bibliography in Barzun (#210).

A. Letters in single volumes.

121.   _Correspondance inédite de Hector Berlioz, 1819-1868_; _avec une notice biographique par Daniel Bernard._ Paris: Calmann-Lévy, 186-?. OCLC 15683216. 3rd ed. Paris: Calmann-Lévy, 1896. 385 p. ML410 B5 A1 OCLC 9628994.

   Translated by H. Mainwaring Dunstan as _The Life and Letters of Berlioz_. Vol. 1. London: Remington & Co., 1882. 2 vols. ML410 B5 A45 OCLC 861496.

122.   _Lettres intimes; avec une préface par Charles Gounod._ 2nd ed. Paris: Calmann-Lévy, 1882. xv, 319 p. 2 vols. ML410 B5 A1 1882 OCLC 2941795.

   Translated by H. Mainwaring Dunstan as _The Life and Letters of Berlioz_. Vol. 2. London: Remington & Co., 1882. 2 vols. ML410 B5 A45 OCLC 861496.

123.   _Briefe hervorragender Zeitgenossen an Franz Liszt._ Edited by La Mara [Ida Maria Lipsius]. Leipzig: Breitkopf & Härtel, 1895-1904. 3 vols. ML410 L7 L52 OCLC 5960797.

   Text in French. Volumes 1 and 2 contain letters written from 1852 through 1867.

124.   _Briefe von Hector Berlioz an die Fürstin Carolyne Sayn-Wittgenstein._ Edited by La Mara [Ida Maria Lipsius]. Leipzig: Breitkopf & Hartel, 1903. vi, 188 p. ML98 B51 OCLC 12094318.

Text in French. Letters date from 1852 through 1867.

125. *Lettres, 1819-55.* Edited by Julien Tiersot. Paris: Calmann-Lévy, 1904-1930. 3 vols.

Vol. 1: *Les années romantiques, 1819-1842.* 1904. xlii, 451 p. ML410 B5 A4 OCLC 2733429.

Vol. 2: *Le musicien errant, 1842-1852.* 1919. xx, 380 p. ML410 B5 A42 OCLC 2229447.

Vol. 3: *Au milieu du chemin, 1852-1855.* 1930. xi, 293 p. ML410 B5 A47 OCLC 5661120.

Best collection of Berlioz's letters prior to the *Correspondance générale,* missing only the last fourteen years of his life.

126. *New Letters of Berlioz, 1830-1868,* with introduction, notes, and English translation by Jacques Barzun. New York: Columbia University Press, 1954. OCLC 401526. 2nd ed. Westport, Conn.: Greenwood Press, 1974. xxxi, 322 p. ISBN 0-837-13251-7 ML410 B5 A33 1974 OCLC 811662.

Text in French with English translation.

127. *Hector Berlioz: a Selection from His Letters,* selected, edited, and translated by Humphrey Searle. London: Gollancz; New York: Harcourt, Brace & World, 1966. OCLC 593466. New York: Vienna House, 1973. 224 p. ML410 B5 A517 1973 OCLC 975168.

A good general collection for the English reader covering the years 1819 through 1868.

128. *Correspondance générale.* Paris: Flammarion, 1972-. (part of Hector Berlioz. Oeuvres littéraires, edition du centenaire). ML410 B5 A3 1972 OCLC 685383.

Vol. 1: *1803-1832,* edited by Pierre Citron. 1972. 595 p.

Vol. 2: *1832-1842,* edited by Frédéric Robert. 1975. 797 p.

Vol. 3: *1842-1850,* edited by Pierre Citron. 1978. 836 p.

Vol. 4: *1851-1855*, edited by Pierre Citron, Yves Gérard, Hugh Macdonald. Paris: Flammarion, 1983.

Volumes 1 through 4 are part of the new and still incomplete critical edition of Berlioz's letters. Even as this series is being published, however, new letters are coming to light. They are being published in various journals (see below) and will eventually be added to a later volume.

B. Letters published in journals and book chapters; listed chronologically

We have included primarily selections that cover the last fourteen years of Berlioz's life which are not yet accounted for in the *Correspondence générale*. These collections comprise letters both to and about Berlioz.

129.   Wilder, Victor, ed. "Vingt lettres inédites d'Hector Berlioz." *Le ménestrel* 45 (June 8 1879): 217-219; (June 15): 233-34; (June 22): 233-34; (June 29): 241-43; (July 6): 249-51; (July 13): 257-59. OCLC 6966764.

Letters written from 1853 through 1866 to the Belgian music critic and composer Adolphe Samuel.

130.   Tiersot, Julien. "La dedicace des *Troyens*.(Lettres inédites de Berlioz). *La revue musicale* 2 (July 1902): 322-27. OCLC 1590287.

Contains extracts of letters to the Princess Carolyne Sayn-Wittgenstein dated 1863 to 1865 concerning the planned dedication to her of the printed score of *Les Troyens*.

131.   "Une page d'amour romantique: lettres à Mme. Estelle Fornier." *Revue politique et littéraire (Revue Bleue)* 40 (April 4 1903): 417-23; (April 11): 457-62; (April 18): 484-88; (April 25): 513-17. OCLC 8339424. Reprint. Paris: Editions de la Revue Bleue et de la Revue scientifique, 1903? xi, 59 p. ML410 B5 A34.

Letters from the last years of Berlioz's life written to his first boyhood love.

132.   Tiersot, Julien. "Lettres inédites de Berlioz." *La revue musicale* 3 (August 15 1903): 426-30. OCLC 1590287.

Letters to a variety of persons, including the famous singer
Pauline Viardot (1859).

133.   Prod'homme, J.-G. "Nouvelles lettres de Berlioz." *Rivista
         musicale italiana* 12 (no. 2 1905): 339-82. OCLC 1773309.

         A collection of letters written between 1828 and 1866 that did
         not appear in the Bernard (#121) and Gounod (#122)
         collections.

134.   _____. "Les lettres de Berlioz à Auguste Morel." *Le guide
         musical* 58 (October 27 1912): 609-12; (November 3): 629-31;
         (November 10): 647-48; (November 17): 667-69; (November
         24): 687-90; (December 1): 707-10. OCLC 1509855.

         A complement to Bernard's *Correspondance inédite* (#121).
         These letters to one of Berlioz's most voluminous
         correspondents cover the period from 1842 through 1868.

135.   "Berlioz et J.W. Davison." *Le guide musical* 59 (February 16
         1913): 128-31; (February 23): 147-50; (March 2): 171-74.
         OCLC 1509855.

         Davison was a music critic for the London *Times* and
         publisher of *The Musical World.* Letters cover the period from
         1848 through 1864.

136.   "Unveroffentlichte Briefe Hector Berlioz an seine Freunde
         Auguste Morel und Lecourt." Translated by Mimi Zoff. *Neue
         Musik Zeitung* 36 (April 1 1915): 150-53. OCLC 11930822.

         Letters from 1847 through 1867 to Auguste Morel, composer
         and music critic for the *Journal de Paris*, and to Lecourt, an
         amateur musician friend. Letters are translated into German.

137.   Lange, Maurice. "Lettres inédites de Berlioz." *Revue
         d'Auvergne* 35 (1918): 1-11.

         Letters to Georges Hainl written between 1845 and 1855.

138.   [Tiersot, Julien]. "Lettres de Berlioz sur *Les Troyens.*" *La
         revue de Paris* 28 (August 1 1921): 449-73; (August 15): 747-
         70; (September 1): 146-71. OCLC 1775173.

         Traces Berlioz's life-long interest in Virgil's *Aeneid* and
         follows with reproductions of letters written to friends and

relatives between 1856 and 1864 concerning plans for and the realization of his ambitious plan to write a Virgilian opera.

139. "Hector Berlioz." In *Lettres de musiciens écrites en français du XVe au XXe siècle (de 1831 à 1885)*, edited by Julien Tiersot. Deuxième série, 154-218. Turin: Bocca frères, 1924-36. 2 vols. ML90 T5 vol. 2 OCLC 1630681. Reprinted in *Rivista musicale italiana* 36 (no. 1 1929): 1-25; (no. 3-4): 408-29; 37 (no. 1 1930): 1-20. OCLC 1773309.

Consists of letters missing in Tiersot's earlier three volumes (#126). Also includes letters to and about Berlioz.

140. Ginsburg, Semjon. "Correspondance russe inédite de Berlioz." *La revue musicale* 11 (May 1930): 417-24. OCLC 1764223.

Three letters written during 1867 and 1868 to Russian patrons and court officials.

141. Clarence, G. "Lettres inédites à Berlioz." *La revue musicale* 11 (May 1930): 400-416. OCLC 1764223.

Letters written from 1858 through 1868 to Berlioz from various friends and colleagues.

142. "Lettres inédites de Berlioz." *La revue musicale* 16 (March 1935): 164-68. OCLC 1764223.

Letters written between 1858 and 1863 to François Schwab, Strasbourg music critic and orchestra conductor.

143. Holde, Arthur. "A Little-Known Letter by Berlioz and Unpublished Letters by Cherubini, Leoncavallo, and Hugo Wolf." *The Musical Quarterly* 37 (no. 3 1951): 340-47. ISSN 0027-4631 OCLC 1642493.

Includes a letter from Berlioz to Hans von Bülow written in 1858, in which he mentions an alternate ending for *Les Troyens*.

144. Delli, Bertrun. "Sechs unbekannte Briefe von Hector Berlioz." *Neue Zeitschrift für Musik* 119 (September 1958): 499-503. ISSN 0028-3509 OCLC 1776104.

Contains letters written from 1853 through 1858 from Berlioz to Baron Wilhelm de Donop, a German music amateur and friend.

145.   ["Letters"]. In *The Literary Clef; an Anthology of Letters and Writings by French Composers*, translated and compiled by Edward Lockspeiser, 15-34. London: John Calder, 1958. 186 p. ML90 L8 OCLC 957959.

Letters to Humbert Ferrand, Berlioz's sister Adèle, Estelle Fornier, and the Princess Carolyne Sayn-Wittgenstein (on *Les Troyens*).

146.   Grindea, Myron, ed. "Sixty-One Letters by Berlioz." *Adam International Review* nos. 331-333 (1969): 48-87. ISSN 0001-8015 OCLC 1965286.

Letters written from 1828 through 1863 to various friends, relatives, and business acquaintances.

147.   Ahouse, John B. "Berlioz and Odoevsky." *Berlioz Society Bulletin* no. 88 (July 1975): 15-20; no. 89 (October): 13-20. OCLC 2386332.

English translation of six letters (four of which are possible forgeries) to Prince Odoyevsky written in 1868.

148.   Locke, Ralph P. "New Letters of Berlioz (with texts of 8 unpublished letters)." *19th-Century Music* 1 (no. 1 1977): 71-85. ISSN 0148-2076 OCLC 3280195. Also published in slightly revised form in *Berlioz Society Bulletin* no. 102 (Winter 1978-79): 2-20; no. 103 (Spring 1979):3. OCLC 2386332.

Review of the *Correspondance générale*, volume 2, which offers detailed corrections and additions, notably several unpublished letters of Berlioz and one by Harriet Smithson. Also includes the first publication of the full poetic text of the *Chansonette de M. Léon de Wailly*, later reworked as the "Choeur des masques" in Act I of *Benvenuto Cellini*. The letters are in French with English translations.

149.   Wella. David Arthur. "Letters of Mendelssohn, Schumann and Berlioz in Belfast." *Music and Letters* 60 (no. 2 1979): 180-85. ISSN 0027-4224 OCLC 1758884.

Reports the discovery of an 1843 letter in which Berlioz solicited an operatic role for his friend and future second wife, Marie Recio. Translation is included.

150. Bloom, Peter. "Berlioz and Officialdom: Unublished Correspondence." *19th-Century Music* 4 (no. 2 1980): 134-46. ISSN 0148-2076 OCLC 3280195.

Letters written by Berlioz between 1833 and 1846 to officials of the French government and not included in the *Correspondance générale.* Also includes three letters by Harriet Smithson.

151. Fauquet, Joël-Marie. "Deux lettres inédites d'Hector Berlioz à Humbert Ferrand et Jean-Baptiste Vuillaume." *Revue musicale de Suisse Romande* 37 (no. 1 1984): 14-20. ISSN 0035-3744 OCLC 9077868.

Includes a letter written in 1835 to Ferrand recommending the violinist Jean Delphin and one written in 1855 to Vuillaume concerning the invention of a new larger double-bass called the octo-basse.

III. General Background

This chapter includes those works which deal with the cultural, intellectual, artistic, or social history of Berlioz's era, including general studies of nineteenth-century Romanticism.

1. AESTHETICS

152.   Bouyer, Raymond.. "Petites notes sans portée: Schumann et la 'musique à programme.'" *Le ménestrel* 69 (September 3 1903): 290-92. OCLC 6966764.

Points out differences in musical temperament that characterize the Germans and the French, stating that the former, as exemplified by Schumann, preferred a purer form of absolute instrumental music.

153.   Bücken, Ernst. "Berlioz." In *Musikalische Charakterköpfe,* 126-36. Leipzig: Quelle & Meyer, 1925. 174 p. ML300 B92 OCLC 5283371.

Discusses Berlioz and Wagner as important musical aestheticians and the significance of the "poetic idea" in Berlioz's program music. Contends that Berlioz failed to appreciate Wagner's music dramas because he misunderstood the operatic theories of Gluck from which they evolved.

154.   Dömling, Wolfgang. "Eine Welt des Phantastischen." In *Hector Berlioz und seine Zeit*, 54-76. Laaber: Laaber-Verlag,

1986. 360 p. bibliography, 347-53. ISBN 3-921-51890-3
ML410 B5 D63 1986 OCLC 15228157.

Argues that the *fantastique* in literature and music are not
equivalent. Relates the musical *fantastique* to earlier concepts
of the fantasia and to the idea of creating musical dissociation
via departures from constructive norms. Demonstrates how
the program of the *Symphonie fantastique* was influenced by
the ideals of the literary *fantastique*, while its music was
influenced by the techniques of the musical *fantastique* which
Berlioz found in the symphonies of Beethoven.

155.   Pinson, Patricia T. "The Shattered Frame: a Study of the
        Grotesque in Nineteenth Century Literature and Music."
        Ph.D. dissertation, University of Ohio, 1971. vii, 209 p.
        bibliography, 200-209. OCLC 1152170.

        Borrows concepts from art and literature to define the
        grotesque in music as the continuous breaking of predictable
        frames of reference. Traces this technique in the music of
        Berlioz (e.g., thematic transformation in the *Symphonie
        fantastique)* and others [from abstract].

156.   Schmidt-Garre, Helmut. "Der Teufel in der Musik."
        Melos/Neue Zeitschrift für Musik 1 (May-June 1975): 174-83.
        ISSN 0343-0138 OCLC 2327912.

        Analyzes the growing fascination with the demonic in early-
        nineteenth-century French music and literature. Discusses in
        this context *Sardanapale*, the *Symphonie fantastique*, *La
        damnation de Faust*, and the *Requiem*, finding "shocking and
        grotesque monstrosities" and a "love of the Demonic as an end
        in itself."

157.   Smith, Martin Dennis. "Antoine Joseph Reicha's Theories on
        the Composition of Dramatic Music." Ph.D. dissertation,
        Rutgers University, 1979. viii, 439 p., bibliography, 407-27.
        OCLC 13463792.

        Compares Reicha's theories on dramatic music with those of
        other aestheticians and composers, including Berlioz [from
        abstract].

2. EXHIBITION CATALOGS

158.   Anon. "A Recollection of Buxton 1980." *Berlioz Society Bulletin* no. 112 (Summer 1981): 2-18. OCLC 2386332.

Lists ninety-six items devoted to Berlioz's "twin passions," Shakespeare and Harriet Smithson. Includes autograph letters and manuscripts, printed music, engravings, programs, and photographs. Part of the Berlioz festival held at Buxton, England, in 1980.

159.   *Berlioz and the Romantic Imagination: an Exhibition Organized by the Arts Council and the Victoria and Albert Museum...* London: Arts Council, 1969. xxiv, 147 p. ISBN 0-90008-512-6 ML141 L6 B5 OCLC 63446.

Includes art works, photographs, music, letters, and books assembled to portray Berlioz's career. Essay, "Berlioz in Perspective," by Edward Lockspeiser (xiv-xviii) emphasizes Berlioz's impact on the evolution of ideas in nineteenth-and twentieth-century arts, especially as regards the use of color and dream images. For a review of this exhibition, see #330.

160.   France. Bibliothèque Nationale. *Hector Berlioz, Paris, 1969. Exposition inaugurée le 5 mars, catalogue publié à l'occasion de l'Exposition Berlioz.* Catalogue par François Lesure, avec le collaboration de Yane Fromrich. Paris: Bibliothèque Nationale, 1969. 178 p. ML141 P18 B4 OCLC 860164.

Juxtaposes catalog entries from the exhibit with relevant excerpts from Berlioz's writings.

161.   Grenoble. Exposition Hector Berlioz, 1953. *Exposition Hector Berlioz, organisée à l'occasion de son 150e anniversaire, Grenoble, 1953.* Grenoble: Imprimerie Allier, 1954. 27 p. ML410 B5 G56.

Lists manuscripts, documents, letters, and pictorial materials assembled for the 150th anniversary of Berlioz's birth.

162.   Institut français d'Ecosse. *Hector Berlioz; exhibition, Edinburgh Festival 1963.* n.p., 1963. 40 p. ML141 E2 B45 OCLC 15264165.

Includes books, scores, pictorial materials in various
mediums, letters, concert seating plans, admission tickets,
concert programs, program notes, scene designs, libretti, and
other miscellaneous memorabilia. Materials are "arranged
chronologically, with a view to showing the various musical
and literary influences that acted upon Berlioz, the
contemporary scene in which he worked, his own musical
achievements, and the significant activities and incidents of
his life."

3. PARISIAN CONCERT LIFE

163.   Cooper, Jeffrey Hawley. "A Renaissance in the Nineteenth
         Century: the Rise of French Instrumental Music and Parisian
         Concert Societies, 1828-1871." Ph.D. dissertation, Cornell
         University, 1981. vii, 555 p. bibliography, 537-55. OCLC
         10962482.

         Surveys the increasing popularity of instrumental music in
         mid-nineteenth-century Paris. Discusses several major concert
         series and the then-common distinction between those
         featuring conservative "art" music and those promoting
         "popular" music [from abstract].

164.   Dandelot, Arthur. *La Société des Concerts du Conservatoire
         de 1828 à 1897*. Paris: G. Havard fils, 1898. viii, 221 p.
         OCLC 5747849. Expanded as *La Société des Concerts du
         Conservatoire (1828-1923)*. Paris: Delagrave, 1923. 267 p.
         ML270.8 P2 D16 OCLC 2881025.

         Presents a complete history of nineteenth-century Parisian
         concert life. Includes discussions of smaller concert series
         modeled after those of the *Société*. Chronicles the works of
         Berlioz performed at such concerts both during his lifetime
         and after his death. Mentions the role of important
         conductor/organizers such as Pasdeloup and Colonne in
         supporting and programming works of Berlioz.

165.   Elwart, Antoine Aimable Elie. *Histoire de la Société des
         Concerts du Conservatoire impérial de musique, avec dessins,
         musique, plans, portraits, notices biographiques, etc.* Paris: S.

Castel, 1860. OCLC 2686194. 2nd ed. Paris: S. Castel, 1864.
438 p. ML270.8 P2 S744 OCLC 3353535.

Presents detailed records of the founding and organization of
this famous concert series, along with programs for every
concert from 1828 to 1859, including performances of some
of Berlioz's works. Also includes a short biography of the
conductor Habeneck.

4. ROMANTIC MOVEMENT

166.　Boschot, Adolphe. "Berlioz et le romantisme." In *Le
romantisme et l'art*, 275-88. Paris. H. Laurens, 1928. iv, 319
p. N6847 R65 OCLC 1002559.

Provides useful information regarding political influences
working against Berlioz's career as well as his influence on
late-nineteenth-century Russian composers.

167.　Bouyer, Raymond. "Petites notes sans portée: note sur la
trinité romantique: Hugo, Delacroix, Berlioz." *Le ménestrel*
69 (July 12 1903): 219-20. OCLC 6966764.

Explains that although from a twentieth-century perspective
these artists seem to share a common aesthetic, the actual
relationship among the so-called "Romantic Trinity" might
better be described as one of "reciprocal misunderstandings."

168.　Evans, Raymond Leslie. "Berlioz, musicien du romantisme
français." In *Les romantiques français et la musique*, 108-22.
Paris: H. Champion, 1934. OCLC 918152. Reprint. Geneva:
Slatkine Reprints, 1976. xiii, 184 p. ML3849 E9 1976 OCLC
3012290.

Calls attention to the existence of a fraternity of Romantic
artists in Paris circa 1830, including Sand, Gautier, Hugo,
Balzac, Deschamps, and Barbier, who counted Berlioz as a
friend and fellow advocate of freedom in the arts.

169.　Fabbro, Beniamino dal. "Berlioz: figlio del secolo." In *I
bidelli dei Walhalla. Ottocento maggiore e minore e altri
saggi*, 69-75. Florence: Parenti, 1954. 171 p.

Examines Berlioz's career in relation to the musical
environment of nineteenth-century Europe. Concludes that his
success in Germany was due to the receptive attitude of
audiences there to serious art music in the new Romantic
style.

170.   Flat, Paul. "Le romantisme de Berlioz." *Le guide musical* 49
(November 29 1903 supplement): 3-4. OCLC 1509855.

Suggests that Berlioz, like Byron, was one of the few
Romantic artists whose work was a direct outgrowth of his
life, i.e., that his life and work were part of one interrelated
Romantic experience.

171.   Goehler, Georg. "Hector Berlioz." *Die Zukunft* 51 (April 1
1905): 433-39. OCLC 4572937.

Reviews Berlioz's career and shows that he was a product of
his own time--a composer who sought musical effects that
were bizarre and previously unheard. Describes him as a
sincere artist whose life and music alike rested on the
foundation of a Romantic spirit.

172.   Grunfeld, Frederic V. "The Discovery of the Mediterranean."
Horizon 16 (no. 1 1974): 96-103. ISSN 0018-4977 OCLC
1752266.

Explains how Romantic writers and musicians such as Goethe,
Byron, Berlioz, and Stendhal took artistic sustenance from
Italy and the overall Mediterranean atmosphere.

173.   Imbert, Hugues. "Berlioz, initiateur de la haute culture
musicale." *Le guide musical* 49 (November 29 1903
supplement): 8-20. OCLC 1509855.

Asserts that the origins of the French Romantic movement in
the arts can be traced to Berlioz, whose insistence on the value
of "beauty" over "mediocrity" was one of its key principles.
Examines this principle in Berlioz's writings.

174.   Locke, Arthur Ware. "Berlioz." In *Music and the Romantic
Movement in France,* 110-44. London: K. Paul, Trench,
Trubner & Co.; New York: E.P. Dutton, 1920. OCLC
1601301. Reprint. Freeport, N.Y.: Books for Libraries Press,
1972. viii, 184 p. ISBN 0-836-96859-X ML270.4 L63 1972
OCLC 297883.

Describes Berlioz's early years in Paris, depicting him as an active participant in a movement of Romantic excess that overtook the arts in early-nineteenth-century France and Germany. Attributes his lack of success in France to the superficiality of audiences who were interested only in easy, entertaining music and pretty sounds.

175. Newman, Ernest. "Berlioz, Romantic and Classic." In *Musical Studies*, 3-67. London and New York: John Lane, 1905. vii, 304 p. OCLC 3238687. Reprint. New York: Haskell House Publishers, 1969. viii, 319 p. ISBN 0-838-30309-9 ML60 N53 1969 OCLC 21550.

Examines the Romantic movement in France and Berlioz's relationship to it. Draws a physiological and psychological profile of Berlioz that portrays him as the only French musician who manifested the characteristics of a Romantic temperament. Counterbalances this depiction by insisting that Berlioz's unorthodox style did not result from a lack of early musical training, and that many of his works represent a Classical balance and restraint that belies the usual caricatures of him as a wild Romantic .

176. _____. "The Potency of Berlioz in Modern Music." In *The Century Library of Music*, edited by Ignacy Jan Paderewski. Vol. 1, 18-22. New York: The Century Co., 1900. 20 vols. M1 C3 OCLC 3979883.

Sketches the early Romantic movement in France and depicts Berlioz as a "true child of his epoch." Measures the significance of his achievement against the emptiness of the French musical tradition from which he grew.

177. _____. "The Work of Berlioz." *Contemporary Review* 79 (February 1901): 212-20. ISSN 0010-7565 OCLC 1564974.

Concisely defines French Romanticism and Berlioz's place in the formulation of its aesthetic. Relates his lack of success in France during his lifetime to the disparity between his new Romantic style and the Classical norms of his French predecessors. Reviews his limited musical background, early training, and "awkward" melodic style, describing him as a composer given to exaggeration of feeling and idea.

178. _____. "The Young Romantics." In *Berlioz, Romantic and Classic*, edited by Peter Heyworth, 69-72. London: Gollancz,

1972. 288 p. ISBN 0-575-01365-6 ML410 B5 N49 OCLC 516762.

Claims that Berlioz was more of a wild Romantic in his life and writings than in his music, where discipline is clearly evident.

179.   Pitrou, Robert. "Le romantisme de Berlioz." *Le correspondant* 322 (February 25 1931): 510-27. OCLC 5258641.

Describes the interdependent relationships of painting, literature, and music in early-nineteenth-century France. States that the Romantic movement in general, and Berlioz in particular, is characterized by exaggerated autobiography.

180.   Primmer, Brian. "Berlioz and a Romantic Image." *Berlioz Society Bulletin* no. 83 (April 1974): 4-13. OCLC 2386332.

Finds in Berlioz's music the continual expression of his passionate preoccupation with that typically Romantic principle--"the eternal feminine."

181.   _____. "Unity and Ensemble: Contrasting Ideals in Romantic Music." *19th-Century Music* 6 (no. 2 1982): 97-140. ISSN 0148-2076 OCLC 3280195.

Differentiates French and German Romanticism by analyzing their respective relationships to the Classical tradition, the relative importance of language to music, and the role of intellect versus intuition in forming national styles in art. Finds that the French concentration on melody is responsible for the importance of color, vagaries of harmony, and lack of development in its music. Illustrates these points with examples from Berlioz's music.

182.   Raynor, Henry B. "Berlioz and His Legend." *The Musical Times* 96 (August 1955): 414-17. ISSN 0027-4666 OCLC 5472115.

Suggests that Berlioz was not as much of a Romantic as his prose writings might lead us to believe. Concludes that his music is Romantic only in so far as it expresses reaction to specific literary stimuli.

183.   Schneider, Marcel. "Berlioz dans le mouvement romantique."
        In *Berlioz*, 69-85. Paris: Réalités-Hachette, 1973. 269 p.
        ML410 B5 B33 OCLC 1011818.

        Discusses the influence on Berlioz of Romantic writers such
        as Goethe, Hugo, Gautier, and Byron, and Berlioz's
        relationship to musicians such as Le Sueur, Cherubini,
        Mendelssohn, Liszt, Schumann, and Paganini.

184.   Schuré, Edouard. "Le génie de Berlioz." *Le guide musical* 49
        (November 29 1903 supplement): 1-3. OCLC 1509855.

        Calls Berlioz the incarnation in sound of the ideals of the
        Romantic movement. Suggests that he was a volcanic
        composer whose music has surprising moments of tranquility.
        Claims that he influenced the style of later French composers.

185.   Scudo, P. "De l'influence du mouvement romantique sur l'art
        musical et du rôle q'a voulu jouer M. H. Berlioz." In *Critique
        et littérature musicales*. Vol. 1, 21-74. Paris: L. Hachette,
        1856. 2 vols. OCLC 2011024. Reprint. Geneva: Minkoff,
        1986. 2 vols in 1. ISBN 2-826-60689-1 ML60 S43 1986
        OCLC 18201448.

        Gives a brief history of the evolution of instrumental music
        followed by a discussion of the roots of French Romanticism
        in eighteenth-century literature. Suggests that Berlioz wished
        to "paint the nervous agitation" of the Romantic age, but that
        as a composer his ambitions outstripped his abilities and that
        he mistook disorder and bizarre exaggeration for Romantic
        liberty.

186.   Shilstone, Frederick W. "Berlioz' 'One Work': an
        Interdisciplinary Approach to Romanticism." In *Images and
        Innovations, Update '70's*, 85-97. Spartansburg, S.C.: Center
        for the Humanities, Converse College, 1979. 175 p. AZ221
        S69 1979 OCLC 6014936.

        Finds in the works of Berlioz, Goethe, Byron, and Delacroix a
        common Romantic desire to create comprehensive,
        organically unified works that dramatically reflect the
        conflicting thoughts and moods of modern man. Views
        Berlioz's most characteristic work in this respect as *La
        damnation de Faust*.

187.   Tiersot, Julien. "Music and the Centenary of Romanticism."
        Translated by Frederick H. Martens. *The Musical Quarterly*
        15 (no. 2 1929): 268-80. ISSN 0027-4631 OCLC 1642493.

        Discusses Berlioz's life and musical style as manifestations of
        Romanticism in nineteenth-century France. Compares the
        Symphonie fantastique with Beethoven's symphonies and calls
        Berlioz his only logical successor.

188.   _____. "Le romantisme musical de 1830 (Hector Berlioz)."
        In *La musique aux temps romantiques*, 68-106. Paris: F.
        Alcan, 1930. OCLC 2901557. Reprint. Paris: Presses
        universitaires de France, Editions d'Aujourd'hui, 1983. 186 p.
        ISBN 2-730-70211-3 ML196 T4 1983 OCLC 12430578.

        Traces Berlioz's musical career from his childhood to 1830.
        Emphasizes his relationship to Romantic trends and writers
        such as Hugo. Extensively discusses the *Symphonie
        fantastique* as musical autobiography.

IV. Research Materials

This chapter includes catalogs, works lists, indexes, guides to manuscript and printed sources, and bibliographies of both primary and secondary source materials relating to Berlioz research.

189. Ahouse, John B. *Berlioz: the Centenary Years; a Bibliography of Articles in the Periodical Literature, 1967-1971.* El Paso: University of Texas Library, 1974. 25 p. ML134 B515 A43 OCLC 5926547.

Lists articles, books, book reviews, scores, and performance reviews. Provides one-line annotations of most items.

190. Barzun, Jacques. "The Latest Berlioz Finds." *Columbia Library Columns* 17 (no. 3 1968): 8-12. ISSN 0010-1966 OCLC 1564233.

Mentions some of the materials acquired for the Columbia University Library Berlioz collection since the publication of Barzun's biography (#210). These include the manuscript of a nocturne for two sopranos and guitar, a composition book for *La captive* (later found to be a forgery-see Holoman, #196), the manuscript of a rejected second prologue for *Roméo et Juliette*, letters, and libretto sketches for *Les Troyens*.

191. Bibliothèques de la Ville de Paris. *Hector Berlioz; [bibliographie].* Edited by Germaine Frigot and Brigitte Le Courbe. Paris: Bibliothèques de la Ville de Paris, 1979. 28 p. ML134 B5 B5 OCLC 5940101.

A short bibliography which includes a biographical timeline, a list of Berlioz's major prose works, a short annotated list of important books and periodicals devoted to Berlioz, and a discography.

192.   Bloom, Peter. "Academic Music: the Archives of the *Academie des Beaux-Arts.*" *19th-Century Music* 7 (no. 2 1983): 130-35. ISSN 0148-2076 OCLC 3280195.

Presents a historical sketch of the *Académie des Beaux-Arts* along with a summary of the types of primary source materials (letters, minutes, and reports) that can be found in its Archives.

193.   Espiau de la Maëstre, André. *Catalogue des manuscrits et documents berlioziens conservés dans les bibliothèques et archives publiques et privées de Vienne.* Vienna: Collections de l'Institut Français de Vienne, 1967. 16 p.*

194.   Holoman, D. Kern. *Catalogue of the Works of Hector Berlioz.* Hector Berlioz. New Edition of the Complete Works. Vol. 25. Kassel: Bärenreiter, 1987. xlv, 527 p. ISBN 3-761-80449-0 ML134 B515 H754 1987 OCLC 17335125.

The definitive scholarly catalogue of Berlioz's works, including those planned but never composed, fragmentary scores, and sketches. Entries are chronological and provide the following information: title, incipit, performance forces, editions, date of composition, autograph or other sources, performances during Berlioz's lifetime, authors of vocal texts, self-borrowings, and a bibliography. Catalogue also contains a list of Berlioz's prose works, including all known feuilletons.

195.   _____. "Orchestral Material from the Library of the *Société des Concerts* (includes inventory of Berlioz' gift to the *Société des Concerts*)." *19th-Century Music* 7 (no. 2 1983): 106-18. ISSN 0148-2076 OCLC 3280195.

Traces the complex history of Berlioz's gift of orchestral performing parts to the *Société des Concerts* and supplies an inventory with indications of their present locations.

196.   _____. "The Present State of Berlioz Research." *Acta musicologica* 47 (no. 1 1975): 31-67. ISSN 0001-6241 OCLC 1460933.

Provides an overview of primary source materials (prose works, correspondence, printed scores, complete editions, manuscript collections, and other documents), research relating to these materials to 1975 (bibliographies, catalogs, sketch and compositional process studies, and biographies), important style analytical studies, and recent recordings and performances.

197. Hopkinson, Cecil. *A Bibliography of the Musical and Literary Works of Hector Berlioz, 1803-1869, with Histories of the French Music Publishers Concerned.* Edinburgh: Edinburgh Bibliographical Society, 1951. OCLC 936871. 2nd ed. Tunbridge Wells: R. Macnutt, 1980. xix, 230 p. ISBN 0-907-18000-0 ML134 B5 H6 1980 OCLC 6860567.

A valuable source for the publication history of Berlioz's works. Contains a section devoted to French publishers who dealt with Berlioz, a list of manuscripts and their present locations, and, in the second edition, an index to the New Berlioz Edition.

198. Macdonald, Hugh. "The Labitte Catalogue: Some Unexplored Evidence." *Berlioz Society Bulletin* no. 69 (October 1970): 5-7; and "The Labitte Catalogue: More Evidence." *Berlioz Society Bulletin* no. 70 (January 1971): 7-8. OCLC 2386332.

Discusses the compositions listed in Berlioz's "Labitte catalog," including those which have never been located. Dates the catalog to 1847. Also uses information in the catalog to date the original ideas for the *Te Deum* and the *Marche funèbre pour la dernière scène d'Hamlet (Tristia)* to before Berlioz's 1847 trip to London. See also #205.

199. Malliot, Antoine Louis. *La musique au théâtre.* Paris: Amyot, 1863. viii, 432 p. ML1727 M15 OCLC 3702931.

Provides a complete history of the major lyric theaters in Paris from their earliest years to 1863, including *L'Opéra, L'Opéra-comique, L'Odéon, Théâtre des Nouveautés, La Renaissance,* and *Les Bouffes-Parisiens.* Includes repertoire lists.

200. Müller-Reuter, Theodor. "Hector Berlioz." In *Lexikon der deutschen Konzertliteratur,* 260-264. Leipzig: C.F. Kahnt Nachfolger, 1909. viii, 238 p. OCLC 5461932. Reprint. New York: Da Capo Press, 1972. xxii, 625 p. ISBN 0-306-70274-6 ML120 G3 M9 1972 OCLC 303551.

Lists first performances of Berlioz's works in Germany, including date, city, theater, soloists, and director. Also provides a historical background of each piece and reproduces full literary programs where appropriate, as well as listing eighteen of Berlioz's most popular orchestral and choral works.

201. Music Library Association. *An Alphabetical Index to Hector Berlioz Werke, hrsg. von Charles Malherbe and Felix Weingartner, Leipzig und Wien, Breitkopf und Härtel, 1900-1907.* Edited by the Bibliography Committee of the New York Chapter, MLA. New York: Music Library Association, 1964. 6 p. ML134 B5 M9 OCLC 3094158.

Index by volume and page number to all of Berlioz's compositions published in the Old Berlioz Edition.

202. Prod'homme, J.-G. "Bibliographie berliozienne." *Sammelbände der Internationalen Musik-Gesellschaft* 5 (no. 4 1904): 622-59. OCLC 1772498. Expanded in in *La revue musicale* no. 233 (1956): 97-147. OCLC 1764223.

A partial list of Berlioz's feuilletons arranged by journal. While extensive, this list includes only thirteen of the approximately forty journals in which articles by Berlioz appeared. Omitted are all seven of the foreign journals and most of the French journals to which he contributed irregularly. This bibliography is superceded by the more complete list in Holoman's thematic catalog (#194).

203. Tiersot, Julien. "Berlioziana: oeuvres diverses publiées du vivant de Berlioz." *Le ménestrel* 71 (October 15 1905): 331-32. OCLC 6966764.

Reproduces the works list from Opus 1 through Opus 25 which appeared on the cover of the *Tristia* score in 1852.

204. Vaillant, P. "Berlioz à la bibliothèque de Grenoble." *Cahiers de l'alpe* no. 46 (1969): 133-36. OCLC 12101098.

A catalog of the Grenoble Library autograph document collection, including manuscript scores (of which only *L'imperiale* is complete), printed scores with autograph annotations, letters, and other documents (e.g., the autograph libretto of *Les Troyens*).

205. Werth, Kent W. "Dating the 'Labitte Catalogue' of Berlioz's Works." *19th-Century Music* 1 (no. 2 1977): 137-41. ISSN 0148-2076 OCLC 3280195.

Firmly establishes the catalog's date as 1846 and discusses the significance of that fact for the chronology of Berlioz's works, especially the *Marche funèbre pour la dernière scène d'Hamlet* (*Tristia*) and the *Te Deum*. A reproduction of the three-page catalog is included. (See also #198.)

206.   Wotton, Tom S. "The Scores of Berlioz and Some Modern Editing." *The Musical Times* 56 (November 1 1915): 649-56. ISSN 0027-4666 OCLC 5472115.

Denounces the Weingartner-Malherbe edition of Berlioz's complete works (the Old Berlioz Edition) for its numerous "alterations and mutilations" of Berlioz's manuscripts, including changes of instruments and voices, transpositions of parts, and mistakes with mutes and metronome marks.

207.   Wright, Michael G.H. "A Bibliography of Critical Writings on Hector Berlioz." Thesis submitted for fellowship of the Library Association, 1967. Revised as *A Berlioz Bibliography: Critical Writing on Hector Berlioz from 1825 to 1986.* Farnborough: Saint Michael's Abbey Press, 1988. xi, 408 p. ISBN 0-909-07734-X ML134 B5 OCLC 17510408.

A chronological listing of major books and articles (mainly in English, French, and German) containing reviews of and critical writings on Berlioz. Divides the history of Berlioz criticism into five periods, and prefaces each section with an essay summarizing attitudes about the composer during that period.

V. Berlioz the Man and Musician

This chapter includes book-length biographies of a general nature, shorter biographical sketches, and articles about more specialized biographical topics. The works listed in the "general studies" section represent only a small percentage of the total number of biographies of Berlioz. Our selection has been based on a desire to include a variety of languages, dates of publication, and levels of scholarly sophistication and comprehensiveness. Within these guidelines, however, the following list admittedly represents our subjective opinions concerning which biographies will be the most useful to a wide range of readers.

1. GENERAL STUDIES

208.   Ballif, Claude. *Berlioz*. Paris: Editions du Seuil, 1968. 192 p. ML410 B5 B14 OCLC 3820173.

Seeks to explain why Berlioz is often considered today as a musical "precursor." Contains some musical analysis but is generally non-technical in approach and language. Includes bibliography (188) and discography (184-87).

209.   Barraud, Henry. *Hector Berlioz*. Paris: Costard, 1955. 286 p. OCLC 5426199. Paris: Fayard, 1979. 506 p. ML410 B5 B17 1979 OCLC 6356723.

Attempts to de-Romanticize Berlioz. Presents him as a hypersensitive artist who reacted strongly to all kinds of external stimuli. Begins with biographical matters and follows

by discussing Berlioz's major works in a non-technical
manner. Contains no bibliography or musical examples.

210.   Barzun, Jacques. *Berlioz and the Romantic Century.* Boston:
         Little, Brown, 1950. 3rd ed. New York: Columbia University
         Press, 1969. 2 vols. SBN 231-03135-1 ML410 B5 B2 1969
         OCLC 50561. Revised and abridged as *Berlioz and His
         Century.* Cleveland: World Publishing Co., 1956. Chicago:
         University of Chicago Press, 1982. 448 p. ISBN 0-226-03861-
         0 ML410 B5 B2 1982 OCLC 7924957.

         Reviews:
         Dean, Winton. "Barzun's Life of Berlioz." *Music and Letters*
         33 (no. 2 1952): 119-31. ISSN 0027 4224 OCLC 1758884.

         Newman, Ernest. "Barzun's *Berlioz and the Romantic
         Century.*" In *Berlioz, Romantic and Classic*, 255-63. London:
         Gollancz, 1972. 288 p. ISBN 0-575-01365-6 ML410 B5 N49
         OCLC 516762

         The first serious biography in English and still one of most
         important studies of Berlioz. Goes beyond simple biography
         to survey the cultural history of the nineteenth century.
         Includes an especially detailed bibliography (missing in
         abridged version) that is unfortunately marred by numerous
         citation errors. Section on the *Symphonie fantastique*
         excerpted as "The Mind of the Young Berlioz" in *The Musical
         Quarterly* 35 (no. 4 1949): 551-64. ISSN 0027-4631 OCLC
         1642493.

211.   _____. "Truth in Biography: Berlioz." *The University
         Review* 5 (no. 4 1939): 275-80. ISSN 0042-0379 OCLC
         4911912. Reprinted in *Biography as an Art*, edited by James
         L. Clifford, 155-61. London and New York: Oxford
         University Press, 1962. xx, 256 p. CT21 C5 1962a OCLC
         316158.

         Deals with the problems of interpreting and untangling
         conflicting biographical evidence to create an accurate picture
         of Berlioz's life and work.

212.   Boschot, Adolphe. *L'histoire d'un romantique: Hector
         Berlioz.* 3 vols.

         Vol. 1: *La jeunesse d'un romantique: Hector Berlioz, 1803-
         1831, d'après de nombreux documents inédits.* Paris: Plon-

Nourrit, 1906. OCLC 2823742. Rev. ed. Paris: Plon, 1946.
316 p. ML410 B5 B737 1946 OCLC 4631502.

Vol. 2: *Un romantique sous Louis-Philippe: Hector Berlioz,
1831-1842, d'après de nombreux documents inédits.* Paris:
Plon-Nourrit, 1906. Rev. ed. Paris: Plon-Nourrit, 1948. 382 p.
ML410 B515 B7 1948 OCLC 497286.

Vol. 3: *Le crepuscule d'un romantique: Hector Berlioz, 1842-
1869, d'après de nombreux documents inédits.* Paris: Plon-
Nourrit, 1906. Rev. ed. Paris: Plon, 1950. 451 p. ML410 B5
B74 1950 OCLC 3386999.

Abridged as *Hector Berlioz, une vie romantique.* Paris: Plon-
Nourrit, 1919. Edition définitive, Paris: Plon, 1951. OCLC
4631468. Reprint. Geneva: Minkoff, 1975. 354 p. ISBN 2-
826-60599-2 ML410 B5 B75 1975 OCLC 1657549.
Extracted in *Cahiers de l'alpe* no. 46 (1969): 119-21. OCLC
12101098.

A monumental biography, long the standard "definitive" work
in French. Flawed, however, by factual contradictions and an
excessively critical stance that borders on carping and causes
the reader to distrust the author's sympathies and sincerity.
For review see Barzun, Supplement 2, 312-20 (#210).

213.   Clarson-Leach, Robert. *Berlioz: His Life and Times.*
        Tunbridge Wells: Midas Books; New York: Hippocrene
        Books, 1983. 124 p. ISBN 0-882-54666-X ML410 B5 C527
        1983 OCLC 10438615.

        A short, non-technical, and copiously illustrated biography
        that is part of a series on the great composers.

214.   Constantin, Léon. *Berlioz.* Paris: Emile-Paul frères, 1934. vii,
        328 p. ML410 B5 C6 OCLC 5346853.

        A good general biography but with little stylistic discussion of
        individual works. No bibliography or index.

215.   Crabbe, John. *Hector Berlioz: Rational Romantic.* London:
        Kahn and Averill; New York: Taplinger, 1980. 143 p.
        bibliography, 133-36. ISBN 0-800-80718-9 ML410 B5 C74
        1980b OCLC 6737190.

        Attempts to establish "the spiritual and intellectual
        framework" within which Berlioz worked and to measure the

social, political, religious, and literary influences at work in his music.

216.   Daniskas, John. *Hector Berlioz.* Amsterdam: H.J.W. Becht, 1948. Translated by W.A.G. Doyle-Davidson. Stockholm: Continental Book Co., 1949. 63 p. ML410 B5 D32 OCLC 3319047.

One of the best short biographies. Limited in scope but generally accurate in facts. Contains many photographs, facsimiles, and musical examples.

217.   Degeorge, Léon. *Hector Berlioz, sa vie et ses oeuvres, "La damnation de Faust," 14 avril 1879 (première exécution complète en Belgique).* Brussels: F. Callewaert père, 1879. 92 p.

Draws on the *Mémoires* and correspondence, as well as contemporary articles and reviews to sketch Berlioz's life and career. Chapter 15 (67-79) describes *La damnation de Faust* and its failure in Paris in 1846.

218.   Dömling, Wolfgang. *Hector Berlioz in Selbstzeugnissen und Bilddokumenten.* Reinbek bei Hamburg: Rowohlt, 1977. 158 p. ISBN 3-499-50254-2 ML410 B5 D6 OCLC 3539187.

A short biography which draws heavily on Berlioz's letters, the *Mémoires*, and other writings. Especially valuable because it includes copious illustrations of people, places, and events in Berlioz's life, as well as facsimiles of letters and scores. Brief bibliography (151-52).

219.   Elliot, J.H. *Berlioz.* London: J.M. Dent; New York, E.P. Dutton, 1938. OCLC 398412. Rev. ed. London: J.M. Dent; New York: Farrar, Straus & Giroux, 1967. xi, 243 p. bibliography, 235-36. ML410 B5 E37 1967 OCLC 4674509.

Review: Mellers, W.H. *Scrutiny* 7 (no. 1 1938): 119-28. OCLC 1765311.

An uneven and occasionally unsympathetic biography with many factual errors. Contains a chapter sketching the historical-political background of France at the beginning of the nineteenth century. Includes a dictionary of important people in Berlioz's life.

220. Hippeau, Edmond. *Berlioz intime*. Paris: La Renaissance
     musicale, 1883. OCLC 12094271. 2nd ed. Paris: E. Dentu,
     1889. vii, 410 p. ML410 B515 H667 1889 OCLC 4903235.
     and *Berlioz et son temps*. Paris: P. Ollendorf, 1890. v, 403 p.
     ML410 B5 H4 OCLC 8915114.

     One of the first biographies to sort fact from fiction in the
     Mémoires. First volume attempts to present a psychological
     study of Berlioz the man. Arranged topically rather than
     chronologically, including discussions of Berlioz's birthplace,
     his family, his character, and his studies. Aims at discovering
     the man behind the composer. Second volume presents a
     critical evaluation of Berlioz the musician. Explores his early
     musical education, finding it weak in basic technical training.
     Analyzes the innovative aspects of his style, and observes that
     he never formulated a compositional system or theory.
     Contains no musical examples and no analyses of individual
     works.

221. Jullien, Adolphe. *Hector Berlioz: la vie, le combat, les
     oeuvres*. Paris: Charavay, 1882. 198 p. ML410 B5 J95 OCLC
     10710108.

     Contains a biographical sketch (revised as "Hector Berlioz."
     Rivista musicale italiana 1 [1894]: 454-82. OCLC 1773309),
     followed by a collection of semi-autonomous chapters
     designed primarily to give an overview of Berlioz's aesthetics
     and a sense of the critical reaction to his ideas and music
     throughout his life and shortly thereafter.

222. _____. *Hector Berlioz: sa vie et ses oeuvres*. Paris: Librairie
     de l'Art, 1888. xvi, 386 p. ML410 B5 J9 OCLC 346705.
     Extracted as "Hector Berlioz; son second voyage à Saint-
     Petersbourg en 1867." *Revue d'art dramatique* tome 12
     (October-December 1888): 159-65. OCLC 5853914.

     Review: Gonse, Louis. *Gazette des beaux-arts* 2nd period,
     tome 38 (1888): 501-6. ISSN 0016-5530 OCLC 1570479.

     The earliest serious biography of Berlioz, based on primary
     sources, including letters and feuilletons, and recollections of
     contemporaries. Appendix contains a list of Berlioz's works
     appearing on Parisian concert series during his lifetime and
     shortly thereafter.

223.   Kapp, Julius. *Berlioz: eine Biographie*. Berlin: Schuster &
        Loeffler, 1917. OCLC 3386515. 7th ed. Berlin: Schuster &
        Loeffler, 1922. 225 p. ML410 B515 K3 OCLC 7983049.

        First edition contains the most comprehensive bibliography of
        Berlioz's feuilletons before the publication of the Holoman
        catalog (#194). Works list, 217-23. Seventh edition does not
        have bibliography or feuilletons list.

224.   Khokhlovkina, A.A. *Berlioz*. Moscow: Gos. muzykal'noe
        izdvo, 1960. 545 p. bibliography, 543-46. ML410 B6 K4 1960
        OCLC 9539630.

        Divides Berlioz's creative life into three periods and discusses
        one pivotal work from each (the *Symphonie fantastique*, *La
        damnation de Faust*, and *L'enfance du Christ*). Includes lists
        of the programs Berlioz presented during his 1867-68 Russian
        tour.

225.   Kroó, György. *Hector Berlioz*. Budapest: Gondolat, 1960.
        2nd ed. published as *Berlioz*. Budapest: Gondolat, 1980. 396
        p. ISBN 9-632-80852-5 ML410 B5 K72 1980 OCLC
        8430056.*

226.   Louis, Rudolf. *Hector Berlioz*. Leipzig: Breitkopf & Härtel,
        1904. 207 p. ML410 B5 L88 OCLC 399175.

        A study of Berlioz arranged topically rather than
        chronologically. Concentrates on establishing the musical and
        intellectual milieu of Paris circa 1830 (Romanticism) and
        measures the strength of Classical influences on Berlioz's life
        and works.

227.   Macdonald, Hugh. *Berlioz*. Master Musicians Series.
        London: J.M. Dent, 1982. 261 p. bibliography, 248-51. ISBN
        0-460-03156-2 ML410 B5 M13 1982 OCLC 9007640.

        One of the most important biographical studies in English to
        appear since Barzun's work (#210). Part I discusses Berlioz's
        life and character. Part II analyzes his works. Included are a
        detailed works list and a dictionary of important people in
        Berlioz's life. The scope of the book is necessarily limited by
        the nature of the series of which it is a part. Nevertheless,
        important new scholarship appears here for the first time in
        book form.

228.   Mathieu de Monter, Emile. "Hector Berlioz." *Revue et
       gazette musicale de Paris* 36 (June 13 1869): 193-95; (June
       20): 201-3; (June 27): 209-11; (July 11): 226-28; (July 18):
       234-36; (August 1): 250-52; (August 8): 258-61; (August 15):
       265-67; (August 22): 273-75; (September 12): 297-300;
       (September 19): 307-9; (October 10): 330-32; (October 17):
       337-38; (October 24): 345-46; (October 31): 353-55;
       (November 7): 361-63; (November 14): 369-70; (November
       21): 378-80; (December 5): 393-95; (December 12): 404-5;
       (December 26): 420-21; 37 (January 16 1870): 17-18;
       (January 23): 25-27; (February 13): 49-50; (February 20): 57-
       59; (March 20): 89-91; (April 10): 113-15; (May 1): 137-38;
       (May 15): 153-54; (June 19): 193-95; (June 26): 201-3; (July
       3): 209-11. OCLC 10231154.

       One of the earliest biographies of Berlioz, apparently based on
       the *Mémoires* and written shortly after the composer's death.
       Contends that Berlioz was a man of great artistic courage but
       also the architect of his own destruction. Includes a useful
       section on the composer's prose writings (February 13-May
       15, 1870).

229.   Mirecourt, Eugène de [C.J.B. Jacquot]. *Berlioz.* Paris:
       Gustave Havard, 1856. Reprint. Paris: La Flûte de Pan, 1979.
       96 p. ML410 B51 M674 OCLC 8549709.

       Short, anecdotal biography written during the composer's
       lifetime. Author strongly defends Berlioz against a hostile
       public.

230.   Pohl, Louise. *Hector Berlioz' Leben und Werke.* Leipzig:
       Leuckart, 1900. vii, 282 p. ML410 B51 P74 OCLC
       12569647.

       Review: Viotta, Henri. "Muzikaal overzicht. Louise Pohl,
       Hector Berlioz' Leben und Werke." *De Gids: nieuwe
       vaderlandsche letteroefeningen* 64 (1900): 563-80. ISSN
       0016-0730 OCLC 1751214.

       Assembled by the author from research materials left after the
       death of her father, Richard. Finds that Berlioz's significance
       consists of a three-fold contribution to music: the development
       of instrumental music based on the "poetic idea," the
       extension of musical forms, and the exploration of new
       technical resources.

231.   Pourtalès, Guy de. *Berlioz et l'Europe romantique*. Paris:
        Gallimard, 1939. OCLC 15267776. Paris, Gallimard, 1979.
        348 p. ML410 B5 P87 1979 OCLC 8047380.

        Excerpted in *Revue des deux mondes* series 8, tome 49
        (January 1 1939): 100-142; (January 15): 284-319; (February
        1): 514-10; (February 15): 831-66. OCLC 8305048.

        A non-scholarly work that divides Berlioz's life into topics
        including French politics of the early-nineteenth century, the
        impact of Beethoven, Berlioz's major compositions, his
        foreign travels, his relationship to Wagner, and his
        reacquaintance with Estelle Fornier. Contains no bibliography
        or musical examples.

232.   Prod'homme, J.-G. *Hector Berlioz (1803-1869): sa vie et ses
        oeuvres*. Paris: Delagrave, 1905. viii, 495 p. OCLC 9165047.
        3rd ed. Paris: Delagrave, 1927. viii, 327 p. OCLC 9130665.

        A useful and detailed biography in which many new primary
        source materials were first presented. Especially valuable is
        the bibliography of nineteenth-century books and articles
        (475-84), as well as the list of pictorial works (484-89).

233.   Tiersot, Julien. *Hector Berlioz et la société de son temps*.
        Paris: Hachette, 1904. iii, 371 p. ML410 B53 T3 OCLC
        2350170.

        Organizes the facts of Berlioz's life into selected topics in
        order to ascertain his personality and his relationship to the
        political, sociological, and artistic environments in which he
        worked. Includes sections devoted to the women in Berlioz's
        life and the Wagner-Liszt-Berlioz circle.

234.   Turner, W.J. *Berlioz, the Man and His Work*. London and
        Toronto: J.M. Dent, 1934. OCLC 8995380. Reprint. New
        York: Vienna House, 1974. viii, 374 p. ISBN 0-844-30096-9
        ML410 B5 T8 1974 OCLC 867376.

        One of the best English-language biographies before the
        appearance of Barzun's work (#210). Appendices include a
        short essay on Berlioz as critic and a chronological list of his
        major works (356-64). Discussion of Berlioz's music is non-
        technical and without musical examples. Intended for a
        general audience. Brief bibliography (viii).

2. SKETCHES AND REMINISCENCES

235.   Anon. [L.E.] "Berlioz." *Temple Bar* 69 (October 1883): 204-25. OCLC 1640150.

An amusing combination of biography (drawn from the *Mémoires*), personal reminiscences, and miscellaneous musings.

236.   Apthorp, William F. [Biographical Sketch]. In *Hector Berlioz: Selections from His Letters, and Aesthetic, Humorous, and Satirical Writings*, 3-77. New York: Holt, 1879. ix, 427 p. ML410 B5 A2 OCLC 747685.

Quotes the *Mémoires* to present Berlioz's character and the major events of his life.

237.   Barbier, Auguste. "Berlioz." In *Souvenirs personnels et silhouettes contemporaines*, 230-33. Paris: E. Dentu, 1883. 378 p. PQ2189 B33 Z52 1883 OCLC 2356325.

Relates that Berlioz was thinking of setting *Roméo et Juliette* to music as early as 1832 when he was working in Italy. Also hints that he may have played the piano better than is usually thought.

238.   Barzun, Jacques. "A Biographical Sketch of the Artist as Musician." In *Critical Questions...*, edited by Bea Friedland, 132-35. Chicago: University of Chicago Press, 1982. xvii, 269 p. ISBN 0-226-03863-7 ML60 B278 1982 OCLC 8032099.

Presents a short overview of Berlioz's life and works, both of which the author says suffered from organized opposition to his unorthodoxy.

239.   Beaunier, André. "Vie d'un romantique: Berlioz." *Revue des deux mondes* series 6, tome 56 (April 1 1920): 687-98. OCLC 8305048.

Suggests that Berlioz was attracted to the poetry of Shakespeare and Virgil to such an extent that he actually began to live out the lives of his literary heroes. One of the most interesting biographical sketches.

240.   Bernard, Daniel. "Notice sur Berlioz." In *Correspondance
         inédite*, 1-61. 2nd ed. Paris: Calmann-Lévy, 1879. 361 p.
         ML410 B5 A1 1879 OCLC 10758286. Translated by H.
         Mainwaring Dunstan as "The Life of Berlioz." In *The Life and
         Letters of Berlioz*. Vol. 1, 1-74. London: Remington & Co.,
         1882. ML410 B5 A45 OCLC 861496.

         A detailed personal account of Berlioz's life which attempts to
         correct and fill in omissions in the *Mémoires* with information
         drawn from contemporary journal articles on Berlioz. Suffers
         from instances of confused facts.

241.   Bondeville, Emmanuel. *Au seuil de l'année Berlioz...* Paris:
         l'Institut, 1968. 16 p. ML410 B5 B65 OCLC 4836546.

         Highlights important aspects of Berlioz's life and career,
         including his work as an opera composer, his music criticism,
         his revolutionary compositional style, and his relationship to
         audiences in France and abroad. An excellent study.

242.   _____. "Berlioz vivant." In Académie des beaux-arts.
         *Hommage national à Hector Berlioz; séance publique du 14
         mai 1969*, 9-18. Paris: Typ de Firmin-Didot, 1969. 21 p.
         ML410 B5 A62 OCLC 12662582.

         A short sketch of Berlioz's life and struggles which concludes
         that the goal of his career was to develop a recognition of the
         beautiful in art.

243.   Boschot, Adolphe. "Berlioz." In *Chez les musiciens*, 70-79.
         Paris: Plon-Nourrit, 1922. 285 p. ML60 B783 OCLC
         4178284.

         Analyzes Berlioz's personality and its relationship to his
         work. Discusses the circumstances surrounding the
         composition and production of *Les Troyens* to demonstrate the
         kinds of problems that typically beset him throughout his
         career.

244.   Castil-Blaze [François Henri Joseph Blaze]. "Caractères et
         portraits du temps--Hector Berlioz." *Revue des deux mondes*
         2nd period, tome 80 (April 15 1869): 1006-22. OCLC
         8305048.

         An obituary that assesses Berlioz's character without drawing
         any conclusive estimates of his work. Admits that he was an

uneven composer who suffered during his lifetime for his
devotion to high musical ideals.

245.   Chantavoine, Jean. "Berlioz." In *De Couperin à Debussy*, 96-
        120. Paris: F. Alcan, 1921. 179 p. ML390 C44 1921 OCLC
        3674325.

        Claims that Berlioz was the author of his own mostly
        Romanticized legend of persecution, but that he was actually a
        composer of considerable success.

246.   Clément, Félix. "Berlioz." In *Les musiciens célèbres depuis le
        seizième siècle jusqu'à nos jours*, 489-98. Paris: L. Hachette,
        1868. OCLC 2536198. 4th ed. Paris, Hachette, 1887. 672 p.
        ML390 C62 1887 OCLC 6973924.

        A short biographical sketch by one who had limited sympathy
        for the Romantic aesthetic. Admires only those aspects of
        Berlioz's work which he finds Classical in style, such as some
        sections of *Les Troyens*.

247.   Combarieu, Jules. "Hector Berlioz--Felicien David." In
        Histoire de la musique. Vol. 3, 63-111. Paris: A. Colin, 1919.
        3 vols. ML160 C72 OCLC 1986910.

        Draws attention to Berlioz's significance as the quintessential
        Romantic artist and as the forefather of the symphonic poem.
        Also explains Le Sueur's influence on Berlioz's conception of
        "imitative" music, and Berlioz's importance as an author and
        critic. One of the best single-chapter surveys of Berlioz
        available.

248.   Diehl, Alice Mangold. Chapter 3 of *Musical Memories*, 54-
        73. London: R. Bentley and Son, 1897. xii, 319 p. ML385
        D55 OCLC 2456450. Excerpted as "A Visit to Berlioz" in
        The Musician 14 (September 1909): 417-19. OCLC 6135261.
        Excerpted as "Berlioz at Home" in *Berlioz Society Bulletin* no.
        66 (January 1970): 14-17. OCLC 2386332.

        Presents a first-hand account of the author's visit to the elderly
        Berlioz, who, contrary to contemporary opinion, proved to be
        most cordial and professionally encouraging to her.

249.   Etex, Antoine. *Les souvenirs d'un artiste*, 120-21. Paris: E.
        Dentu, 1877. 313 p. ND553 E8 E8 OCLC 11354355.

Describes an episode in 1831 in which the author roamed the
Italian countryside with Berlioz in search of and meeting
brigands.

250. Fétis, François-Joseph. "Hector Berlioz." In *Biographie
universelle des musiciens et bibliographie générale de la
musique*. Vol. 2, 150-52. Brussels: Leroux, 1837. 8 vols.
OCLC 15516027. 2nd ed. Vol. 1, 362-65. Paris: Firmin-
Didot, 1860. 8 vols. ML105 F422 OCLC 1440218. Reprint.
Brussels: Culture et Civilisation, 1972. 8 vols. ML105 F42
1972 OCLC 3108252.

Fétis completely rewrote his biographical and critical note on
Berlioz for the second edition of his dictionary. The later entry
expresses a renewed admiration for and more objective
evaluation of the composer's music quite different from the
vituperative hostility expressed in the first edition.

251. Gautier, Théophile. "Hector Berlioz." In *Histoire du
romantisme*, 259-70. 2nd ed. Paris: Charpentier et Cie., 1874.
vi, 410 p. PQ287 G3 1874 OCLC 356275. Reprinted as "Mort
d'Hector Berlioz." In *La musique*. 166-78. Paris: Fasquelle,
1911. 310 p. PN2636 P2 G28m OCLC 10736748. Translated
by F.C. de Sumichrast as "Hector Berlioz." In *The Works of
Théophile Gautier*, Vol. 16: *A History of Romanticism*, 207-
21. New York and Chicago: E.R. Dumont, 1902. 360 p.
PQ2258 A26 (16) OCLC 9259515.

A biographical sketch of the composer written as an obituary.
Summarizes his career as a constant struggle against
mediocrity, asserting that his refusal to pander to popular
opinion was characteristic of the Romantic movement.
Originally appeared in *Journal officiel*, March 16, 1869.

252. Gavoty, Bernard. "Ma vie est un roman qui m'intéresse
beaucoup." In *Berlioz*, 7-23. Paris: Réalités-Hachette, 1973.
269 p. ML410 B5 B33 OCLC 1011818.

Based primarily on Henry Barraud's work, this sketch
emphasizes Berlioz's quintessentially Romantic spirit, fiery
and iconoclastic.

253. Glinka, Mikhail Ivanovich. *Memoirs*, 191-93. Translated by
Richard B. Mudge. Norman: University of Oklahoma Press,
1963. OCLC 602218. Reprint. Westport, Conn.: Greenwood
Press, 1980. xi, 264 p. ISBN 0-313-22331-9 ML410 G46 A25
1980 OCLC 594212.

Reports on Berlioz's help in getting Glinka's music performed in Paris.

254.   Goldbeck, Fred. "Berlioz." In *Encyclopédie de la musique.* Vol. 1, 398-403. Paris: Fasquelle, 1958. 3 vols. ML100 E48 OCLC 860571.

A useful short sketch that makes a point of relating Berlioz's self-sufficient melodies to his early training as a flutist.

255.   Gounod, Charles. Preface to *Lettres intimes*, i-ix. 2nd ed. Paris: Calmann-Lévy, 1882. xv, 319 p. ML410 B5 A1 1882 OCLC 2941795. Translated by H. Mainwaring Dunstan in *The Life and Letters of Berlioz.* Vol. 2, 1-13. London: Remington & Co., 1882. 2 vols. ML410 B5 A45 OCLC 861496. Reprinted in *Mémoires d'un artiste*, 329-42. Paris, Calmann-Lévy, 1896. 361 p. ML410 G71 OCLC 12749092. Translated by W. Hely Hutchinson as "Berlioz." In *Charles Gounod; Autobiographical Reminiscences*, 195-205. London: W. Heinemann, 1896. OCLC 1936009. Reprint. New York, Da Capo Press, 1970. ix, 267 p. ML410 G7 G75 1970 OCLC 6513250.

Recounts the composer's appreciation of Berlioz's work, which he came to know while studying at the Paris *Conservatoire.* Describes him as a "volcano" equivalent to Beethoven in stature and spirit.

256.   Hadow, W.H. "Hector Berlioz and the French Romantic Movement." In *Studies in Modern Music.* Series 1. *Berlioz, Schumann, Wagner*, 71-146. London: Seeley, Service, & Co., 1893. Reprint. Port Washington, N.Y.: Kennikat Press, 1970. ISBN 0-804-60755-9 ML390 H132 1970 OCLC 53701.

A lengthy and detailed sketch marred by many factual errors and encumbered by outmoded critical thinking (e.g., "His thought is sometimes impared and degraded by the touch of defilement which pathologists note as a possible symptom of insanity."). Also calls the programmatic element in instrumental music a "false ideal."

257.   Hallé, Charles. "Life in Paris 1838-48." In *The Life and Letters of Sir Charles Hallé*, 52-100. London: Smith, Elder & Co., 1896. OCLC 2286496. Published as *The Autobiography of Charles Hallé.* Edited by Michael Kennedy. London: Paul

Elek, 1972. New York: Barnes & Noble, 1973. 215 p. ISBN 0-064-93634-1 ML422 H18 A3 1973 OCLC 627183.

This is the source of the famous story of how Berlioz leapt onto the conductor's podium when Habeneck put down his baton to take a pinch of snuff during the first performance of the *Requiem*. Hallé also blames Berlioz's lack of piano skills for his unfamiliarity with much of the standard musical repertoire and for some of his "compositional crudities." Also comments on Berlioz's extraordinary ability as a conductor.

258.   Hanslick, Eduard. "Berlioz." In *Aus dem Concertsaal; Kritiken und Schilderungen aus den letzten 20 Jahren des Wiener Musiklebens*, 483-87. Vienna: W. Braumüller, 1870. xii, 534 p. ML246.8 V6 H2 OCLC 8829290.

Reports that what most impressed the author about the young Berlioz were his high artistic ideals and the sincerity of his art. But on seeing Berlioz in 1860, he found a broken old man whose fire had gone out and who had given up his life-long artistic battles.

259.   Hiller, Ferdinand. "Hector Berlioz." *Westermann's Illustrierte Deutsche Monatshefte* 45 (February 1879): 554-93. OCLC 11085344. Reprinted in *Künstlerleben*, 63-143. Cologne: M. Du Mont-Schauberg, 1880. 302 p. ML410 H654 OCLC 12065854.

Contains a detailed sketch of Berlioz's life based on the author's personal association with the composer. Attempts to establish an objective appraisal of Berlioz's career by pointing out his many successes and concluding that the hardships he endured were not uncommon among composers of his era. Also contains an evaluation of Berlioz's compositional style which blames his musical irregularities on his having begun serious training too late in life.

260.   Jong, J. de. "Berlioz." *De Gids: nieuwe vaderlandsche letteroefeningen* 43 (July 1879): 138-73. ISSN 0016-9730 OCLC 1751214.

Especially useful in its treatment of Berlioz's opinions of his contemporaries, including Mendelssohn, Verdi, and Rossini, his disavowal of any association with the principles of Wagner and "the music of the future," his relationship with his son Louis, and his love-hate relationship with the city of Paris.

261.   Jullien, Adolphe. "Berlioz." In *Famous Composers and Their Music*, edited by Theodore Thomas, John Knowles Paine, and Karl Klauser. Vol. 5, 675-90. Boston: J.B. Millet, 1901. 6 vols. ML390 F26 1901 OCLC 17515424.

Divides Berlioz's career into two periods: the years of struggle before 1842, and the years of success abroad after 1842. Describes him as one of the few French musicians to cast his lot with the new Romantic movement. Also includes a review of critical opinion circa 1901 of the Berlioz style.

262.   _____. "Hector Berlioz." *Revue contemporaine* 19 (March 14 1870): 64-94. OCLC 1696043. Reprinted in *Airs variés; histoire, critique, biographie musicales et dramatiques*, 1-64. Paris: Charpentier et Cie., 1877. viii, 360 p. ML60 J99 OCLC 11375917.

A short life and works which finds the same passion and impetuosity in Berlioz's prose as in his music. Sees him as one who supported lofty, noble ideals throughout his life.

263.   La Mara [Ida Maria Lipsius]. "Hector Berlioz." In *Musikalische Studienköpfe*. Vol. 2. *Ausländische Meister*, 263-342. Leipzig: H. Schmidt & C. Günther, 1881. 5 vols. ML60 L47 OCLC 4187501.

Depicts Berlioz as a misunderstood and unappreciated martyr in his own country and as an artist whose temperament was more in tune with the Germanic spirit.

264.   Lamber, Juliette. "Wagner, Berlioz and Edmond Adam." *Berlioz Society Bulletin* no. 123 (Winter 1984-85): 12-18. OCLC 2386332.

Juliette Lamber (Mrs. Edmond Adam) was an acquaintance of Liszt, Wagner, von Bülow, and Berlioz. She reports opinions of each of them about the others as well as her own reactions to all four men.

265.   Lancellotti, Arturo. "Ettore Berlioz." *Musica d'oggi* 13 (July 1931): 302-10. OCLC 9238646.

Presents a good general biographical sketch, with special emphasis placed on Berlioz's role as music critic and his relationships with Harriet Smithson and Mendelssohn.

266.   Legouvé, Ernest. "Hector Berlioz." In *Soixante ans de souvenirs*. Vol. 1, 278-330. Paris: J. Hetzel, 1886. 2 vols. PQ2377 L23 Z5 1886 OCLC 2870410. Reprinted in *Le ménestrel* 52 (August 29 1886): 309-10; (September 5): 317-18; (September 12): 325-26; (September 19): 333-34; (September 26): 341-43. OCLC 6966764.

         Translated by Albert D. Vandam as "Hector Berlioz." In *Sixty Years of Recollections*. Vol. 1, 203-66. London: Eden, Remington & Co., 1893. 2 vols. PQ2337 L23 Z51 OCLC 5304197. Extracted in *Berlioz Society Bulletin* no. 42 (April 1963): 2-5; no. 43 (July 1963): 10-12. OCLC 2386332.

         Other extracts translated by Emile F. Bauer as "A New Glimpse of Berlioz." *Musical World* (Boston) 3 (August 1903): 134-36. OCLC 7970554; by Alistair Bruce in *Berlioz Society Bulletin* no. 108 (Summer 1980): 2-9. OCLC 2386332; and in Appendix I of Cairns's translation of the *Mémoires* (#109d).

         The most thorough account of Berlioz's personality given by a life-long friend. Establishes the sincerity and truthfulness of Berlioz's wildly passionate and intensely suffering character throughout his life. Includes valuable comments on such diverse subjects as Harriet Smithson, Marie Recio, Chopin, Berlioz attending opera performances, the relationship of Berlioz's musical genius to his technical ability, Berlioz's alleged egoism and spitefulness, and Berlioz as guitarist.

267.   Lockspeiser, Edward. *Berlioz*. London: Novello, 1939. 16 p. ML410 B5 L7 OCLC 5000789.

         Brief but well-written introduction to the composer's life and works.

268.   Lüning, Otto. "Hector Berlioz; ein Pionier der Tonkunst." *Neujahrsblatt der allgemeinen Musikgesellschaft in Zürich* 81 (1893): 4-26; 82 (1894): 3-24. OCLC 6926929.

         Claims that Berlioz is chiefly significant as an orchestrational genius who fought against outmoded rules of form and process as well as the frivolity and superficiality of public taste.

269.   Macdonald, Hugh. "Berlioz." In *The New Grove Dictionary of Music and Musicians*. Edited by Stanley Sadie. Vol. 2, 579-610. London: Macmillan; Washington, D.C.: Grove's

Dictionaries of Music, 1980. 20 vols. ISBN 0-333-23111-2
ML100 N48 OCLC 5676891. Reprinted in *The New Grove
Early Romantic Masters 2: Weber, Berlioz, Mendelssohn*, 85-
195. London: Macmillan, 1985. OCLC 13834713. New York:
W.W. Norton, 1985. 314 p. ISBN 0-393-01692-7 ML390
W18 1985 OCLC 12775309.

An excellent, up-to-date summary of Berlioz's life and career
by one of the most eminent scholars in the field. First presents
a biographical sketch, then follows with an overview of
Berlioz's works arranged and discussed by genre. Divides the
analysis of his musical style into separate sections devoted to
melody, harmony, counterpoint, rhythm, orchestration, space,
form, and programs. The reprint updates the bibliography to
1984.

270. Malherbe, Charles. "Une autobiographie de Berlioz." *Rivista
musicale italiana* 13 (1906): 506-21. OCLC 1773309.

Describes the manuscript of autobiographical notes prepared
by Berlioz and given to his friend Joseph d'Ortigue to serve as
the basis for a biographical sketch of the composer which
appeared in the *Revue de Paris*, December 23, 1832 (#272).
Illustrates by parallel columns the changes that d'Ortigue
made in Berlioz's original text.

271. Maréchal, Henri. "Souvenirs d'un musicien." *Le ménestrel*
72 (September 23 1906): 293-94; (September 30): 301-2.
OCLC 6966764. Reprinted and slightly expanded in *Paris--
souvenirs d'un musicien*, 273-89. Paris: Hachette, 1907. xv,
306 p. ML410 M324 OCLC 6180206. Extracted as "Hector
Berlioz vu par un élève du Conservatoire de l'année 1868."
Journal musical français musica-disques no. 179 (April
1969): 21-23. OCLC 9888150.

Gives a resumé of Berlioz's innovations in and contributions
to the field of music, both as composer and critic. Presents a
picture of the composer at the end of his life as a tired warrior
who had devoted his entire career to the battle against
Philistinism.

272. Ortigue, Joseph d'. "Galerie biographique: Hector Berlioz."
Revue de Paris 45 (December 23 1832): 281-98. OCLC
1645749. Reprinted in *Le balcon de l'Opéra*, 295-324. Paris:
E. Renduel, 1833. xv, 414 p. ML1704 O77 OCLC 15356838.

A biographical note with perceptive and favorable reviews of the *Symphonie fantastique* and *Le retour à la vie* by an important contemporary of Berlioz. Calls these works revolutionary in instrumental music and asserts that they cannot be compared to earlier works by Classical composers. Prepared from notes made by Berlioz (see #115, #116, #270).

273.   Osborne, G.A. "Berlioz." *Proceedings of the Royal Musical Association* 5 (1879): 60-75. ISSN 0080-4452 OCLC 1764602.

Berlioz's career sketched by one who knew him well. Contains the interesting report that at the suggestion of the author, Berlioz had considered leaving his first wife as early as the late 1830s.

274.   Puttmann, Max. "Hector Berlioz zu seinem 100. Geburtstage." *Allgemeine Musik-Zeitung* 30 (December 11 1903): 793-95; (December 18/25): 813-15. OCLC 1641284.

Evaluates Berlioz's importance in the history of nineteenth-century music and presents a biographical sketch. The author's attitude is that Berlioz's program music derived from Beethoven and that, while he was a great composer of instrumental music, he could not compare to Wagner as a composer of vocal music.

275.   Reyer, Ernest. "Hector Berlioz: Biographical Notes and Personal Reminiscences." *Century Magazine* 47 (December 1893): 305-10. OCLC 4453029. Also in *The Century Library of Music*, edited by Ignacy Jan Paderewski. Vol. 1, 1-17. New York, The Century Co., 1900. 20 vols. M1 C3 OCLC 3979883.

Contains miscellaneous biographical facts concerning Berlioz's last years in Paris and discusses his posthumous reputation as observed by this close friend and fellow composer.

276.   _____. "Hector Berlioz." In *Notes de musique*, 264-76. 2nd ed. Paris: Charpentier et Cie, 1875. 438 p. ML60 R457 OCLC 9072525.

Contains a short reminiscence of Berlioz written in 1869 which laments the fact that this great and innovative composer was so misunderstood and unappreciated by Frenchmen of his day.

277.   . "*Mémoires* d'Hector Berlioz." In *Notes de musique*,
           305-57. 2nd ed. Paris: Charpentier et Cie, 1875. 438 p. ML60
           R457 OCLC 9072525.

           A detailed resumé of Berlioz's career drawn from the
           Mémoires.

278.   Rimsky-Korsakov, Nikolay. *My Musical Life*. Translated
           from the revised second Russian edition by Judah A. Joffe;
           edited with an introduction by Carl Van Vechten. New York:
           Alfred .A. Knopf, 1923. xxiv, 389 p. ML410 R525 OCLC
           891388. London: Ernst Eulenburg, 1974. xliv, 480, xxi p.
           ISBN 0-903-87313-3 ML410 R52 A33 1974 OCLC
           2839684. Translation of *Letopis' moei musykal' noi zhizni*.

           Relates that Berlioz was completely uninterested in Russian
           music and musicians when he visited St. Petersburg to
           conduct concerts in 1867-68. Also comments on the clarity of
           Berlioz's conducting technique. Attests to the respect held for
           Berlioz by the older generation of Russian composers such as
           Balakirev, Musorgsky, and Cui, and critics such as Stasov,
           and to the importance the *Traité d'instrumentation* had for
           them. Remarks about Berlioz appear throughout the book.

279.   Saint-Saëns, Camille. "Discours de M. Saint-Saëns." *Le
           guide musical* 49 (September 6 & 13 1903): 626-27. OCLC
           1509855.

           Comments on the change in French public opinion of Berlioz
           between 1830 and 1903. Reports on the overwhelming effect
           that the *Requiem* had on the author when he first heard it. Also
           relates the story of Saint-Saëns's final visit to the dying
           Berlioz.

280.   . "Hector Berlioz." In *Portraits et souvenirs*, 3-14.
           Paris: Société d'édition artistique, 1900. viii, 246 p. ML60
           S156 OCLC 2714621.

           Contains a short portrait of Berlioz as composer and critic and
           an evaluation of the *Traité d'instrumentation*. Calls Berlioz
           "un paradoxe fait homme."

281.   Schlösser, Louis. "Gedenkblätter an Hektor Berlioz."
           Allgemeine Deutsche Musik-Zeitung 9 (April 21 1882): 136-
           38. OCLC 1641284.

Recalls a performance of Gluck's *Orphée et Eurydice* which the author attended with Berlioz and describes his intensely emotional reaction to the music.

282.   Stasov, V.V. "The Letters of Berlioz." In *Selected Essays on Music*, 52-61. Translated by Florence Jonas. London: Barrie & Rockliff, 1968. OCLC 8029593. New York: F.A. Praeger, 1968. OCLC 2420. Reprint. New York: Da Capo Press, 1980. 202 p. ISBN 0-306-76033-9 ML60 S823 S42 1980 OCLC 6043127.

Quotes many letters with the intent of creating a character sketch. Reprint of Stasov's 1879 review of Bernard's *Correspondance inédite de Berlioz* (#121). Originally appeared in *Novoe Vremya*, January 18 and 30, 1879.

283.   Villemer, Marquis de [Charles Emile Yriarte] "Hector Berlioz." In *Les portraits cosmopolites*, 181-216. Paris: E. Lachaud, 1870. vii, 240 p. CT144 Y7 OCLC 3987572.

Presents the major highlights of Berlioz's life and works. Depicts him as a fiery and uncompromising musical spirit whose works met with greater approval abroad than in Paris. Suggests that this Parisian apathy eventually broke his spirit.

3. PERSONALITY

284.   Feis, Oswald. "Hector Berlioz, eine pathographische Studie." *Grenzfragen des Nerven-und Seelenlebens* 12 (1911): 1-28. OCLC 2261655.

Analyzes Berlioz's personality from a medical point of view and concludes that the physical pain he suffered throughout his life was psychological rather than neurological in origin, and that Berlioz was a pathologically disturbed man who suffered from hysteria. Finds that this disorder is reflected in his life and works.

285.   Foix, Pierre. "Etude graphologique; le caractère de Berlioz d'après son écriture." *Journal musical français musica-disques* no. 179 (April 1969): 16. OCLC 9888150.

Analyzes the handwriting of Berlioz in a letter dated June 25, 1861. Finds the composer to be hyperemotional, hypersensitive, vain, and haughty.

286.   Ironfield, Susan Elizabeth. "Creative Developments of the *mal de l'isolement* in Berlioz." *Music and Letters* 59 (no. 1 1978): 33-48. ISSN 0027-4224 OCLC 1758884.

Analyzes excerpts from Berlioz's writings to demonstrate and define his lifelong concern with the "sickness of isolation" (a kind of hypersensitive Romantic loneliness and feeling of vague passions). Discusses musical manifestations of this psychic malady in the *Symphonie fantastique* and other works.

287.   Keeton, A.E. "Hector Berlioz 1803-1869." *The Fortnightly Review* 80 (December 1903): 928-40. OCLC 1781612.

Attempts to analyze Berlioz's "fiery, energetic" personality to find the source of his feverish, volcanic musical style. A good general survey of Berlioz's character, marred perhaps by the author's implication that the composer was a man whose passions ran out of control in his life and music.

288.   Klein, John W. "Berlioz's Personality." *Music and Letters* 50 (no. 1 1969): 15-24. ISSN 0027-4224 OCLC 1758884.

Surveys the enigma of Berlioz's contradictory personality traits: the naïve optimist versus the bitter pessimist and the generous, supportive critic versus the acrid satirist. Also delves into the paradoxes of Berlioz's relationship with his son Louis.

289.   Knepler, Georg. "Hector Berlioz." In *Musikgeschichte des 19. Jahrhunderts*. Vol. 1, 288-315. Berlin: Henschelverlag, 1961. 1033 p. ML196 K67 OCLC 2292175.

Studies Berlioz's character as manifested in his music. Contains especially good discussions of his life-long war with society, his interest in the Saint-Simonian movement, and his concern with the themes of isolation and heroism.

290.   Landormy, Paul. "Berlioz auf Reisen." *Die Musik* 25 (December 1932): 176-78. OCLC 1696908.

Hypothesizes that Berlioz was a man of passion but not of love, and that the love that was missing from his life was

reflected by his inability to write truly tender and sympathetic
love music.

291.   Newman, Ernest. "A Man of the South." In *Berlioz, Romantic
         and Classic*, edited by Peter Heyworth, 89-96. London:
         Gollancz, 1972. 288 p. ISBN 0-575-01365-6 ML410 B5 N49
         OCLC 516762.

         Explores the influence of the Dauphiné on Berlioz's character.
         Suggests that he may have had some Italian blood in his
         distant ancestry, which might account for his Latin outlook on
         life and music.

292.   Salas Viú, Vicente. "Berlioz, paradigma del artista
         romantico." *Revista musical chilena* no. 89 (July-September
         1964): 15-42. ISSN 0035-0192 OCLC 1590560.

         Surveys most of the major works of Berlioz to define his true
         personality. Concludes that he was the heir of Beethoven, but
         also a composer whose intellect was incapable of controlling
         his passions. Also discusses Berlioz's influence on Liszt and
         Wagner.

293.   Schuré, Edouard. "Les concerts du dimanche et les maîtres
         symphonistes: Beethoven, Berlioz, Richard Wagner." *Revue
         des deux mondes* series 3, tome 62 (April 15 1884): 789-816.
         OCLC 8305048.

         Claims that the music of Beethoven, Berlioz, and Wagner
         became popular in Paris thanks mainly to several series of
         "concerts populaires" directed by Pasdeloup, Colonne, and
         Lamoureux. Follows with a sketch of each of the composers
         mentioned. Characterizes Berlioz as the quintessentially fiery,
         volcanic spirit of Romanticism, and finds evidence of this in
         the *Symphonie fantastique*, *Roméo et Juliette*, and *La
         damnation de Faust*.

4. FAMILY

294.   Chaulin, N.P. "Miss Smithson." In *Biographie dramatique
         des principaux artistes anglais venus à Paris: précédée de
         souvenirs historiques du théâtre anglais à Paris en 1827 et*

1828, 44-45. Paris: J. Pinard, 1828. 166 p. PN2597 C45
OCLC 12109293.

Briefly describes the early stages of Harriet Smithson's acting
career in Ireland and England.

295. Chenley, Brian. "Marie Recio." *Berlioz Society Bulletin* no.
39 (July 1962): 12-14. OCLC 2386332.

Biographical sketch of Berlioz's second wife, a mediocre
opera singer, who, much to Berlioz's distress, always wanted
to sing his music.

296. Guichard, Léon. "Quels furent les témoins du premier
mariage de Berlioz?" *Revue de musicologie* 52 (no. 2 1966):
211-14. ISSN 0035-1601 OCLC 1773306.

Identifies witnesses to Berlioz's marriage to Harriet Smithson.
Includes facsimile of marriage record.

297. Raby, Peter. *Fair Ophelia; Harriet Smithson Berlioz.*
Cambridge and New York: Cambridge University Press, 1982.
xiii, 216 p. ISBN 0-521-24421-8 PN2598 B577 R3 1982
OCLC 8034756.

Depicts Harriet Smithson as a competent young actress, and
disposes of the common theory that she did not do well in
England because of her Irish accent. Contains a chapter
detailing the history of Shakespeare translations and
productions in France, observing that antagonisms between
Classical French drama and the new Romantic ideas about
Shakespearean drama had by no means been settled at the
time of Harriet Smithson's Paris engagements in the late
1820s.

298. Sablière, Françoise de la. "Quel père fut Hector Berlioz." *La
revue de Paris* 76 (February 1970): 94-103. OCLC 1775173.

Explores the relationship between Berlioz and his son Louis
through previously unpublished letters of the latter. Presents
Louis as somewhat jealous of his father's devotion to his
music and Hector as unable to allow his son to choose and
lead his own life.

299. Wright, Michael G.H. "The Genealogy of the Berlioz
Family." *Berlioz Society Bulletin* no. 126 (Autumn-Winter
1985): 13-18. OCLC 2386332.

History of the Berlioz family from 1590 to the birth of the composer in 1803.

5. BERLIOZ'S YOUTH AND EDUCATION

300.   Association Nationale Hector Berlioz. *Berlioz, sa jeunesse, son adolescence, 1803-1821: 18 ans de vie familiale dans son pays natal.* St. Etienne: Editions Foréziennes, 1969. 44 p.

Draws on the work of earlier authors, including Tiersot, Boschot, and Jullien, to present an overview of Berlioz's early years in La Côte-St-André. Contains a description of the town, history of the Berlioz family, a sketch of Berlioz's early education, descriptions of his physiology, and a list of events that shaped his early life. Also enumerates festivals and special performances of Berlioz's music held in La Côte-St-André between 1903 and 1969, and a history of the statue erected there in Berlioz's honor in 1890.

301.   Blondel, Raoul. "La jeunesse médicale de Berlioz." *Chronique médicale* 15 (April 1 1908): 209-13. OCLC 1554544. Reprinted in *Propos variés de musique et de médecine: histoire, critique, esthétique, physiologie, etc.*, 1-13. Paris: Editions d'art et médecine, 1934. 188 p. ML3800 B654 1934 OCLC 14746210.

Discusses the medical studies that Berlioz pursued during 1821 and 1822 in Paris in the company of his cousin Alphonse Robert. Hypothesizes that their separation, along with the closing of the medical school for eight months in 1823, pushed Berlioz into abandoning medicine for music. Fails, however, to explain why Berlioz took examinations for the bachelor of science degree in 1824 if he had already terminated his medical studies. See #302 and #303 for more current research on this subject.

302.   Donnet, V. "Hector Berlioz et la médecine." *La vie medicale: lettres et médecins* 1er semestre (January 1969): 31-34; (February): 32-36; (March): 23-32; (April): 33-40. OCLC 10734028.

The most detailed examination of Berlioz's years as a medical student in Paris (1821 through 1823). Contradicts Boschot by suggesting that Berlioz abandoned his studies in 1823 and corrects some details concerning his academic records previously offered by Blondel (#301).

303. Donnet, V., and C. Moureaux. "Le baccalauréat-ès-sciences d'Hector Berlioz." *Marseille médical* 106 (no. 3 1969): 277-83. ISSN 0025-4053 OCLC 10436961.

Suggests that parental pressure and concerns about the continuation of his allowance from home may have been responsible for Berlioz's taking the bachelor of science examination in 1824, even though he had apparently already decided against a medical career.

304. Holoman, D. Kern. "Berlioz au Conservatoire: notes biographiques." *Revue de musicologie* 62 (no. 2 1976): 289-92. ISSN 0035-1601 OCLC 1773306.

Quotes registration and examination registers belonging to Luigi Cherubini to document remarks made by Berlioz in the *Mémoires* concerning his student years at the *Conservatoire de Paris*.

305. Kurtz, Lynn. "Connections Between Education and Creativity: the Composer Hector Berlioz (1803-1869)." Ed.D. dissertation, Columbia University Teachers College, 1979. vi, 119 p. bibliography, 113-19. OCLC 7346627.

Formulates the theory that Berlioz's unique creativity was the product of his early musical and academic experiences which were independent of prevailing modes of educational thought. Also suggests that his musical style was shaped early in his life and remained consistent throughout his career [from abstract].

306. Tiersot, Julien. "Un pélerinage au pays de Berlioz." *Le ménestrel* 51 (October 4 1885): 345; (October 11): 353; (October 18): 361-63. OCLC 6966764.

Concerns the influence of Berlioz's birthplace and early childhood experiences on his later compositional style. Mentions the strong Classical influence of Pleyel and Devienne on his earliest works. Reconstructs the original form of the vocal melody Berlioz borrowed from himself for use in the introduction to the *Symphonie fantastique* by setting to it the relevant text from Florian's *Estelle et Némorin*. Concludes with an exploration of the influences of the countryside near Grenoble and Estelle Duboeuf Fornier on Berlioz's later works, especially *Les Troyens*. Occasioned by the author's visit in 1883 to La Côte-St-André. (See also #362.)

6. BERLIOZ AND THE SAINT-SIMONIANS

307.   Espiau de la Maëstre, André. "Berlioz, Metternich et le Saint-Simonisme." *La revue musicale* no. 233 (1956): 65-78. OCLC 1764223.

Explains Berlioz's association with Saint-Simonianism while he was residing in Rome in 1831 and his failure to continue this association after his return to Paris in 1832.

308.   _____. "Hector Berlioz et Metternich." *Österreichische Musikzeitschrift* 8 (December 1953): 365-71. ISSN 0029-9316 OCLC 2113066.

Suggests that Metternich's early view of Berlioz as a dangerous revolutionary tied to the radical philosophies of the Saint-Simonians was altered in later years after Berlioz distanced himself from the movement.

309.   Locke, Ralph P. "Autour de la lettre à Duveyrier: Berlioz et les Saint-Simoniens." *Revue de musicologie* 63 (no. 1-2 1977): 55-77. ISSN 0035-1601 OCLC 1773306.

Uses Berlioz's letter to one of the leading Saint-Simonians and other evidence to demonstrate that he was interested in the social, but not the religious, tenets of this utopian movement. His interest is said to date from the late 1820s and to be reflected in the libretto for the unfinished choral work, *Le dernier jour du monde*. Also discusses other musician friends (including Liszt) who might have influenced Berlioz in his interest.

310.   _____. "Berlioz and the Saint-Simonians." In *Music, Musicians and the Saint-Simonians*, 114-21. Chicago: University of Chicago Press, 1986. xvi, 399 p. bibliography,

375-84. ISBN 0-226-48901-9 ML270.4 L65 1986 OCLC 12669584.

Explores in detail Berlioz's brief association with the Saint-Simonian movement circa 1830, the possible relationship between its social ideals and the scenario of his projected choral work, *Le dernier jour du monde*, and his mixed feelings about the movement from 1832 on.

7. BERLIOZ AS CONDUCTOR

311. Appert, Donald L. "Berlioz, the Conductor." D.M.A. dissertation, University of Kansas, 1985. iii, 72 p. bibliography, 70-72. OCLC 15102874.

Draws on the *Mémoires*, the *Traité d'instrumentation*, and reports and reviews contemporaneous with Berlioz's activity as a conductor in order to formulate a complete picture of his career on the podium and his importance in the evolution of nineteenth-century orchestral conducting techniques [from abstract].

312. Galkin, Elliott W. "Berlioz as Conductor." *Journal of the American Liszt Society* 9 (1981): 19-30. ISSN 0147-4413 OCLC 3162965. Translated as "Hector Berlioz, chef d'orchestre." *Revue de musicologie* 63 (no. 1-2 1977): 41-54. ISSN 0035-1601 OCLC 1773306. Excerpted from the author's "The Theory and Practice of Orchestral Conducting Since 1752." Ph.D dissertation, Cornell University, 1960. ix, 650 p. OCLC 10820537. Revised as *The History of Orchestral Conducting: Its Theory and Practice*. New York: Pendragon Press, in press. ISBN 0-918-72844-4 ML457 G3 1988 OCLC 12943551.

Establishes that Berlioz was the first virtuoso conductor, that he exercised a Classical restraint in his approach to tempos (as opposed to Wagner's more exaggerated rallentendos), and that he "invented" the idea of the sectional rehearsal.

313. Tiersot, Julien. "Berlioziana. Chapitre IV: Berlioz, directeur de concerts symphoniques." *Le ménestrel* 75 (October 16 1909): 332-33; (October 23): 339-41; (October 30): 347-48;

(November 13): 363-64; (November 27): 379-80; (December 11): 394-96; (December 25): 410-11. 76 (January 8 1910): 11-12; (January 15): 20; (January 22): 27-28; (January 29): 34-36; (February 12): 50-51; (March 5): 75-76; (March 19): 91-92; (March 26): 99-100; (April 2): 107-8. OCLC 6966764.

Gives a detailed account of Berlioz's involvement with various European orchestras and concert series, both as conductor and composer, throughout his career. Traces his activities from his early sponsorship of concerts of his own music in Paris in the late 1820s through his many engagements with foreign orchestras and his direction of several "public festival" concerts in Paris. Also documents Berlioz's relationship with the *Société des Concerts du Conservatoire*.

8. BERLIOZ AS CONCERT ORGANIZER

314.   Bloom, Peter A., and D. Kern Holoman. "Berlioz's Music for *L'Europe littéraire*." *The Music Review* 39 (no. 2 1978): 100-109. ISSN 0027-4445 OCLC 1758893.

Discusses Berlioz's involvement as composer and organizer in the last in a series of four concerts presented on June 6, 1833, by the Parisian journal, *L'Europe littéraire*. Works discussed include *Le pêcheur*, *La captive*, and Berlioz's arrangement of Weber's *Lützow's wilde Jagd* as *La chasse de Lützow*.

315.   Fauquet, Joël-Marie. "Hector Berlioz et l'Association des Artistes Musiciens; lettres et documents inédits." *Revue de musicologie* 67 (no. 2 1981): 211-36. ISSN 0035-1601 OCLC 1773306.

Explains that Berlioz was a founding member of and remained active as a concert organizer from 1843 to 1853 in the *Association des Artistes Musiciens*, a society devoted to the economic security of its members. Includes many previously unpublished letters.

316.   Husson, Thérèse. "Hector Berlioz, l'inventeur des festivals." *Musica* no. 90 (September 1961): 16-21. OCLC 9888150.

Chronicles Berlioz's organization of two huge public concerts ("festivals") of choral and instrumental music in Paris in 1840 and 1844, at which were assembled first 400 and later more than 1000 performers.

9. BERLIOZ AND THE INSTITUT

317.   Bloom, Peter. "Berlioz à l'Institut Revisited." *Acta musicologica* 53 (no. 2 1981): 171-99. ISSN 0001-6241 OCLC 1460933.

Presents documentation from Academy archives relating to Berlioz's candidacy for the *Institut* and his actions as a member. Includes texts of previously unpublished letters of candidacy (1842, 1851, 1854, 1856) and reports written by Berlioz.

318.   Boschot, Adolphe. "Berlioz et l'Institut." *Le monde français* 15 (August 1949): 220-36. OCLC 1607277.

Chronicles Berlioz's association with the *Institut* from his student years as a *Prix-de-Rome* competitor to the time he was elected as a member in 1856.

319.   Celle, Jean. "Berlioz à l'Institut (deux lettres inédites)." *Revue politique et littéraire: (Revue Bleue)* 5th series, tome 6 (August 18 1906): 219-22. OCLC 8339424.

Quotes letters written by Berlioz at the time of his election to the *Insitut* in 1856 which contradict the impression given in the *Mémoires* that the election meant little to him. In one of these letters Berlioz called his election an "unbelievable joy for all the young generation of artists."

320.   Tiersot, Julien. "Berlioziana: Berlioz à l'Institut." *Le ménestrel* 77 (August 19 1911): 259-61; (August 26): 269-70; (September 2): 276-77; (September 9): 283; (September 16): 291-22. OCLC 6966764.

Examines the careers of some of the students who competed with Berlioz for the *Prix de Rome* in the late 1820s, as well as Berlioz's unethical submission of works composed prior to

1829 as examples of work done as *pensionnaire* in Rome in
1830. Also presents the history of his numerous attempts
between 1839 and 1856 to be elected to the *Institut*.

10. BERLIOZ AS LIBRARIAN OF THE CONSERVATOIRE

321.   Prod'homme, J.-G. "Hector Berlioz, bibliothécaire du
        Conservatoire." *Le guide musical* 59 (December 14 1913):
        783-88; (December 21): 803-5. OCLC 1509855.

        Reproduces letters to and from various government officials
        concerning Berlioz's tenure as librarian of the *Conservatoire*.
        Most of these documents are related to his frequent requests
        for leaves of absence so that he could travel abroad for
        concerts of his music.

322.   Tiersot, Julien. "Berlioziana. Chapitre V: Berlioz,
        bibliothécaire du Conservatoire." *Le ménestrel* 77 (July 22
        1911): 226-27; (July 29): 235-36; (August 5): 244-45; (August
        12): 252-53. OCLC 6966764.

        Chronicles the history of the Paris Conservatory Library up to
        1821, when Berlioz began using it. Follows with an account of
        Berlioz's appointments first as *conservateur* in 1839 and then
        as *bibliothécaire* in 1850. States that his duties were minimal,
        his absences frequent, and his principal concern that of
        increasing the library's holdings of works by Liszt,
        Schumann, and Wagner.

11. BERLIOZ CENTENARY 1903

323.   Anon. "The Centenary of Berlioz." *The Athenaeum* no. 3957
        (August 29 1903): 295. OCLC 15641593.

        Reports on the August 16, 1903, centenary celebration in
        Grenoble. Includes abstracts of speeches by Maréchal and
        Reyer.

324.   Bouyer, Raymond. "Petites notes sans portée: pour le
        centenaire d'un maître français." *Le ménestrel* 69 (February 8
        1903): 42-43. OCLC 6966764.

        Complains that reliable sources of information about Berlioz's
        life and works are difficult to find and that the centenary of his
        birth should mark the beginning of a new era of Berlioz
        research.

325.   Jullien, Adolphe. "Le centenaire de Berlioz." In *Musiciens
        d'hier et d'aujourd'hui*, 132-47. Paris: Fischbacher, 1910.
        371 p. ML390 J95 OCLC 4795075.

        Reports on concerts and other centennial commemorations in
        Grenoble, La Côte-St-André, Paris, and elsewhere in Europe.

326.   *Le livre d'or du centenaire Hector Berlioz*. Paris: G. Petit,
        1907. vi, 224 p. ML410 B5 L59 OCLC 5781226.

        Commemorative volume of the 1903 Grenoble centennial
        celebration of Berlioz's birth. Contains texts of speeches,
        concert programs, excerpts of reviews and reports from
        contemporary journals, a biographical sketch by Adolphe
        Jullien, other general appreciations and eulogies by various
        authors, short descriptive analyses of major works by Berlioz,
        a catalog of an exhibition assembled in Frankfurt, Germany, in
        1901, and an annotated bibliography of English-language
        materials. See also #337; #375; #433; #637; #977.

327.   Maclean, Charles. "The Country of Berlioz." *The Musical
        Times* 44 (September 1903): 594-96. ISSN 0027-4666 OCLC
        5472115.

        Provides a description and history of the southern Dauphiné
        where Berlioz grew up. Points to Latin elements in this region
        of France and to their probable influence on Berlioz's
        personality. Also briefly describes the 1903 centennial
        celebrations held at Grenoble and La Côte-St-André.

328.   Tiersot, Julien. "Berlioziana. I: au Musée Berlioz." *Le
        ménestrel* 70 (April 17 1904): 123-24. OCLC 6966764.

        Describes the circumstances surrounding Gabriel Fauré's
        dedication of a Berlioz statue at the 1903 centenary
        celebration in Grenoble.

329.   Weingartner, Felix. "Die Zentenarfeier für Hector Berlioz in
         Grenoble." In *Akkorde: gesammelte Aufsätze*, 218-30.
         Leipzig: Breitkopf & Härtel, 1912. OCLC 2608838. Walluf-
         Nendeln: Sändig, 1977. iv, 304 p. ISBN 3-500-30490-7
         ML60 W45 1977 OCLC 4190155.

         Reports on the programs and festivities of the 1903 Berlioz
         Centenary Festival in Grenoble; includes concert reviews.

                    12. BERLIOZ CENTENARY 1969

330.   Bird, Alan. "Berlioz and the Romantic Imagination."
         Contemporary Review 216 (January 1970): 41-46. ISSN 0010-
         7565 OCLC 1564974.

         Offers a critique of the 1969 exhibit at the Victoria and Albert
         Museum (#159), singling out for special praise some of the
         evocative set pieces designed to capture the ambiance of
         Berlioz's time and place. Also presents a general critical
         evaluation of his music, claiming that while Berlioz was not as
         innovative as Liszt, there is nonetheless great originality in his
         use of orchestral color and space.

331.   Boschot, Henriette. "Renovation de la maison natale d'Hector
         Berlioz." *Cahiers de l'alpe* no. 46 (1969): 125-26. OCLC
         12101098.

         Describes the 1969 restoration of Berlioz's birthplace in La
         Côte-St-André, which had been the home of the Hector
         Berlioz Museum since 1935.

332.   *Bulletin de liaison* (Association Nationale Hector Berlioz) no.
         6-7 (1969-70): entire issue. OCLC 6952566.

         Gives details of all commemorative concerts, broadcasts, etc.,
         in France during the 1969 centenary of Berlioz's death.

333.   Macdonald, Hugh. "Hector Berlioz 1969: a Centenary
         Assessment." *Adam International Review* nos. 331-333
         (1969): 35-47. ISSN 0001-8015 OCLC 1965286. Translated
         by Peter Schmidt as "Hector Berlioz 1969; zur 100.

Wiederkehr seines Todestages am 8. März." *Musica* 23 (no. 2
1969): 112-15. ISSN 0027-4518 OCLC 2362604.

Describes centenary publishing projects of both the musical
and literary works. Summarizes the controversy involving
Tiersot and Boschot over the origin of the "Marche au
supplice," finally proving the validity of Boschot's claim that
the work was borrowed from the "Marche des gardes" in *Les
francs-juges*. Analyzes Berlioz's role in the 1861 Paris *Opéra
Tannhäuser* fiasco. Concludes with a description of Berlioz
orchestral performance materials in the library of the *Société
des Concerts*.

13. ICONOGRAPHY

334.   Bischoff, Friedrich A. "Dire que maintenant,...Eine Daumier-
Karikatur von Berlioz, Wagner und Rossini." *Die
Musikforschung* 38 (no. 1 1985): 22-26. ISSN 0027-4801
OCLC 2669982.

Interprets a lithograph by Daumier which appeared in *Le
charivari*, January 10, 1856, depicting Berlioz as a writer,
Wagner as a grocer, and Rossini as a butcher. The caricature
was based on a satiric vaudeville then playing in Paris.

335.   Boschot, Adolphe. "Les romantiques à Versailles." In *Carnet
d'art*, 187-94. Paris: Bloud & Cie., 1911. viii, 264 p. ML60
B78 OCLC 15309410.

Describes a portrait of Berlioz housed in the Musée de
Versailles, attributed to Daumier, and dated circa 1850-60, in
which the composer appears as an "irascible, hideous specter."

336.   Imbert, Hugues. "Hector Berlioz au Palais de Versailles." *Le
guide musical* 46 (June 24 1900): 499-501. OCLC 1509855.

Reports the discovery of a previously unknown portrait of the
composer by Daumier in the Musée de Versailles. Also lists
twenty-one additional portraits and busts of Berlioz. Reprinted
as part of #337.

337. _____. "Histoire d'un buste et portrait de Berlioz." In *Le livre d'or du centenaire Hector Berlioz*, 113-21. Paris: G. Petit, 1907. vi, 224 p. ML410 B5 L59 OCLC 5781226.

Explains the circumstances leading to Jean-Joseph Perraud's 1875 commission for a bust of Berlioz for the Grenoble library and describes a little-known portrait of the composer by Daumier, circa 1852, which is housed in the Musée de Versailles.

338. Imbert, Hugues and N. Liez. "Nos gravures." *Le guide musical* 49 (November 29 1903 supplement): 39-40. OCLC 1509853.

Describes the portraits and lithographs reproduced throughout this special supplement to *Le guide musical*, including the portrait of Berlioz by Daumier in the Musée de Versailles and a lithograph by Baugniet of Berlioz with famous musician colleagues in London.

339. Rénier, Francis. "Les caricatures françaises et étrangères sur Richard Wagner et Hector Berlioz." *Le livre (Bibliographie rétrospective)* 10 (April 1889): 98-111. OCLC 1756056.

Discusses caricatures of Wagner and Berlioz that were reprinted by Jullien in his biographies of the two composers, noting that such art work can be a serious and useful tool for music historians.

340. Riat, Georges. "Berlioz dans l'art et la caricature." *Le monde moderne* 18 (1903): 671-80. OCLC 9169982.

Describes caricatures of Berlioz (aimed mostly at his noisy orchestrations), official portraits, and lithographs by Fantin-Latour of scenes from his dramatic works.

341. Tiersot, Julien. "Le premier portrait de Berlioz." *Le ménestrel* 75 (April 3 1909): 105-6; (April 10): 113-14. OCLC 6966764.

Presents the history of the first official portrait of Berlioz painted by Dubufe after Berlioz won the *Prix de Rome* in 1830. Compares this portrait with two others from 1831, noting discrepancies among all three.

342. Wright, Michael G.H. "Berlioz's Physiognomy." *Berlioz Society Bulletin* no. 43 (July 1963): 3-9. OCLC 2386332.

Surveys the evidence of various portraits and descriptions by
contemporaries to assemble a picture of Berlioz's physical
appearance.

14. OTHER

343. Bone, Philip James. "Berlioz." In *The Guitar and Mandolin;
      Biographies of Celebrated Players and Composers for These
      Instruments*, 30-35. London: Schott, 1914. 2nd ed. London
      and New York: Schott, 1954. Reprint. London: Schott, 1972.
      388 p. ISBN 0-403-01910-9 ML399 B6 1972 OCLC 631595.

      Draws from Berlioz's letters, *Mémoires*, and the *Traité
      d'instrumentation* to explain the composer's involvement with
      the guitar, which he both played and wrote for from his
      student days until the end of his career.

344. Boschot, Adolphe. "Berlioz à Montmartre." In *Carnet d'art*,
      77-82. Paris: Bloud & Cie., 1911. viii, 264 p. ML60 B78
      OCLC 15309410.

      Depicts Montmartre as a place of special significance for
      Berlioz--where he first made his home after marrying Harriet
      Smithson and where both are buried.

345. _____. "Le témoin d'un siècle," In *Carnet d'art*, 113-21,
      Paris: Bloud & Cie., 1911. viii, 264 p. ML60 B78 OCLC
      15309410.

      Explains that one of the reasons Berlioz disliked Fétis so
      much was that Fétis had interfered with his plans to marry
      Camille Moke by convincing her to accept an alternate suitor
      with more money.

346. Cairns, David. "The Pinch of Snuff." *Berlioz Society Bulletin*
      no. 40 (October 1962): 3-7; no. 41 (January 1963): 3-10.
      OCLC 2386332.

      Reviews all the evidence relating to Berlioz's story (related in
      the *Mémoires*) of the premiere of the *Requiem*, during which

the conductor Habeneck put down his baton to take a pinch of
snuff. Concludes that the story is most likely true.

347.   Dell'ara, Mario. "Hector Berlioz, il signor che suona la
        chitarra francese." *Il Fronimo; rivista trimestrale di chitarra
        e liuto* 5 (January 1977): 6-14. OCLC 1788283.

        Presents an overview of Berlioz's lifelong involvement with
        the guitar. Discusses the role of this instrument in his early
        childhood musical education. Quotes his letters and the
        Mémoires to depict the joy he experienced while wandering
        with his guitar among the mountain villagers of the Italian
        Subiaco in 1831 and 1832. Also includes an analysis of the
        technical aspects of Berlioz's discussion of the guitar in the
        Traité d'instrumentation.

348.   Gavot, Jean. "Berlioz à Nice." *Cahiers de l'alpe* no. 46
        (1969): 122-24. OCLC 12101098.

        Examines Berlioz's fondness for the city of Nice as
        demonstrated by his several visits there throughout his life.
        Presents detailed coverage of his 1831 stay, where he gave up
        his plan to return to Paris from Rome to murder Camille Moke
        and her mother, and where he was arrested by Italian police on
        suspicion of being an undercover revolutionary.

349.   Gérard, Bernadette. "L'inventaire après déces de Louis-
        Hector Berlioz." *Bulletin de la Societé de l'Histoire de Paris*
        (1979): 185-91.

        An inventory and appraisal of the furnishings of Berlioz's
        home, auctioned from March 9 to May 19, 1869 (from RILM
        abstract).

350.   Goléa, Antoine. "Un coeur ardent et déchiré." In *Berlioz*, 53-
        67. Paris: Réalités-Hachette, 1973. 269 p. ML410 B5 B33
        OCLC 1011818.

        Discusses the women in Berlioz's life. Points to his lack of
        true love relationships and suggests that his were cerebral
        attachments.

351.   Lenneberg, Hans. "The First 'Unappreciated' Genius." *The
        Journal of Musicological Research* 4 (no. 1-2 1982): 145-57.
        ISSN 0141-1896 OCLC 6273983.

Reviews the emergence of the idea of "genius" in musical historiography of the nineteenth century and the concomitant idea that genius implies lack of contemporary appreciation and understanding. Classifies Berlioz as the first such unappreciated genius and suggests that he willingly accepted and even cultivated this role.

352. Lesure, François. "Le testament d'Hector Berlioz. *Revue de musicologie* 55 (no. 2 1969): 219-33. ISSN 0035-1601 OCLC 1773306.

Presents the full text of Berlioz's will, which demonstrates his concern for the future integrity of his three operas (which he wanted published without cuts), as well as his continued support for his mother-in-law and his life-long affection for Estelle Duboeuf Fornier.

353. Pontmartin, A. de. "Berlioz." In *Souvenirs d'un vieux critique*. Vol. 2, 305-21. Paris: Calmann-Lévy, 1881-89. 10 vols. PQ282 P8 OCLC 7096847.

A review of Berlioz's *Lettres intimes* which isolates and explores the composer's volcanic, incendiary love relationships with Harriet Smithson and Camille Moke.

354. Pougin, Arthur. "Berlioz et l'Exposition Universelle de 1867." *Le ménestrel* 69 (December 20 1903): 403-4. OCLC 6966764.

Reproduces a letter from d'Ortigue to Madame Moët de Crèvecoeur asking for help in obtaining a commission for Berlioz to write an overture for the opening of the 1867 *Exposition Universelle*.

355. _____. "Inauguration de la statue de Berlioz le dimanche 17 octobre 1886." *Le ménestrel* 52 (October 24 1886): 373-77. OCLC 6966764.

Presents a detailed account of the ceremony celebrating the unveiling of a bronze statue of Berlioz by Alfred Lenoir in Paris on October 17, 1886. Includes texts of speeches given, most notably that of Berlioz's friend Reyer, and a poem written for the occasion by Grandmougin.

356. Prod'homme, J.-G. "Hector Berlioz à Montmartre." *Guide du concert* 1 (no. 18 1910-11): 97-98. OCLC 1507082.

Describes the exact location and structure of Berlioz's
residence in Montmartre and what works he composed while
living there immediately after his marriage to Harriet
Smithson.

357.   Royer, Louis. "Les chroniques: Stendhal et Berlioz." *Le
divan* 21 (January-February 1935): 365-69. OCLC 4676275.

Draws attention to a passage in Stendhal's novel, *Le rouge et
le noir*, which parodies the real-life episode during Berlioz's
1831-32 Italian sojourn, when he bought two pistols and a
female disguise for the purpose of returning to Paris to kill his
former fiancée, Camille Moke, and her mother.

358.   Savic, Gertrud. "Berlioz und die Frauen." *Die Musik* 3
(December 1 1903): 348-57. OCLC 1696908.

Describes Berlioz's relationships with women throughout his
life but offers little evidence of how they affected his work.
Illustrated.

359.   Stier, Ernest. "Berlioz' erste und letzte Liebe." *Neue Musik-
Zeitung* 25 (December 3 1903): 88-89. OCLC 11930822.

Quotes Berlioz's letters to Estelle Duboeuf Fornier to
formulate a psychological picture of the aging composer
during the last five years of his life.

360.   Tiersot, Julien. "Berlioziana. I: au Musée Berlioz." *Le
ménestrel* 70 (January 3 1904): 3-4. OCLC 6966764.

Describes the house where the museum is located and the
village of La Côte-St-André. Reproduces Berlioz's internal
passport obtained when he first went to Paris as a medical
student in October 1821.

361.   _____. "Berlioziana. I: au Musée Berlioz." *Le ménestrel* 70
(March 13 1904): 83-84; (March 27): 99-100. OCLC
6966764.

Describes documents relating to the establishment of a
military band in La Côte-St-André in 1803. Reproduces a
letter from Berlioz to *Janet et Cotelle* music publishers dated
March 25, 1819. Also quotes a series of letters written to his
family while a medical student in Paris describing his life.

362.   _____. "Berlioziana. I: au Musée Berlioz." *Le ménestrel* 70 (April 3 1904): 107-8. OCLC 6966764.

Describes Berlioz's attitude towards his birthplace in his later years (sarcasm). Follows with a discussion of the proposed formation of the *Association Berlioz*. Describes contemporary attitudes of his compatriots toward Berlioz. Mentions Tiersot's first visit to La Côte-St-André (described at greater length in #306).

363.   _____. "Berlioziana. I: au Musée Berlioz." *Le ménestrel* 70 (April 10 1904): 116. OCLC 6966764.

Describes Berlioz's visit to Grenoble in August 1868, his final trip before his death. Includes quotes from Mathieu de Monter's description of the banquet at which Berlioz appeared.

VI. Berlioz's Foreign Travels and Associations

Most of the major successes in Berlioz's career came as a result of his
extensive concertizing abroad. This chapter contains studies devoted to
aspects of these foreign affiliations, arranged by country.

1. AUSTRIA

364. Schenk, Erich. "Berlioz in Wien." *Bastei* 1 (no. 5 1946): 9-
13. Reprinted in *Österreichische Musikzeitschrift* 24 (April
1969): 217-24. ISSN 0029-9316 OCLC 2113066.

Details the positive reception of Berlioz and his works in
Vienna in 1845-46, where, after he directed several concerts
of his own music, the *Neue Zeitschrift für Musik* hailed him as
"a new musical Messiah."

2. BELGIUM

365. Closson, Ernest. "Hector Berlioz à Bruxelles." *Le guide
musical* 49 (November 29 1903 supplement): 33-39. OCLC
1509855.

A detailed study of Berlioz's trips to Brussels in 1842 and
1855, where, under the sponsorship of the *Société royale de la*

Grande Harmonie, he organized and conducted concerts, mostly of his own music. Compares favorable reviews in *L'emancipation* with unfavorable critiques by Fétis in *L'independant*. Includes lists of concert programs.

366.   Vander Linden, Albert. "En marge du centième anniversaire de la mort d'Hector Berlioz (8 mars 1869)." *Académie royale des sciences, des lettres et des beaux-arts de Belgique, Classe des beaux-arts. Bulletin de la classe des beaux-arts* 51 (1969): 36-75. OCLC 1460688.

Provides a history of the changing relationship (from friendly to hostile and back to friendly) between Berlioz and Fétis. Also gives detailed information about Berlioz's 1842 and 1855 trips to Brussels and the concerts he conducted there. Mentions Berlioz's opinions of people in the Belgian musical world such as Vieuxtemps, Sax, Seghers, and Snel.

3. CZECHOSLOVAKIA

367.   Emingerova, Katinka. "Hector Berlioz à Prague." Translated and adapted from Czech by "J.H." and "J.P." *La revue française de Prague* 12 (March 15 1933): 167-86. OCLC 1645826.

Describes the successful reception of Berlioz's music in Prague in 1846, where he presented several concerts that were supported by a group of young Czech musical revolutionaries. Quotes extensively from Czech newspaper reviews.

4. ENGLAND

368.   Beale, William. "Berlioz and the New Philharmonic Society." *Berlioz Society Bulletin* no. 72 (July 1971): 7-11; no. 73 (October 1971): 11-16; no. 74 (January 1972): 15-17. OCLC 2386332.

Extracts all announcements and reviews of Berlioz's London concerts from the *Illustrated London News*, January through June 1852.

369. Cook, Dutton. "Berlioz and Jullien." *Belgravia* 41 (May 1880): 285-96. OCLC 1519465.

Gives a short biographical sketch of Jullien, who assumed the directorship of the Drury Lane Theatre in London in 1847 with the well-intentioned but ill-conceived mission of founding an English Grand Opera. To this purpose he engaged Berlioz as his orchestra conductor.

370. Edwards, F.G. "Berlioz in England: a Centenary Retrospect." *The Musical Times* 44 (July 1903): 441-48. ISSN 0027-4666 OCLC 5472115.

Presents an overview of Berlioz's experiences in England by quoting many primary sources, including newspaper reviews of his conducting, as well as his letters on England and English musicians.

371. Ganz, A.W. *Berlioz in London.* London: Quality Press, 1950. OCLC 399218. Reprint. Westport, Conn., Hyperion Press, 1979. OCLC 4490445. Reprint. New York: Da Capo Press, 1981. 222 p. ISBN 0-306-76092-4 ML410 B5 G24 1981 OCLC 7276411.

An in-depth account of Berlioz's five trips to London between 1847 and 1855, where his music was much better received than in Paris.

372. Hueffer, Francis. "Berlioz in England." In *Half a Century of Music in England, 1837-1887*, 151-234. London: Chapman & Hall; Philadelphia: Gebbie, 1889. OCLC 3055311. Reprint. Boston: Longwood Press, 1977. ix, 240 p. ISBN 0-893-41025-X ML286.4 H8 1977 OCLC 2423395.

Reviews all of Berlioz's personal and professional connections with England, including discussions of his relationship with Harriet Smithson, concerts of his music in London, and his love of Shakespeare.

373. Klein, Herman. "Rediscovering Berlioz." *The Monthly Musical Record* 64 (February 1934): 31; (March-April): 59-60. OCLC 1605021.

Chronicles the decline of Berlioz's popularity in England after his appearances there in the 1850s. This trend was reversed in 1880 when Charles Hallé directed several complete performances of *La damnation de Faust*.

374.   Lack, Leo. "Berlioz à Londres." *La revue musicale* no. 233 (1956): 87-90. OCLC 1764223.

Reproduces the program of Berlioz's concert with the New Philharmonic Society on May 30, 1852.

375.   Maclean, Charles. "Berlioz and England." *Sammelbände der Internationalen Musik-Gesellschaft* 5 (no. 2 1904): 314-28. OCLC 1772498. Reprinted in *Le livre d' or du centenaire Hector Berlioz*, 143-57. Paris: G. Petit, 1907. vi, 224 p. ML410 B5 L59 OCLC 5781226.

Examines chronologically all of Berlioz's dealings with England, including the first performances of his works in 1840, his direction of the 1847-48 Jullien concerts, his tenure as conductor of the New Philharmonic Society in 1852 and 1855, and the 1853 production of *Benvenuto Cellini*. Gives an overview of changing critical opinion of Berlioz in England and a selective bibliography of English writings on Berlioz.

376.   Maretzek, Max. Chapter 7 of *Sharps and Flats*. Vol. 1, supplement, 71-81. New York: American Publishing Co., 1890. OCLC 891539. Reprinted as *Revelations of an Opera Manager in 19th-Century America. Crochets and Quavers & Sharps and Flats*. New York: Dover Publications, 1968. xxxv, 346, 94 p. ML429 M32 A3 OCLC 1082. Reprinted in *Berlioz Society Bulletin* no. 80 (July 1973): 6-19. OCLC 2386332.

Reminiscences by the chorus-master of Jullien's new English opera company at the Drury Lane Theatre in London, where Berlioz was hired to conduct the 1847-48 season. Describes Berlioz's gradual change from hopeful optimism to disappointment as Jullien's ambitious project began to fail.

377.   Wright, Michael G.H. "Berlioz and the Great Exhibition." *Berlioz Society Bulletin* no. 38 (April 1962): 2-7. OCLC 2386332.

Explains how Berlioz used his appointment to the jury for musical instruments at the 1851 Great Exhibition in London as an opportunity to further his own reputation and career abroad.

5. GERMANY

378. Baser-Heidelberg, Friedrich. "Hector Berlioz und die germanische Seele." *Die Musik* 26 (January 1934): 259-63. OCLC 1696908.

Traces the connections between Germany and various aspects of Berlioz's life, including his ancestral roots, his musical preferences, and his greatest professional triumphs.

379. Bloom, Peter. "La mission de Berlioz en Allemagne; un document inédit." *Revue de musicologie* 66 (no. 1 1980): 70-85. ISSN 0035-1601 OCLC 1773306.

Presents a previously unpublished report from Berlioz to the French Minister of the Interior prepared while traveling through Germany in 1843. It gives his impressions of the state of musical life there, including conducting, orchestras, amateur choral societies, opera choruses, and wind bands.

380. Bouyer, Raymond. "Petites notes sans portée: romantiques bravos et jugements classiques." *Le ménestrel* 69 (September 27 1903): 306-8. OCLC 6966764.

An overview of critical reaction to Berlioz's music in Germany. Explains that Romantic supporters such as Liszt and Schumann saw him as the continuation of the tradition of Beethoven, while Classical detractors such as Hanslick and Jahn decried the programmatic excesses of his music.

381. Brenet, Michel [Marie Bobillier]. "Les oeuvres de Berlioz en Allemagne." In *Deux pages de la vie de Berlioz*, 3-41. Paris: L. Vanier, 1889. 72 p. ML410 B51 B66 OCLC 12737478.

Reviews critical opinion of Berlioz in Germany and shows that, while predominantly favorable, German attitudes were split, with Liszt, von Bülow, and Pohl in support, Wagner, Hanslick, and Jahn in opposition. The source of much of the conflict lay in the perceived relationship of Berlioz's new

program symphonies to the German symphonic tradition.
Concludes that the enthusiastic reception of Berlioz's work in
Germany has been exaggerated and that in reality there were
few performances of his works other than those he conducted
while on tour.

382.   Cornelius, Peter. "Hector Berlioz in Weimar." *Revue et
        gazette musicale de Paris* 22 (May 27 1855): 163-64; (June 3):
        169-71. OCLC 10231154. Translated in *Die Musik* 4
        (February 1905): 159-68. OCLC 1696908.

        Reviews Berlioz's first two Weimar concerts in 1855. Praises
        L'enfance du Christ and *La captive* and gives a detailed
        account of the *Symphonie fantastique* with *Lélio*,
        demonstrating that German critics considered Berlioz to be the
        logical continuation of a musical tradition stemming from
        Beethoven, Schubert, and Weber.

383.   "A.F." "Berlioz vor 60 Jahren in Stuttgart." *Neue Musik-
        Zeitung* 25 (December 3 1903): 87. OCLC 11930822.

        A report of the not altogether enthusiastic reception of
        Berlioz's music at his first concert in Stuttgart in 1842.

384.   Fischer, Georg. *Musik in Hannover*, 133-35, 230-31.
        Hannover: Hahn'sche Buchhandlung, 1903. xiii, 288 p.
        ML279.8 H25 F5 OCLC 15937647.

        Chronicles the concert activity of the court orchestra in
        Hannover up to 1866. Describes Berlioz's appearances as
        guest conductor-composer in 1843 and 1853. Lists all works
        performed and summarizes critical opinion of Berlioz's
        conducting as "admirably accomplished" and his music as
        daring and exciting in its effects but often weak in musical
        ideas. Also quotes Berlioz's letter to the *Journal des débats*
        concerning his impressions of the orchestra in Hannover.

385.   Helms, F. "Musikalische Wanderung durch Deutschland. Im
        Briefen von Hector Berlioz" *Kleine Musik-Zeitung* 9 (June
        1848): 142-44; (July): 150-52. OCLC 2448141.

        A review of the *Voyage musical en Allemagne et en Italie*,
        which defends Germany and German musicians against
        Berlioz's critical observations.

386.   Mönch, Walter. "Hector Berlioz auf der ersten Deutschland-
        Tournee. Ein Kapitel musikalischer Landeskunde." In

Perspektiven zur Frankreichkunde; Ansätze zu einer interdisziplinär orientierten Romanistik, edited by R. Picht, 101-14. Tübingen: Max Niemeyer, 1974. x, 274 p. ISBN 3-484-50078-6 DC33.9 P47 OCLC 4884950.

Traces the route of Berlioz's first concert tour of Germany in 1842-43, paying special attention to his relations with important people he met, including Mendelssohn and Wagner. Also suggests that Wagner and Berlioz developed similarly anticapitalist views on the relationship between music and politics.

6. ITALY

387. Bailbé, Joseph-Marc. "Berlioz, Janin et les *Impressions d'Italie*." *Revue de littérature comparée* 45 (no. 4 1971): 489-513. ISSN 0035-1466 OCLC 1764063.

Explains that despite different reasons for traveling in Italy, both Janin and Berlioz viewed their sojourns as a Romantic dream come true--a chance to experience first-hand the Italian adventures so vividly portrayed in the writings of some of their favorite authors such as Byron, Dante, Virgil, and Shakespeare.

388. Boschot, Adolphe. "Berlioz: un Prix de Rome réfractaire." In *Chez les musiciens (de XVIIIe siècle à nos jours); troisième série*, 83-94. Paris: Plon-Nourrit, 1926. 243 p. ML60 B786 OCLC 15309396. Also in *Carnet d'art*, 187-94. Paris: Bloud & Cie., 1911. viii, 264 p. ML60 B78 OCLC 15309410.

Recounts Berlioz's elaborate attempts to circumvent the required two-year stay in Italy that was part of the *Prix de Rome*. Quotes his letters to the authorities and a note from his doctor testifying to Berlioz' "nervous disorders." Originally appeared in *Le figaro*, July 1908.

389. Cuvillier-Fleury, Alfred-Auguste. "M. Hector Berlioz en Italie." In *Dernières études historiques et littéraires*. Vol. 2, 346-59. Paris: Michel Lévy, 1859. 2 vols. OCLC 9705963.

Recalls that Berlioz was unhappy during his 1831 Italian stay. He had just achieved his first successes in Paris and had grandiose dreams for future musical projects which were thwarted by his required stay in Italy as a *Prix de Rome* winner.

390.   Guichard, Léon. "Berlioz et l'Italie." *Bulletin mensuel de l'Académie delphinale* 8th series, tome 8 (December 1969): 320-26. OCLC 1961247.

Recounts Berlioz's experiences in Italy as a young man and his fondness for the countryside and its people. States that his condemnation of Italian Renaissance music reflected his misunderstanding of the style and that his dislike of nineteenth-century Italian opera arose from his inherently greater interest in the effects of orchestration than of vocal display. Closes with comments on how Italy inspired Berlioz's music from *Lélio* to *Les Troyens*.

7. RUSSIA

391.   Anon. "One Hundred Years Ago: the Russian Tour 1867-68." *Berlioz Society Bulletin* no. 59 (April 1968): 15-19. OCLC 2386332.

Describes Berlioz's final trip to Russia, including programs of all six of the concerts he conducted and a report by Rimsky-Korsakov testifying to Berlioz's lack of interest in the younger generation of Russian composers.

392.   Boschot, Adolphe. "Musique russe: la musique russe et Berlioz." In *Chez les musiciens (du XVIIIe siècle à nos jours); deuxième série*, 128-36. Paris: Plon-Nourrit, 1924. viii, 274 p. ML60 B785 OCLC 15309440. Revised as "Berlioz et la musique russe." In *Portraits de musiciens*. Vol. 1, 85-94. Paris: Plon, 1947. ML385 B8 OCLC 2685310.

Summarizes Berlioz's experiences in Russia. Includes an 1868 letter from Balakirev to Berlioz urging Berlioz to write a symphony based on Byron's *Manfred*, even supplying a complete programmatic outline. The author concludes that

Berlioz's greatest influence was in helping Russian composers avoid the domination of German music.

393.   Bourmeyster, Alexandre. "Berlioz et ses héritiers russe." *Silex* no. 17 (September 1980): 101-113. ISSN 0151-2315 OCLC 3739044.

Discusses Berlioz's relationship to Russian composers and their music between 1847 and 1868. Explains that he found himself in the middle of a battle between supporters of Italian music and advocates of the German style. Concludes that Berlioz's major influence was on Stasov and the younger generation of Russian nationalists who saw him as the founder and spiritual leader of the new school of program music.

394.   Covell, Roger. "Berlioz, Russia and the Twentieth Century." *Studies in Music* no. 4 (1970): 40-51. ISSN 0081 8267 OCLC 1792275.

Summarizes Berlioz's influence on Russian composers of the nineteenth century, nearly all of whom knew his music well and responded to the newness of his rhythmic and orchestrational technique.

395.   Fouque, Octave. "Berlioz en Russie." In *Les révolutionnaires de la musique*, 185-256. Paris: Calmann-Lévy, 1882. 358 p. ML390 F7 F72 OCLC 5314173.

Gives detailed information on Berlioz's 1847 and 1867-68 trips to Russia and his friendship with Glinka. Includes lists of concert programs. Quotes correspondence.

396.   Hofmann, Michel R. "Hector Berlioz en Russie." *Journal musical français musica-disques* no. 179 (April 1969): 28-30. OCLC 9888150.

Details Berlioz's earliest contact with Russian music through his first meeting with Glinka in Paris in 1845. Also describes his 1847 and 1867-68 concert trips to Russia and the enthusiastic reception he received.

397.   Newmarch, Rosa. "Berlioz in Russia." *Musical Leader and Concert-Goer* 6 (July 30 1903): 12-13. OCLC 10074089.

Describes the friendly relations between Berlioz and Glinka in Paris and how the latter helped pave the way for Berlioz's successful 1847 tour of Russia. Suggests that Berlioz was not

as thoroughly understood or appreciated in Russia as his
reports indicated.

398.   Sahlberg, M. "Berlioz et les russes." dissertation, University
        of Paris, 1944.*

399.   Stasov, V.V. "List, Shuman i Berlioz v Rossii." *Sievernyi
        viestnik* no. 7 (1889) pt. 1: 115-57; no. 8 (1889) pt. 1: 73-110.
        OCLC 8097022. Translated by Florence Jonas as "Liszt,
        Schumann and Berlioz in Russia." In *Selected Essays on
        Music*, 117-94. London: Barrie & Rockliff, 1968. OCLC
        8029593; New York: F.A. Praeger, 1968. OCLC 2420.
        Reprint. New York: Da Capo Press, 1980. 202 p. ML60 S823
        S42 1980 OCLC 6043127.

        Presents a detailed account of Berlioz's warm reception in
        Russia in 1847. Concludes, however, that he had no effect on
        Russian composers of his generation other than Glinka.

400.   Svyet, G. "Gektor Berlioz i Rossiya." *Russkaia mysl'* 20
        (March 2 1967): 4. OCLC 1968946.

        Presents some interesting details concerning Berlioz's 1847
        trip to Russia, including the report of a mixed language
        performance (French and German) of *La damnation de Faust*
        in St. Petersburg, Berlioz's surprise at the quality of Russian
        choristers who learned his music without the aid of a piano,
        and the story of his short-lived romance with a Russian chorus
        girl in Moscow.

VII. Berlioz in Relation to Others

Berlioz's life and career intersected in a variety of ways with those of
many late-eighteenth and early- nineteenth-century artists, writers, and
musicians. This chapter includes works devoted to the study of these
relationships.

1. LUDWIG VAN BEETHOVEN

401.   Boschot, Adolphe. "Un propagateur de Beethoven: Hector
        Berlioz." *La revue musicale* 8 (April 1 1927): 60-76. OCLC
        1764223.

        Draws on Berlioz's essays and feuilletons to show how he
        promoted the appreciation of Beethoven's symphonies in
        France. Berlioz found in these works the application of the
        "poetic idea" to instrumental music, and he assigned specific
        dramatic intentions to each symphony he wrote about.

402.   Comini, Alessandra. "Beethoven Interpreted: the Musicians'
        Musician. Part 2, Berlioz to Brahms." In *The Changing Image
        of Beethoven; a Study in Mythmaking*, 226-52. New York:
        Rizzoli International, 1987. 480 p. ISBN 0-847-80617-0
        ML410 B4 C73 1987 OCLC 14068476.

        Surveys Berlioz's total absorption in the music of Beethoven
        from 1828 on. Finds his characterization of Beethoven as a
        "soaring eagle" and his music as "poetical" to be
        characteristically Romantic responses. Discusses his analyses
        of Beethoven's symphonies in the *Journal des débats*, which

contain elaborate descriptions of the emotional effects of the
music on the listener. Attempts to show how the Romantic
image of Beethoven was fashioned in France by Berlioz's
proselytizing.

2. NATHAN BLOC

403.   Baud-Bovy, Samuel. "Berlioz et Nathan Bloc." *Revue
         musicale de Suisse Romande* 37 (no. 1 March 1984): 2-9.
         ISSN 0035-3744 OCLC 9077868.

         Explains how and why Berlioz asked Bloc, principal
         conductor of the *Odéon* orchestra, to conduct the first all-
         Berlioz program at the *Conservatoire* in 1828.

3. LUIGI CHERUBINI

404.   Bellasis, Edward. Chapter 6: 1825-1830; Chapter 8: 1836-42
         of *Cherubini: Memorials Illustrative of His Life*, 297-316;
         353-57. London: Burnes & Oates, 1874. OCLC 1327885.
         New ed. Birmingham: Cornish Brothers, 1912. OCLC
         11386074. Reprint. New York: Da Capo Press, 1971. xv, 356
         p. ISBN 0-306-70071-9 ML410 C5 B4 1971 OCLC 162944.
         Reprint. Wilmington: International Academic Pub., 1979.
         ISBN 0-897-65400-5 ML410 C5 B4 1979 OCLC 4638559.

         Describes the poor relations between Berlioz, while he was a
         student at the *Conservatoire*, and Cherubini, at that time its
         director. Also explains Cherubini's role in eliminating Berlioz
         from consideration for the position of professor of harmony at
         the *Conservatoire* in 1833 and in hindering the performance of
         the *Requiem* in 1837.

4. PETER CORNELIUS

405.   Irmen, Hans-Josef. "Cornelius und Hector Berlioz." In *Peter
        Cornelius als Komponist, Dichter, Kritiker und Essayist*, 65-
        79. Regensburg: Gustav Bosse, 1977. 237 p. ISBN 3-764-
        92125-0 ML410 C8 P5 OCLC 5891235.

        Explains how the German poet-composer became familiar
        with the music of Berlioz through Liszt's 1852 Weimar
        production of *Benvenuto Cellini*. Thereafter Cornelius became
        an ardent supporter of the new German school of Liszt and
        Wagner and the translator of many of Berlioz's vocal works
        for performance in Germany. Mentions the influence of
        Benvenuto Cellini on Cornelius's opera, *Der Barbier von
        Bagdad*.

406.   Istel, Edgar. "Berlioz und Cornelius." *Die Musik* 3
        (December 1 1903): 366-72. OCLC 1696908.

        Describes the relationship between Berlioz and Cornelius,
        who was responsible for the German translations of *Benvenuto
        Cellini* and other Berlioz vocal works. He also wrote a
        favorable review of a December 1853 concert in Leipzig of
        Berlioz's music in the journal *Echo*, which is excerpted here.

5. JAMES WILLIAM DAVISON

407.   Davison, Henry, comp. *Music During the Victorian Era.
        From Mendelssohn to Wagner: Being the Memoirs of J.W.
        Davison, Forty Years Music Critic of "The Times,"* 93-101;
        148-59; 176-81; 270-75. London: William Reeves, 1912.
        xviii, 539 p. ML423 D18 OCLC 3850115.

        Includes correspondence between Berlioz and Davison dating
        from 1847 through 1864. Also reports on Berlioz's 1847-48
        and 1851 visits to England, the 1853 failure of *Benvenuto
        Cellini* in London, and Berlioz's tenure as conductor of the
        New Philharmonic Society in 1855.

6. EUGENE DELACROIX

408.   Sear, H.G. "Delacroix and Berlioz." *The Music Review* 4
         (November 1943): 216-23. ISSN 0027-4445 OCLC 1758893.

         Demonstrates that as a music critic, Delacroix was mired in
         the Classical thinking of the late-eighteenth century.
         Documents his objections to the use of thematic repetition and
         development as unifying techniques and his antipathy for
         Berlioz's music.

409.   Thompson, Joan. "The *Chaos Man* and the *Colossal
         Nightingale*: a Comparative Study of Eugène Delacroix and
         Hector Berlioz." *Berlioz Society Bulletin* no. 124 (Spring
         1985): 10-24; no. 125 (Summer-Autumn 1985): 12-23. OCLC
         2386332.

         Analyzes similarities and differences between two of the
         greatest French Romantics. Concludes that Delacroix and
         Berlioz were temperamentally very different, and that
         Delacroix neither understood nor liked Berlioz's music.

7. HUMBERT FERRAND

410.   Wright, Michael G.H. "Humbert Ferrand." *Berlioz Society
         Bulletin* no. 22 (September 1957): 5-6; no. 23 (December
         1957): 3-4. OCLC 2386332.

         Biographical sketch of Berlioz's lifelong friend who was first
         a writer and later a lawyer. Concludes that Ferrand was more
         conventional, more inhibited, and less of a genius than
         Berlioz.

8. FRANÇOIS-JOSEPH FETIS

411.   Bloom, Peter. "Berlioz and the Critic: 'La damnation de
        Fétis.'" In *Studies in Musicology in Honor of Otto E. Albrecht*,
        edited by John Walter Hill, 240-65. Kassel: Bärenreiter;
        Clifton, N.J.: European American Music Distribution Corp.,
        1980. viii, 287 p. ISBN 0-913-57427-9 ML55 A38 1980
        OCLC 7502231.

        A detailed account of the change in relations (from cordial to
        antagonistic) between Berlioz and Fétis after Berlioz
        publically humiliated Fétis, accusing him, in one of the spoken
        monologues of *Lélio*, of rewriting Beethoven's symphonies to
        "correct" obvious copyists' errors.

412.   _____. "François-Joseph Fétis and the *Revue musicale*
        (1827-1835)." Ph.D. dissertation, University of Pennsylvania,
        1972. xxxiii, 451 p. bibliography, xii-xxix. OCLC 995866.

        Contains much valuable information about the relationship
        between the influential teacher, composer, conductor, and
        critic and the young Berlioz. Fétis expressed a reserved
        admiration for some of Berlioz's early works in his journal,
        the *Revue musicale* [from abstract].

9. THEOPHILE GAUTIER

413.   Spencer, Michael. "Théophile Gautier, Music Critic." *Music
        and Letters* 49 (no. 1 1968): 4-17. ISSN 0027-4224 OCLC
        1758884.

        States that the music criticism of this famous writer and poet
        was more intuitive than technically informed and that some of
        his more erudite ideas may have been suggested by
        professional musician friends such as Berlioz or Reyer.

10. MIKHAIL IVANOVICH GLINKA

414.   Brown, David. "Paris and Spain." In *Mikhail Glinka; a
         Biographical and Critical Study*, 237-56. London and New
         York: Oxford University Press, 1974. 340 p. ISBN 0-193-
         15341-4 ML410 G46 B76 OCLC 811449.

         Discusses Glinka's visit to Paris in 1844-45, pointing out how
         valuable Berlioz's support was to the Russian composer. Also
         mentions Glinka's admiration for the novelty of Berlioz's
         music.

11. CHRISTOPH WILLIBALD GLUCK

415.   Barsham, Eve. "Berlioz and Gluck." In *C.W. von Gluck:
         "Orfeo,"* compiled by Patricia Howard, 84-97. Cambridge
         Opera Handbooks. Cambridge and New York: Cambridge
         University Press, 1981. ix, 143 p. ISBN 0-521-22827-1
         ML410 G5 C2 1981 OCLC 7838886.

         Reviews Berlioz's love of Gluck's operas, which he
         discovered in Paris during his student years. Cites many
         instances of Berlioz's defense in print of Gluck in the face of
         the growing popularity of Italian opera in Paris in the 1820s.
         Suggests that what Berlioz most admired about Gluck was his
         use of the orchestra for dramatic effect. Also discusses
         Berlioz's revision of *Orfeo* for an 1859 production at the
         Théâtre-lyrique, in which he restored the lead part to the alto.

12. CHARLES GOUNOD

416.   Bailbé, Joseph-Marc. "Autour de *La Reine de Saba*: Nerval et
         Gounod." In *Regards sur l'opéra*, 113-27. Paris: Presses
         universitaires de France, 1976. 259 p. ML1700.1 R43 OCLC
         2820334.

Contrasts Berlioz's favorable opinion of Gounod's opera, *La reine de Saba*, as reported in the *Journal des débats*, March 8, 1862, with critiques by Scudo and Jouvin.

417. Harding, James. *Gounod.* New York: Stein & Day, 1973. 251 p. ISBN 0-812-81541-6 ML410 G7 H4 OCLC 722886. London: Allen & Unwin, 1973. ISBN 0-047-80021-6 ML410 G7 H4 1973b OCLC 3241984. Reprint. New York: Da Capo Press, 1986. ISBN 0-306-79712-7 OCLC 15863437.

Describes Gounod's favorable opinion of *Roméo et Juliette* (34-36), his first meeting with Berlioz, Berlioz's review of *Sapho* (72-73), and Berlioz's release of Scribe's libretto, *La nonne sanglante*, which was subsequently set by Gounod (83-89).

13. HEINRICH HEINE

418. Guichard, Léon. "Berlioz et Heine." *Revue de littérature comparée* 41 (no. 1-3 1967): 5-23. ISSN 0035-1466 OCLC 1764063.

Quotes correspondence and journal articles by both men to establish that they enjoyed friendly relations for over twenty years. Berlioz seems to have understood Heine better than Heine did Berlioz, the poet being impressed only by the grandiose element in Berlioz's music.

419. Kolb, Jocelyne. "Heine's Amusical Muse." *Monatshefte* 73 (no. 4 1981): 392-404. ISSN 0026-9271 OCLC 1758529.

Determines that one of Heine's favorite modes of expression in his music criticism was the technique of reducing music to suggestive poetic images, thus concealing his lack of musical knowledge. Berlioz, who was frequently the subject of Heine's criticism, realized better than most how incompetent Heine really was as a music critic.

14. VICTOR HUGO

420.   Tiersot, Julien. "Victor Hugo musicien." *La revue musicale*
        16 (September-October 1935): 167-96. OCLC 1764223.

        Traces Hugo's involvement with music and musicians of his
        time, including Berlioz. Attests to the mutual respect,
        admiration, and support these two artists showed for one
        another throughout their careers.

15. FRANZ LISZT

421.   Brenet, Michel [Marie Bobillier]. "L'amitié de Berlioz et de
        Liszt." *Le guide musical* 50 (August 14-21 1904): 595-600;
        (September 18): 659-66; (September 25): 679-87. OCLC
        1509855.

        Describes the friendship of Berlioz and Liszt from their first
        meeting in 1830 to the end of Berlioz's life. Includes
        information on Liszt's piano transcriptions of Berlioz's works
        and a synopsis of Liszt's article on *Harold en Italie* (#874).
        Demonstrates that the dissolution of the friendship was mainly
        the result of Liszt's continuing support for Wagner's "music
        of the future." The most extensive treatment of this subject.

422.   Kapp, Julius. "Die Kampfgenossen (Berlioz/Liszt)." In *Das
        Dreigestirn: Berlioz, Liszt, Wagner*, 27-54. Berlin: Schuster
        & Loeffler, 1920. 179 p. ML390 K17 OCLC 11061021.

        Details the history of the relationship between Berlioz and
        Liszt which began in Paris in 1830. Initially each man
        supported the artistic endeavors of the other, but in later years,
        when Berlioz became jealous of Liszt's attachment to Wagner,
        the friendship gradually deteriorated. Implies that Berlioz was
        interested in Liszt only as long as he was actively
        campaigning in support of Berlioz's music.

423.   Perényi, Eleanor. Chapters 8, 36, 39 of *Liszt, the Artist as
        Romantic Hero*, 68-75; 342-45; 375-95. Boston: Little,

Brown, 1974. x, 466 p. ISBN 0-316-69910-1 ML410 L7 P3
OCLC 914888.

Describes the relationship between Berlioz and Liszt from
Liszt's point of view, claiming that his professional
admiration and support for Berlioz was much greater and
more genuine than was Berlioz's for him. Later chapters
explain how Liszt got caught in the ideological crossfire
between Berlioz and Wagner.

16. GIACOMO MEYERBEER

424.   Besnier, Patrick. "Berlioz et Meyerbeer." *Revue de
musicologie* 63 (no. 1-2 1977): 35-40. ISSN 0035-1601
OCLC 1773306.

Extracts passages from the letters and feuilletons to prove that
Berlioz had a great deal of respect for Meyerbeer, probably
because he found much of his own spectacular style in the
German composer's works.

425.   Stuart, Charles. "Did Berlioz Really Like Meyerbeer?"
Opera 3 (December 1952): 719-25. ISSN 0030-3526 OCLC
2574662.

Contends that most Berlioz scholars have misrepresented the
composer's favorable review of Meyerbeer's *Le prophète* as a
professional courtesy extended in repayment of favors
received. However, an impartial examination of the evidence
shows that Berlioz was both genuinely complimentary *and*
severely critical of Meyerbeer's style.

17. WOLFGANG AMADEUS MOZART

426.   Boschot, Adolphe. "Mozart et Berlioz." In *Portraits de
musiciens*. Vol. 1, 168-73. Paris: Plon-Nourrit, 1947. ML 385
B8 OCLC 2685310.

Notes that Berlioz, like most of the French musical world of
the early nineteenth century, knew little of the works of
Mozart. It was not until his 1853 trip to London that he
"discovered" Mozart.

18. GERARD DE NERVAL

427.   Jensen, E.F. "Berlioz and Gérard de Nerval." *Soundings: a
        Music Journal* no. 11 (1983-84): 46-51. ISSN 0081-2080
        OCLC 1948031.

        Explains that despite Berlioz's enthusiasm for Nerval's
        translation of *Faust*, no direct collaboration between the two
        men ever materialized, primarily because of "aesthetic and
        personal differences which separated them." Suggests that
        Berlioz may have preferred a more restrained and Classical
        style of writing to the shockingly avant-garde style of Nerval
        and his circle.

19. NICOLO PAGANINI

428.   Kolon, Victor. "Die Pariser Gitarre von Paganini-Berlioz."
        Zeitschrift für die Gitarre 5 (April 15 1926): 50-53.

        Explains that Berlioz made a gift of his guitar to Paganini
        circa 1840 as a sign of his admiration for the friendship and
        talent of the great virtuoso.

20. ERNEST REYER

429.   Boschot, Adolphe. "Reyer ami de Berlioz." In *Chez les musiciens (du XVIII siècle à nos jours); deuxième série*, 93-99. Paris: Plon-Nourrit, 1924. viii, 274 p. ML60 B785 OCLC 15309440.

Neatly summarizes the relationship between the two composers, who met in 1848. Berlioz was impressed by Reyer's ballet *Sacountalâ*, whose orchestrational originality he especially praised in an 1850 review in the *Journal des débats*.

21. GEORGE SAND

430.   Lubin, Georges. "Drame perdu pour une étoile sans emploi; George Sand et Hector Berlioz." In *Homage à George Sand*, 18-23. Paris: Presses universitaires de France, 1969. 150 p. PQ2412 H55 OCLC 1105135.

Concerns Berlioz's request that George Sand write a play specifically for his wife, Harriet Smithson, who, because of her poor French, could find no work as an actress in Parisian theaters. This proposed play was to include among its *dramatis personae* the character of an English woman who spoke little French.

22. ROBERT SCHUMANN

431.   Tiersot, Julien. "Schumann et Berlioz." *La revue musicale* no. 161 (December 1935): 89-102. OCLC 1764223.

Documents Schumann's knowledge and active support of Berlioz's music in the *Neue Zeitschrift für Musik*, citing particularly his analysis of the *Symphonie fantastique*. States

that Berlioz, on the other hand, knew Schumann's music less
well and had to ask Liszt to write an article about it in 1837
for the *Revue et gazette musicale de Paris.*

23. EUGENE SCRIBE

432.   Bonnefon, Paul. "Les avatars de Faust." *Revue politique et*
         littéraire (Revue Bleue) 55 (May 12 1917): 292-95. OCLC
         8339424.

         Includes correspondence between Berlioz and Scribe written
         in 1847 concerning a possible adaptation of *La damnation de*
         Faust for the London operatic stage and Scribe's withdrawal
         of his libretto for *La nonne sanglante* from Berlioz.

24. P. SCUDO

433.   Dorville, Alexis. "Berlioz and Scudo." In *Le livre d'or du*
         centenaire Hector Berlioz, 96-99. Paris: G. Petit, 1907. vi,
         224 p. ML410 B5 L59 OCLC 5781226.

         Sketches the unsympathetic reaction of Scudo, music critic for
         the *Revue des deux mondes* and ardent supporter of Italian
         opera in Paris, to Berlioz's works. Includes excerpts from his
         reviews.

25. STENDHAL

434.   Guichard, Léon. "Berlioz et Stendhal." *Cahiers de l'alpe* no.
         46 (1969): 114-18. OCLC 12101098.

Explains that although there were many parallels between their lives and artistic temperaments, Berlioz and Stendhal probably never met. Berlioz showed nothing but sarcastic antipathy for Stendhal as a writer on music, mainly because of Stendhal's ardent support for Italian *opera buffa*.

26. PAULINE VIARDOT

435.   Waddington, Patrick. "Pauline Viardot-Garcia as Berlioz's Counselor and Physician." *The Musical Quarterly* 59 (no. 3 1973): 382-98. ISSN 0027-4631 OCLC 1642493.

Chronicles the relationship between Berlioz and Pauline Viardot from 1859, the period of their collaboration on Gluck's *Orphée*, until the production of *Les Troyens à Carthage* in November 1863. Extensively quotes correspondence of both.

27. ALFRED DE VIGNY

436.   Court, Glyn. "Hector Berlioz and Alfred de Vigny." *Music and Letters* 37 (no. 2 1956): 118-27. ISSN 0027-4224 OCLC 1758884.

Quotes Berlioz's correspondence to trace the professional and personal relationship between him and the famous poet-dramatist from circa 1830 to de Vigny's death in 1863. Suggests that they were alike in their serious artistic temperaments and that they continually supported and defended one another's work. Mentions de Vigny's connection with the *Benvenuto Cellini* libretto, to which he contributed anonymously.

437.   Dupuy, Ernest. "Alfred de Vigny et Hector Berlioz." *Revue des deux mondes* 6th period, tome 2 (April 15 1911): 837-65. OCLC 8305048. Reprinted in *Alfred de Vigny, ses amitiés, son rôle littéraire*. Vol. 2, 291-331. Paris: Société française

d'imprimerie et de librairie, 1912. 2 vols. PQ2474 Z3 D82
OCLC 2418046.

Uses previously unpublished correspondence between Berlioz
and de Vigny to establish the exact nature of their lifelong
relationship of mutual artistic support and personal
admiration.

28. RICHARD WAGNER

438.   B. [Richard Batka?] "Richard Wagner über Wagner."
        Kunstwart 17 (December 1 1903): 333-36. OCLC 15712421.

        Neatly summarizes Wagner's changing opinions of Berlioz,
        from his first favorable impressions of the symphonies,
        through his critical attack in *Oper und Drama* (where Wagner
        accused Berlioz of drowning himself in a flood of his own
        effect-oriented technical apparatus), to the final peacemaking
        in Berlioz's later years.

439.   Boschot, Adolphe. "Le conflit Berlioz-Wagner." *La revue de
        Paris* 19 (November-December 1912): 717-47. OCLC
        1775173. Reprinted in *Portraits de musiciens*. Vol. 1, 1-38.
        Paris: Plon-Nourrit, 1947. ML385 B8 OCLC 2685310.

        Demonstrates that although Berlioz and Wagner were bound
        by a mutual respect for serious music and a common
        abhorrence of everything commonplace and "popular" in
        opera, they often misunderstood or were simply ignorant of
        one another's true goals and ideals. Also elucidates the role
        that Marie Recio Berlioz played in turning her husband
        against Wagner.

440.   Bouyer, Raymond. "Berlioz et Wagner en 1903." *La nouvelle
        revue* new series, tome 24 (October 1 1903): 417-23. OCLC
        1717084.

        Briefly reviews the points of contention between Berlioz and
        Wagner and tries to re-evaluate their relative positions in the
        history of nineteenth-century music. Concludes that while
        Wagner was the "uncontested master" of opera, Berlioz's true
        genius manifested itself in the "dramatic symphony."

441. _____. "Petites notes sans portée: Berlioz jugé par Wagner." *Le ménestrel* 69 (September 20 1903): 300-301. OCLC 6966764.

Summarizes the various contacts between Berlioz and Wagner. Establishes that in the breakdown of friendly relations between them, it was Wagner who first publically attacked Berlioz in 1841, criticizing both the man and his music in the *Revue et gazette musicale de Paris*.

442. Dahlhaus, Carl. "Wagners Berlioz-Kritik und die Asthetik des Hasslichen." In *Festschrift für Arno Volk*, 107-23. Cologne: Hans Gerig, 1974. 146 p. ISBN 3-872-52077-6 ML55 V55 1974 OCLC 1205673.

States that Wagner accused Berlioz of obscuring the essence of music with elements of superficial decoration. In Wagner's opinion, Berlioz's music was therefore "in error," and represented only a transitional stage in the evolution of music towards its final redemption in the music drama.

443. Ernst, Alfred. "Wagner corrigé par Berlioz." *Le ménestrel* 50 (September 28 1884): 348-49. OCLC 6966764.

Lists some of the harmonic "errors" that Berlioz identified in the score of *Tristan und Isolde* given to him by Wagner. Ironically, most of these "corrections" were of unusual and unresolved dissonances similar to those Berlioz himself used.

444. Hurlimann, Martin, compiler. "Berlioz." In *Richard Wagner in Selbstzeugnissen und im Urteil der Zeitgenossen*, 167-74. Zurich: Manesse Verlag, 1972. 411 p. ISBN 3-717-51442-3 ML410 W1 H84 OCLC 847677.

Presents excerpts from Wagner's writings and letters which show the sympathetic and understanding side of his relationship with Berlioz.

445. Kapp, Julius. "Die feindlichen Brüder (Berlioz/Wagner)." In *Das Dreigestirn: Berlioz, Liszt, Wagner*, 55-107. Berlin: Schuster & Loeffler, 1920. 179 p. ML390 K17 OCLC 11061021.

Uses extensive excerpts from the writings of Wagner to document the complex evolution of the relationship between him and Berlioz, which began with a mutual sympathy for

their common plight as unappreciated artists in Paris circa
1840, but which quickly broke down over differences of
opinion on musical style during Berlioz's visit to Dresden in
1843. Includes a discussion of Liszt's role as mutual friend
and arbitrator.

446.   Kufferath, Maurice. "Wagner et Berlioz." *Le guide musical*
        49 (November 29 1903 supplement): 24-27. OCLC 1509855.

        Attributes the problems between Berlioz and Wagner to
        jealousy on Berlioz's part. Offers the unusual theory that their
        disagreement was one of musical aesthetics, Wagner taking
        the part of Classical balance and order against the "unbridled
        caprice" of Berlioz.

447.   Macdonald, Hugh. "Berlioz and the 1861 *Tannhäuser*."
        Berlioz Society Bulletin no. 34 (April 1961): 2-6. OCLC
        2386332.

        Describes Berlioz's ambivalence toward the Paris *Opéra*
        production of Wagner's *Tannhäuser* and his indirect role in its
        failure.

448.   Mache, François-Bernard. "Deux frères ennemis issus de
        Beethoven." In *Berlioz*, 111-35. Paris: Réalités-Hachette,
        1973. 269 p. ML410 B5 B33 OCLC 1011818.

        Finds the cause of the troubled relationship between Berlioz
        and Wagner not in professional rivalry but in irreconcilable
        differences in their artistic temperaments.

449.   Massougnes, Georges de. "Berlioz et Wagner." *Revue d' art
        dramatique* 15 (January 1900): 5-22. OCLC 5853914.

        Takes the unusual position that the animosity between Berlioz
        and Wagner was more the product of fanatical partisans on
        both sides than of ill will on the part of the composers
        themselves. Support for this hypothesis is drawn from Mottl's
        testimony that Wagner defended Berlioz's music as
        vigorously circa 1860 (after their "feud") as he had circa 1840.

450.   Newman, Ernest. "The Relations of Wagner and Berlioz." In
        Berlioz, Romantic and Classic, edited by Peter Heyworth, 97-
        101. London: Gollancz, 1972. 288 p. ISBN 0-575-01365-6
        ML410 B5 N49 OCLC 516762.

Notes that Wagner criticized many of Berlioz's works without having the slightest knowledge of them, and that many eminent Wagner scholars have deliberately glossed over this fact.

451.   Tiersot, Julien. "Hector Berlioz and Richard Wagner." Translated by Theodore Baker. *The Musical Quarterly* 3 (no. 3 1917): 453-92. ISSN 0027-4631 OCLC 1642493.

Shows that Berlioz and Wagner were at one point brothers in the war against philistinism, but that each composer's personal suspicions about the other's intention to dominate the musical world, along with strongly held differences of opinion about the role of music in relation to drama, formed the basis for most of the ill will and misunderstanding that characterized their relationship in later years. One of the most thorough accounts of the Berlioz-Wagner relationship.

452.   Turner, W.J. "The Problem of Berlioz." *The New Statesman and Nation* 24 (October 25 1924): 78-79; (November 8): 138-39. ISSN 0952-102X OCLC 4589119.

Takes issue with Rolland's contention that Wagner was a greater man than Berlioz because, unlike Berlioz, he ended his life in the solace of his sincere religious convictions.

453.   Willy [Henry Gauthier-Villars]. "Berlioz et Wagner." In *Propos d'ouvreuse*, 85-99. Paris: Les Editions Martine, 1928. 146 p. ML60 G38 1928 OCLC 10155226.

Suggests that the hostility between Berlioz and Wagner was due to more than simple jealousy: that at heart they had fundamentally different musical principles and temperaments, Berlioz being more of a Classicist, Wagner more a radical. Originally appeared in *Renaissance latine*, May 15, 1903.

29. VINCENT WALLACE

454.   Klein, John W. "Berlioz and Vincent Wallace." *The Music Review* 30 (no. 2 1969): 138-44. ISSN 0027-4445 OCLC 1758893.

Explains that Wallace, an Irish composer whom Berlioz met in London in 1847 and in whom he found a kindred and impetuous spirit, was the source for one of the stories in *Les soirées de l'orchestre.*

VIII. Berlioz As Writer and Critic

One of the most important aspects of Berlioz's career was his work as a professional writer and music critic. This chapter includes general surveys of his writing, analyses of his style and technique, studies of his critical aesthetics, and essays devoted to individual prose works.

1. GENERAL STUDIES

455.   Bailbé, Joseph-Marc. "Le sens de l'espace dans les textes littéraires de Berlioz." *Romantisme* no. 12 (1976): 35-42. ISSN 0048-8593 OCLC 931119.

Attempts to draw a connection between references to the vast spaces of nature in Berlioz's literary works and the use of colossal performing forces in large acoustic ambiances in his music. Also draws attention to the fact that much of Berlioz's music implies or was inspired by specific geographic locations.

456.   Boschot, Adolphe. "Hector Berlioz, critique musical." *Académie royale des sciences, des lettres et des beaux-arts de Belgique. Classe des beaux-arts. Bulletin de la classe des beaux-arts* 20 (1938): 34-42. OCLC 1460688.

Traces Berlioz's early involvement with music criticism. Depicts him as a fiery young composer consumed by an ardent love of his art, and sees in his writing a spontaneous reaction to the wrongs of the musical world around him. Concludes that his journalism was not so much a burdensome duty (as he himself often described it) as it was an inner necessity.

457.   Cohen, Howard Robert. "Berlioz on the Opéra (1829-1849): a Study in Music Criticism." New York University dissertation, 1973. 338 p. bibliography, 310-28. OCLC 5215621.

Surveys Berlioz's critical writing on opera in order to discover the presence of a prevailing aesthestic. Follows with annotated translations of fifteen of his articles on opera and the *Opéra*.

458.   _____. "Hector Berlioz, critique musical; ses écrits sur l'Opéra de Paris de 1829 à 1849." *Revue de musicologie* 63 (no. 1-2 1977): 17-34. ISSN 0035-1601 OCLC 1773306.

Defines several of Berlioz's critical principles concerning opera through a study of his feuilletons. Follows by attempting to show that he applied these principles to his own work as a music journalist in a logical and systematic fashion.

459.   Conati, Marcello. "La Strepponi insegnante di canto a Parigi e un giudizio sconosciuto di Berlioz." *Rassegna musicale Curci* 32 (no. 2 1979): 25-28. ISSN 0033-9806 OCLC 2266766.

Reports on the concerts Giuseppina Strepponi gave in Paris in 1846 and 1847 in preparation for beginning her career there as a voice teacher. Berlioz reviewed one of these concerts and was favorably impressed by the new dramatic style of Italian singing initiated by the works of Verdi.

460.   Curzon, Henri de. "Les débuts de Berlioz dans la critique." *Le guide musical* 49 (November 29 1903 supplement): 28-31. OCLC 1509855.

Describes Berlioz's first two years (1835 and 1836) as music critic for the *Journal des débats*, during which he reviewed different kinds of concerts but not opera. Like Hallays (#465), the author finds no system to Berlioz's critical method.

461.   Dean, Winton. "Critic and Composer." *Opera* 3 (March 1952): 154-61. ISSN 0030-3526 OCLC 2574662.

Differentiates between composers who were successful critics and those who merely put their opinions into words from time to time. Finds that Berlioz and Schumann are the only nineteenth-century examples of the former type. Compares their styles and assesses the effects of their writing on their composing.

462. Didier, Béatrice. "Berlioz conteur et ecrivain." *La revue de Paris* 77 (February 1970): 88-93. OCLC 1775173.

Claims for Berlioz the distinction of being equally gifted as a writer and a musician. Suggests his prose demonstrated the same concern for the elements of rhythm and formal structure as did his music.

463. _____. "Berlioz librettiste." *Silex* no. 17 (September 1980): 52-56. ISSN 0151-2315 OCLC 3739044.

Claims that Berlioz was forced to become his own librettist because of what he saw to be the lack of suitably dramatic librettos by professional writers. Also suggests that the more natural style of the language of his librettos resulted from his frequent use of literary sources in foreign languages which he felt freer to adapt creatively. Draws examples from Berlioz's adaptation of Nerval's translation of *Faust*.

464. Elliott, John R., Jr. "Berlioz the Critic." *Adam International Review* nos. 331-333 (1969): 88-92. ISSN 0001-8015 OCLC 1965286.

Presents Berlioz as the father of modern criticism whose philosophy of music and attempts to elevate public taste and awareness can be found throughout his reviews.

465. Hallays, André. "Hector Berlioz, critique musical." Introduction to *Les musiciens et la musique*, i-xlviii. Paris: Calmann-Lévy, 1903. OCLC 9623344. Reprinted in *La revue de Paris* 10 (April 1 1903): 560-95. OCLC 1775173. Excerpted as "L'esthétique de Berlioz." *Le guide musical* 49 (June 14-21 1903): 483-86. OCLC 1509855.

Analyzes Berlioz's attitudes toward music journalism and the style and technique of his writing. Concludes that he was the first critic to bring a working knowledge of music to journalism, and that he used his position with the *Journal des débats* as a podium from which he could proselytize for "the grand, the true and the beautiful" in music. Nevertheless, the author finds little consistency in Berlioz's writing.

466.   Hauman, Lucien. "Hector Berlioz--l'homme dans l'écrivain."
        Le guide musical 49 (November 29 1903 supplement): 31-32.
        OCLC 1509855.

        Contends that Berlioz was a man of uncompromising musical
        principles who hated mediocrity and everything "easy" or
        common in music, and that these principles are apparent in his
        writings.

467.   Hofer, Hermann. "Barbey d'Aurevilly et Hector Berlioz." *La
        revue des lettres modernes* nos. 285-89 (1972): 73-100. ISSN
        0035-2136 OCLC 1764111.

        Finds many similarities between the music criticism of Barbey
        and that of Berlioz, including a continual battle against
        mediocrity and bad taste, as well as an interest in the
        fantastique.

468.   Ironfield, Susan Elizabeth. "L'art et l'artiste dans les écrits de
        Berlioz." Dissertation, University of Liverpool, 1971.*

469.   Jong, J. de. "Berlioz als Criticus." *Onze Eeuw* 4 (January
        1904): 41-67.

        Discusses and extensively quotes several feuilletons that
        appear in Hallays's collection (#113) to provide an overview
        of Berlioz's critical career.

470.   Jullien, Adolphe. "La critique musicale au *Journal des
        débats*." In *Musique: mélanges d'histoire et de critique
        musicale et dramatique*, 376-88. Paris: Librairie de l'Art,
        1896. 462 p. ML270.1 J94 OCLC 5913288.

        Reviews the publication of *Le livre du centenaire du Journal
        des débats, 1789-1889*. Observes that Berlioz's music
        criticism was marked by a blend of passionate personal
        pleading and amusing witticisms.

471.   Lebois, André. "Hommage à Berlioz ecrivain." *Le bayou* no.
        58 (Summer 1954): 52-65. ISSN 0731-647X OCLC 2923319.

        Suggests that a picture of Berlioz the man and artist is
        revealed in his critical writings where one meets the gods of
        his musical world and encounters both the barbed sarcasm of
        his wit and the profundity of his musical insights.

472. Mey, Kurt. "Hector Berlioz als Schriftsteller." *Neue Musik-Zeitung* 25 (December 3 1903): 79-81. OCLC 11930822.

    Compares Berlioz's and Wagner's writing. Claims that, unlike Wagner, Berlioz never developed into a musical philosopher, and that this prevented him from creating the new music-drama.

473. Mönch, Walter. "Hector Berlioz: 'Voila un ecrivain!'" In *Festgabe für Julius Wilhelm zum 80. Geburtstag,* 106-19. Wiesbaden: Steiner, 1977. viii, 138 p. ISBN 3-515-02626-6 PC2026 W5 F4 OCLC 3747376.

    Divides Berlioz's literary works into two categories, serious and anecdotal, describing some of the latter genre as Hoffmannesque. Also claims that Berlioz's reputation as a writer waned after his death because of the ephemeral nature of his feuilletons. Discusses primarily *Les grotesques de la musique* and *Les soirées de l'orchestre.*

474. Mongrédien, Jean. "La théorie de l'imitation en musique en début du romantisme." *Romantisme* no. 8 (1974): 86-91. ISSN 0048-8593 OCLC 931119.

    Shows that the eighteenth-century theory of music as imitation of nature, which was the point of departure for Berlioz's essay, "De l'imitation musicale" (*Revue et gazette musicale de Paris,* January 1, 8, 1837), was by no means as universally accepted among aestheticians of that time as has previously been suggested.

475. Monselet, Charles. "Hector Berlioz." In *Petits mémoires littéraires,* 347-51. Paris: G. Charpentier, 1885. 356 p. PQ282 M69 1885 OCLC 2844118.

    Claims that Berlioz's music criticism was a combination of bad puns and closed-mindedness. States that his career was far more successful than he or his admirers ever admitted.

476. Morillot, Paul. "Berlioz écrivain." *Annales de l'Université de Grenoble* 15 (no. 2 1903): 369-416. OCLC 18356967. Reprint. Grenoble, Allier, 1903. 50 p.

    Discusses the complementary nature of writing music and writing prose and suggests that this relationship was well understood by Berlioz when he wrote his own librettos. Follows with comments on Berlioz's adaptations of famous

literary works as musical texts. Assesses the effect of the
Dauphiné, Berlioz's birthplace, on the passionate style of
writing found in the *Mémoires*. Concludes that Berlioz's
writing, like his music, is founded on the principle of contrasts
and oppositions.

477.   Murphy, Kerry R. "Attribution of Some Unsigned Articles of
Berlioz in the *Revue et gazette musicale de Paris* (1834-1837).
Musicology Australia 8 (1985): 39-49. ISSN 0814-5857
OCLC 12714872.

Identifies several stylistic characteristics typical of Berlioz's
writing in his signed articles: a fondness for particular
subjects, unique critical opinions, and vocabulary. Using a
comparative analysis of these characteristics, the author then
proceeds to attribute twenty-three unsigned articles to Berlioz.

478.   _____. "The Formation of the Music Criticism of Hector
Berlioz (1823-1837)." Ph.D. dissertation, Melbourne
University, 1984, 437 p. bibliography, 409-30. OCLC
19013166. Revised as *Hector Berlioz and the Development of
French Music Criticism*. Ann Arbor: UMI Research Press,
1987. 306 p. ISBN 0-835-71821-2 ML3880 M85 1988
OCLC 17209797.

Examines Berlioz's early years as a music critic in the context
of the scope and style of French criticism from 1800 to 1850.
Concentrates on Berlioz's opinions of contemporary
composers, particularly those of opera [from abstract].

479.   Niecks, Friedrich. "Hector Berlioz as Musical Critic." *The
Monthly Musical Record* 45 (December 1 1915): 341-43.
OCLC 1605021.

Claims that Berlioz lacked the impartiality of a true music
critic. Lists some of the approximately forty journals to which
Berlioz contributed.

480.   Oliver, Robert E. "Hector Berlioz, the Man and His
Writings." Ph.D. dissertation, University of Illinois, 1952.*

481.   Pleasants, H. "Berlioz as Critic." *Stereo Review* 23 (October
1969): 89-93. ISSN 0039-1220 OCLC 1766502.

Calls Berlioz a literary caricaturist who was more a "belletrist"
than a critic. Maintains that he upheld his ideals of truth and
beauty throughout his writing about music.

482.   Reeve, Katherine Kolb. "Hector Berlioz." In *European
       Writers: the Romantic Century*, edited by Jacques Barzun.
       Vol. 6. *Victor Hugo to Theodor Fontane*, 771-812. New
       York: Charles Scribner's Sons, 1985. 7 vols. ISBN 0-684-
       17915-6 PN501 E9 1983 OCLC 9826161.

       Within the context of a detailed biographical sketch, the
       author highlights Berlioz's life-long association with the
       creative process of writing. All of his prose works (feuilletons
       [including reviews and essays], libretti, memoirs, and letters)
       are analyzed for philosophical content, style, and writing
       technique. An important theme of this analytical essay is the
       constant intersection of and relationship between Berlioz's
       musical and literary careers.

483.   _____. "The Poetics of the Orchestra in the Writings of
       Hector Berlioz." Ph.D. dissertation, Yale University, 1978.
       viii, 350 p., bibliography, 334-50. OCLC 10053538.

       Studies Berlioz's critical writings and artistic principles in the
       context of eighteenth- and nineteenth-century French musical
       aesthetics. Discusses the theory of music as imitation, the
       expressive instrumental music of Beethoven and Berlioz, the
       relationship of composer and audience in the nineteenth
       century, and the Romantic vogue for the *fantastique* in music.

484.   Roberts, W. Wright. "Berlioz the Critic." *Music and Letters* 7
       (no. 1 1926): 63-72; (no. 2 1926): 133-42. ISSN 0027-4224
       OCLC 1758884.

       Evaluates Berlioz's critical stance, discussing his "idols"
       (Beethoven, Gluck, Weber, and Shakespeare) and "aversions"
       (philistinism, bad orchestration, pedants, and prima donnas) in
       relation to his own music. Marred by the author's inaccurate
       assessment of Berlioz's musical style, especially when
       speaking of his "weak counterpoint" and formal problems.

485.   Samuel, Claude. "Les écrits du compositeur." In *Berlioz*, 197-
       209. Paris: Réalités-Hachette, 1973. 269 p. ML410 B5 B33
       OCLC 1011818.

       Provides a survey of Berlioz's career as a writer, emphasizing
       how much he hated having to waste time reviewing concerts.
       Quotes from his letters to demonstrate the volcanic and
       explosive facets of his personality, and from his feuilletons to

explain his philosophy of music (based on the abhorrence of
anything superficial, easy, or popular).

486.   Williams, Roger Lawrence. "The Grotesque in the Writings
        of Hector Berlioz." Ph.D. dissertation, University of
        California at Berkeley, 1958.*

2. INDIVIDUAL WORKS

a. *Le chef d'orchestre*

487.   Matesky, Michael Paul. "Berlioz on Conducting". D.M.A.
        dissertation, University of Washington, 1974. 130 p.
        bibliography, 127-29. OCLC 6908926.

        Uses Berlioz's treatise as the basis for a discussion of
        conductors and conducting in the nineteenth century [from
        abstract].

b. Correspondence

488.   Woesler, Winifried. "Miszelle zum Briefwechsel Berlioz-
        Heine." *Heine-Jahrbuch* 13 (1974): 103-4. ISSN 0073-1692
        OCLC 923884.

        Redates some correspondence concerning complimentary
        tickets for the premiere of *L'enfance du Christ* on December
        10, 1854.

c. *Grande traité d'instrumentation et d'orchestration modernes*

489.   Bruce, Alastair. "Berlioz's Treatise on Instrumentation."
        Berlioz Society Bulletin no. 104 (Summer 1979): 2-13. OCLC
        2386332.

General summary of the work's contents and a history of its publication.

490. Closson, Ernest. "Richard Strauss et le *Traité d'orchestration* d'Hector Berlioz." *Le guide musical* 55 (September 26-October 3 1909): 591-94; (October 10): 607-11. OCLC 1509855.

Uses Strauss's textual revisions of the work to demonstrate his obvious admiration for Wagner. Throughout his revisions, he advised discretion in the application of the massive forces of the Berlioz-Wagner orchestra.

491. Lockspeiser, Edward. "The Berlioz-Strauss Treatise on Instrumentation." *Music and Letters* 50 (no. 1 1969): 37-44. ISSN 0027-4224 OCLC 1758884.

Describes Richard Strauss's 1905 revision of the *Traité d'instrumentation* with particular attention to his introductory comments. Compares musical examples used by Berlioz (drawn mostly from the music of Gluck, Beethoven, and Weber) with those added by Strauss (drawn mostly from the music of Wagner). Reprinted as Appendix A of #614.

d. *Les grotesques de la musique*

492. Hevelyne. *"Les grotesques* de Théophile Gautier, *Les grotesques de la musique* d'Hector Berlioz." *Bulletin de la société Théophile Gautier* no. 2 (1980): 61-76. ISSN 0221-7945 OCLC 7261538.

Describes Berlioz and Gautier as artists in the vanguard of the Romantic movement. In their respective works, *Les grotesques...*, each defends beauty in art--Gautier by praising the French language, Berlioz by satirizing the destiny of French music.

e. *Mémoires*

493.   Bailbé, Joseph-Marc. *Berlioz, artiste et ecrivain dans les
        "Mémoires."* Paris: Presses universitaires de France, 1972.
        172 p. ML410 B5 B13 OCLC 669335.

        Analyzes the *Mémoires* as a mirror of Berlioz's artistic
        personality. Discusses extensively the techniques of humor
        used in his writing, including caricature and exaggeration, the
        use of language for poetic effect, and the manifestation of an
        affinity for Classical antiquity. A separate section takes up the
        related subject of the *Traité d'instrumentation* as an
        illustration of Berlioz's practical understanding of the
        orchestra.

494.   Bate, A. Jonathan. "Berlioz's *Memoirs*: a Shakespearean
        Autobiography." *Berlioz Society Bulletin* no. 118 (Autumn
        1983): 8-11. OCLC 2386332.

        Demonstrates how the influence of Shakespeare was a primary
        organizing force in the writing of the *Mémoires*, manifesting
        itself not only in direct quotations from the bard, but also in
        the autobiographical adoption of the identities of specific
        Shakespearean characters.

495.   Labie, Jean-François. "Berlioz: verité et mensonge."
        Diapason harmonie no. 313 (February 1986): 98-100. OCLC
        7955544.

        Uses the historical facts surrounding the commissioning and
        performance of the *Requiem* to demonstrate the extent of their
        exaggeration and misrepresentation by Berlioz in the
        Mémoires.

f. *Les soirées de l'orchestre*

496.   Didier, Béatrice. "Hector Berlioz et l'art de la nouvelle."
        Romantisme no. 12 (1976): 19-26. ISSN 0048-8593 OCLC
        931119.

        Points to correlations between Berlioz's writing style in *Les
        soirées de l'orchestre* and *Les grotesques de la musique* and
        techniques found in the Romantic literature on musical

subjects, including plot development, variation of voice, and a non-technical vocabulary, used by such writers as Hoffmann and Balzac.

497.   Haar, James. "Berlioz and the 'First Opera.'" *19th-Century Music* 3 (no. 1 1979): 32-41. ISSN 0148-2076 OCLC 3280195.

Demonstrates that the source for much of the historical information in Berlioz's tale, *Le premier opéra*, was the *Dictionnaire historique des musiciens* of Alexandre Choron and François Fayolle (Paris, 1811).

498.   Newman, Ernest. "Berlioz As Journalist." In *Berlioz, Romantic and Classic*, edited by Peter Heyworth, 237-45. London: Gollancz, 1972. 288 p. ISBN 0-575-01365-6 ML410 B9 N49 OCLC 516762.

Surveys *Les soirées de l'orchestre* to demonstrate how Berlioz survived the drudgery of music criticism by treating the absurdities of journalistic life humorously.

IX. Literary Sources

No other composer before Berlioz was so directly motivated in his work by the great authors of the Western world. This chapter includes studies that analyze the influence of such writers on Berlioz's music in general or on a selected group of works. Articles dealing with the relationship of specific literary works to specific compositions of Berlioz can be found in Chapter 13.

499.   Cockrell, William Dale. "Hector Berlioz and 'le système Shakespearien.'" Ph.D. dissertation, University of Illinois, 1978. ix, 304 p. bibliography, 224-34. OCLC 11327091.

Examines the influence of Shakespeare on the French Romantics in general and on Berlioz in particular. Special attention is paid to their fascination with Shakespeare's deliberate violation of the Classical unities of time, place, and action [from abstract].

500.   _____. "A Study in French Romanticism: Berlioz and Shakespeare." *The Journal of Musicological Research* 4 (nos. 1-2 1982): 85-113. ISSN 0141 1896 OCLC 6273983.

Attempts to define Berlioz's concept of the "Shakespearean system" by analyzing the importance of de Vigny, Dumas, and Hugo in the dissemination of ideas about Shakespearean form in French Romantic literature (primarily the disregard of the unities of time, place, and action), and by showing the numerous manifestations of Shakespearean techniques in *Les Troyens*, including tableaux structure, the appearance of ghosts with supernatural knowledge, and the mixing of comic and tragic genres.

501.   Court, A.W.G[lyn]. "Hector Berlioz: the Role of Literature in His Life and Work." Ph.D. dissertation, University of London, 1961.*

502.   Elliott, John R., Jr. "The Shakespeare Berlioz Saw." *Music and Letters* 57 (no. 3 1976): 292-308. ISSN 0027-4224 OCLC 1758884.

         Describes in detail a souvenir program issued by F.J. Moreau in 1827 which contained lithographs of and commentary about the Kemble company productions of *Hamlet* and *Romeo and Juliet*. The author uses this program and contemporary acting texts to reconstruct the types of play that Berlioz would have seen on his attendance of the 1827 performances of *Hamlet* and *Romeo and Juliet*, both of which remained major influences on him throughout his creative life.

503.   Fiske, Roger. "Shakespeare in the Concert Hall." In *Shakespeare in Music*, edited by Phyllis Hartnoll, 182-97. London: Macmillan; New York: St. Martin's Press, 1964. ix, 333 p. ML80 S5 H37 OCLC 598395.

         Provides histories and descriptive analyses of the *Fantaisie dramatique sur La Tempête (Lélio)*, the *Roi Lear* overture, the Hamlet pieces from *Tristia*, and *Roméo et Juliette*. The author points to Garrick's version of *Romeo and Juliet* as performed by the Kemble company in Paris in 1827 as the source of all of Berlioz's modifications of the original play: "Roméo seul," "Convoi funèbre de Juliette," and "Roméo au tombeau du Capulets." Also mentions Mendelssohn's possible influence on Berlioz's interest in musical adaptations of Shakespeare.

504.   Guichard, Léon. "Librettistes." In *La musique et les lettres au temps du romantisme*, 220-54. Paris: Presses universitaires de France, 1955. OCLC 878179. Reprint. Plan de la Tour, Editions d'Aujourd'hui, 1984. 423 p. ISBN 2-730-70242-3 ML196 G96 1984 OCLC 12697813.

         Surveys the literary sources of all of Berlioz's works based on prose or poetic texts. Includes discussions of his adaptations of *Faust*, *Romeo and Juliet*, and the *Aeneid* as well as his use of works by less well-known authors.

505.   Kling, H. "Goethe et Berlioz." *Rivista musicale italiana* 12 (1905): 714-33. OCLC 1773309.

Traces Berlioz's involvement with Goethe's *Faust* during the late 1820s. Mentions an 1827 production of Béancourt's opera *Faust* at the *Théâtre des Nouveautés* where Berlioz was singing in the chorus, as well as his 1828 composition of a Faust ballet. Discusses at greater length the *Huit scènes de Faust*, quoting favorable reviews by Fétis (in *La revue musicale*) and Marx (in *Berliner allgemeine musicalische Zeitung*).

506.   Laster, Arnaud. "Berlioz et Victor Hugo." *Romantisme* no. 12 (1976): 27-34. ISSN 0048-8593 OCLC 931119.

Points to the influence of Hugo's poems, *Les orientales*, and his novel, *Le dernier jour d'un condamné*, on the program of the *Symphonie fantastique* and the text of *Lélio*. Also explores the relationship of Berlioz, Hugo, and Louise Bertin, whose opera *Esmeralda*, based on Hugo's *Notre-Dame de Paris*, was revised and produced with Berlioz's help.

507.   Mendl, R.W.S. "Berlioz and Shakespeare." *The Chesterian* 29 (April 1955): 95-101; 30 (July 1955): 1-5. OCLC 8182289.

Gives a brief sketch of Berlioz's lifelong worship of Shakespeare and describes those compositions based on the playwright's works.

508.   Plantinga, Leon B. "Berlioz' Use of Shakespearean Themes." *Yale French Studies* no. 33 (1964): 72-79. ISSN 0044-0078 OCLC 1770272.

A short, basic survey of Berlioz's works based on Shakespearean drama. The author is occasionally critical in his analysis of Berlioz's style, especially in *Lélio* and parts of *Béatrice et Bénédict*.

X. Critical Evaluations

Critical opinions of Berlioz and his music have differed widely from person to person, country to country, and age to age. This tremendous diversity is reflected in the articles in this chapter under the heading "General Studies," each offering an estimate of the success of Berlioz's career or the value of his music in general. Concert reviews and reviews of individual Berlioz works have not, as a rule, been included. The section of this chapter entitled "History" is devoted to studies that present an overview of the evolution of critical thought about Berlioz.

1. GENERAL STUDIES

509.   Adam, Adolphe. "Lettres sur la musique française (1836-1850)." *La revue de Paris* 10, tome 4 (August 1 1903): 449-81; (August 15): 726-62; tome 5 (September 1): 136-76; (September 15): 275-320; (October 1): 604-52. OCLC 1775173.

A collection of letters from Adam to his German friend Spiker, which represents a valuable source of first-hand information pertaining to operatic life in mid-nineteenth-century Paris. Comments on Berlioz are interspersed throughout. For the most part, Adam attacks Berlioz as a critic who damns the music of some of the best composers active in Paris (Auber, Rossini, and Adam), and as a composer with no talent who obtains government commissions only because of the support of the powerful Bertin family, publishers of the *Journal des débats*.

510.   Aldrich, Richard. "Berlioz Today." In *Musical Discourse from the New York Times*, 183-201. London and New York: Oxford University Press, H. Milford, 1928. OCLC 377641. Reprint. Freeport: Books for Libraries Press, 1967. 304 p. ML60 A4 1967 OCLC 854491.

Argues that despite a wealth of performances over the years, Berlioz's works remain unpopular, and that "the most interesting things about Berlioz are literary, historical, technical, personal, psychological--almost anything but musical."

511.   Amy, Gilbert. "Hector Berlioz: serait-il, après tout, un moderne?" *Le courrier musical de France* no. 26 (2e trimestre 1969): 90-96. ISSN 0011-0620 OCLC 1565352.

Contends that Berlioz's musical style is not the product of a "syntatical musical language," but is rather the result of combining various "functions of sound production." He is therefore a truly modern composer in the manner of Varèse.

512.   Bailbé, Joseph-Marc. "Berlioz dans son siècle," In *Le roman et la musique sous la Monarchie de juillet*, 135-48. Paris: M.J. Minard, 1969. viii, 446 p. ML270.4 B25 OCLC 577381.

Extracts contrasting opinions of Berlioz circa 1830 from newspaper reviews and memoirs. Also shows how Berlioz served as a model for the protagonists of several works of contemporary French fiction, including works by Reybaud, David, and Calvimont.

513.   Barzun, Jacques. "Berlioz a Hundred Years After." *The Musical Quarterly* 56 (no. 1 1970): 1-13. ISSN 0027-4631 OCLC 1642493. Reprinted in *Critical Questions...*, edited by Bea Friedland, 101-14. Chicago: University of Chicago Press, 1982. xvii, 269 p. ISBN 0-226-03863-7 ML60 B278 1982 OCLC 8032099.

Explains the neglect of Berlioz in his own time as the result of his having to compete first with Meyerbeer and then with Wagner, and in this century as the result of too few accurate scores and recordings of his works.

514.   Batka, Richard. "Berlioz." *Kunstwart* 17 (December 1 1903): 329-32. OCLC 15712421.

Finds Berlioz's historical significance in his development of orchestral color and the invention of the *idée fixe*. Concludes that his dramatic works (especially his "distortion" of Goethe's *Faust*) do not measure up to the quality of works by Meyerbeer, Halévy, and Gounod.

515. *Berlioz: Being the Report of a Discussion Held on December 17, 1928.* London: Oxford University Press, 1929. 43 p. ML410 B51 D67 OCLC 12488000. Reprinted in *Berlioz Society Bulletin* no. 13 (May-June 1955): 4-8; no. 14 (August-September 1955): 4-6; no. 15 (November-December 1955): 5-8. OCLC 2386332.

Reports on the exchange of opinions about Berlioz by several leading English musicians and critics, including Michel Calvocoressi, Edwin Evans, Hamilton Harty, and Percy Scholes. Chiefly interesting for the picture it gives of the wide divergence of critical thought about such basic issues as whether Berlioz was primarily a literary or a musical talent, whether he ever mastered the basic craft of composition, and whether his originality was the source of his greatness or the cause of his unpopularity. See also #519; #556.

516. Bertrand, Jean Edouard Gustave. "Berlioz: le romantisme musical en France." In *Les nationalités musicales étudiées dans le drame lyrique*, 260-88. Paris: Didier et Cie., 1872. xxxi, 364 p. ML1700 B37 OCLC 15156491.

Claims that Berlioz's primary failures as a composer lay in his lack of native ability as a composer of opera and in his unwillingness to write music for amusement.

517. Brent Smith, A.E. "Hector Berlioz." *Music and Letters* 7 (no. 4 1926): 340-46. ISSN 0027-4224 OCLC 1758884.

Characterizes Berlioz as a composer who worked from the specific to the general, i.e., from powerful individual musical effects to complete musical subjects in which those effects could suitably be employed. Concludes that this technique resulted in works of uneven quality.

518. Brussel, R. "Hector Berlioz." *Le manuscrit autographe* 6 (January-February 1931): 62-64. OCLC 1586596.

Attempts to explain the resurgence of Berlioz's popularity circa 1931 as the result of the similarity between his aesthetic principles and those of a new generation of twentieth-century composers, particularly with regard to the mixing of traditional genres to create new hybrid forms.

519.   Calvocoressi, M.-D. "Berlioz: a Postscript to a Discussion."
        The Musical Times 70 (April 1 1929): 305-7. ISSN 0027-4666
        OCLC 5472115.

        Concludes through a series of unsupported critical maneuvers
        that everyone agrees that Berlioz's music is full of technical
        defects, especially in the areas of form and harmony. Written
        in response to #515.

520.   Charnacé, Guy de. "Hector Berlioz." In *Musique et musiciens*.
        Vol. 1, 33-40. Paris: E. Lethielleux, 1874. 2 vols. ML60 C53
        OCLC 16160345.

        An obituary that suggests that Berlioz will never be well
        known because he wrote for impractical performance media
        rather than for chamber ensembles or solo piano, and further
        that the "rudeness" of his style will always offend audiences.
        Also criticizes his career as a writer, complaining of the
        "strange moral nature" underlying his criticism and pointing
        out "errors" in his thinking.

521.   Comettant, Jean Pierre Oscar. "Hector Berlioz." *Le ménestrel*
        52 (October 17 1886): 368-69. OCLC 6966764.

        Claims that Berlioz's lack of success results from his music
        being more a means to an end than an end in itself, and from
        his imagination frequently overpowering his heart, resulting in
        a style full of poetic and philosophical allusions, "intellectual
        speculations," and "ingenious calculations."

522.   Cooper, Martin. "Music." *The London Mercury* 33 (April
        1936): 628-29. OCLC 1756136.

        Calls Berlioz a composer of uneven inspiration some of whose
        works show a "deliberate indecision and a violent
        clumsiness." Predicts that these works will never rank in the
        first class but will only achieve a continued *succès de
        scandale*.

523.   Copland, Aaron. "Berlioz Today." In *Copland on Music*, 108-
        16. Garden City: Doubleday, 1960. OCLC 376663. Reprint.
        New York: Da Capo Press, 1976. 285 p. ISBN 0-306-70775-6
        ML63 C48 1976 OCLC 3017789. Excerpted in *Saturday
        Review* 43 (August 27 1960): 33-34. ISSN 0036-4983 OCLC
        1588490.

        Sympathetically evaluates Berlioz as an innovative composer
        whose reputation is due for a reassessment in 1960. Points out

some of his unusual orchestral techniques and his influence on
later-nineteenth-century composers.

524.   Cornelius, Peter. "Musikbericht." In *Literarische Werke*. Vol.
        3. *Aufsätze über Musik und Kunst*, edited by Edgar Istel, 240-
        44. Leipzig: Breitkopf & Härtel, 1904. 4 vols. ML410 C8 A1
        OCLC 4400501.

        Cites the natural affinity that Berlioz felt for the German
        musical spirit (his idols having been Gluck, Beethoven, and
        Weber) as the reason his music was better appreciated in that
        country than in France.

525.   Delacroix, Eugène. *Journal*. Paris: E. Plon, Nourrit, et Cie.,
        1893-95. 3 vols. OCLC 7052310. Paris: Plon, 1981. xxxvi,
        942 p. ISBN 2-259-00646-9 ND553 D33 A2 1981 OCLC
        8667595. Translated by Walter Pach. New York: Hacker Art
        Books, 1980. 731 p. ISBN 0-878-17275-0 ND553 D33 A2
        1980 OCLC 6998428.

        Interspersed throughout the journal are comments about music
        and composers of the nineteenth century, including Berlioz,
        which demonstrate Delacroix's lack of sympathy for and
        understanding of the new Romantic style in music.

526.   Elliot, J.H. "Berlioz and His Critics." *Music and Letters* 17
        (no. 2 1936): 140-144. ISSN 0027-4224 OCLC 1758884.

        States that the continuing controversy over the merits of the
        Berlioz style is the result of the inconsistent and unpredictable
        nature of his music, which thoroughly confounds attempts to
        discover a logical system behind his compositions.

527.   _____. "The Berlioz Enigma." *The Musical Times* 70 (July
        1 1929): 602-4. ISSN 0027-4666 OCLC 5472115.

        Contends that "the art of Berlioz was not an entirely musical
        one," and that when stripped of its programs his music
        becomes vapid and meaningless.

528.   Gautier, Théophile. "Festival en l'honneur de Berlioz." In *La
        musique*, 179-84. Paris: Fasquelle, 1911. 310 p. PN2636 P2
        G28m OCLC 10736748.

        Uses an 1870 Parisian festival of Berlioz's music as the
        inspiration for this review of his career and assessment of his
        achievements in the face of the continual hardships that forced

him to devote extensive time to music criticism. Originally appeared in *Journal officiel*, March 28, 1870.

529.   Griepenkerl, Wolfgang Robert. *Ritter Berlioz in Braunschweig. Zur Charakteristik dieses Tondichters.* Brunswick: E. Leibrock, 1843. Reprint. Brunswick: Literarische Vereinigung Braunschweig, 1974. 71 p. ML410 B5 G24 1974 OCLC 8134622.

An early appraisal of Berlioz's music from Brunswick, which he visited on his first German tour in 1842-43. The author compares the newness of his style with that of Beethoven thirty years earlier.

530.   Guillaume. Institut impérial de France. Académie des Beaux-Arts. *Discours de M. Guillaume, président, prononcé aux funérailles de M. Berlioz, le jeudi 11 mar 1869.* Paris: Didot, 1869. Translated in Apthorp, Appendix A, 405-8 (#112).

A remarkably astute summation and evaluation of Berlioz's career and musical philosophy which mentions his hatred of the easy, frivolous music so much in favor with French audiences of his time and his love for the grand tradition of Gluck and Beethoven.

531.   Hanslick, Eduard. [Reviews]. In *Aus den Concertsaal. Kritiken und Schilderungen aus den letzten 20 Jahren des Wiener Musiklebens.* Vienna: W. Braumüller, 1870. OCLC 8829290. 2nd ed. Vienna: W. Braümuller, 1897. xvi, 604 p. ML246.8 V6 H2 1897 OCLC 1880330.

Contains short reviews of the "Reine Mab" scherzo from *Roméo et Juliette* (79-80), the "Marche de pèlerins" from *Harold en Italie* (226), *Roméo et Juliette* (289), the "Choeur de soldats, choeur d'étudiants" from *La damnation de Faust* (312), and the *Benvenuto Cellini* overture (317). In these reviews Hanslick speaks of the mixed quality of Berlioz's music--some parts "forced, empty and trivial," others full of "powerful impulses." Hanslick recognized the passionate inner being of Berlioz but suggested that such a personality led to unorganized musical thinking.

532.   Harty, Hamilton. "The Approach to Berlioz." *Music Teacher* 7 (September 1926): 521-23. ISSN 0027-4461 OCLC 2680409.

Claims that Berlioz's musical originality was the result of his having developed his first ideas about music more or less in a vacuum, and that his earliest impressions were literary rather than purely musical in nature.

533.   Jahn, Otto. "Hector Berlioz in Leipzig." In *Gesammelte Aufsätze über Musik*, 95-111. Leipzig: Breitkopf & Härtel, 1866. OCLC 1401710. Reprint. Farnborough: Gregg International, 1969. 337 p. ISBN 0-576-38160-3 ML60 J25 1969 OCLC 830167.

Reviews an 1853 concert of Berlioz's music in Leipzig and finds that his concern with extra-musical considerations often prevented him from creating satisfying musical forms. Originally appeared in *Die Grenzboten: Zeitschrift für Politik, Literatur und Kunst*, vol. 4, 1853.

534.   Klein, John W. "Verdi's Attitudes to His Contemporaries." *The Music Review* 10 (no. 4 1949): 264-76. ISSN 0027-4445 OCLC 1758893.

Briefly quotes Verdi's comments on Berlioz along with his opinions of several other nineteenth-century composers.

535.   Koechlin, Charles. "Le cas Berlioz." *La revue musicale* 3 (February 1922): 118-34. OCLC 1764223.

Tries to account for widely divergent opinions on Berlioz. Disposes of arguments about lack of "true beauty," "false basses," and "strange harmonies."

536.   La Laurencie, L. de. "Hector Berlioz et le public de son temps." *Le courrier musical* 7 (January 1 1904): 1-10. OCLC 8320486.

Analyzes the veracity of Berlioz's contention that Parisian audiences understood his music less well than those outside France. Finds that the Parisian public responded favorably to the elements of instrumental color and the *fantastique* in his music, but was perplexed by its complexity, resulting from poetic-pictorial associations, and what they saw as a "lack of melody."

537.   Lobe, J.C. "Ein Märtyrer der Tonkunst." In *Consonanzen und Dissonanzen*, 55-69. Leipzig: Baumgärtner's Buchhandlung, 1869. vi, 463 p. ML60 L79 OCLC 3351156.

Depicts Berlioz as a musical martyr whose ideas were too new for his time and whose fame, as a consequence, could only come after his death.

538.   Louis, Rudolf. "Hector Berlioz." *Neue Musik-Zeitung* 25
        (December 3 1903): 75-77. OCLC 11930822.

        Contrasts the narrow understanding of Berlioz as primarily an
        innovative orchestrator which was common in France during
        his lifetime with the broader German appreciation of Berlioz
        as a complete Romantic musician.

539.   Massougnes, Georges de. "Scudo et la critique." In *Hector
        Berlioz; son oeuvre*, 79-86. Paris: Calmann-Lévy, 1919. 143
        p.

        Lays part of the responsibility for the poor reception of
        Berlioz's works in France on the Parisian critic Scudo, who
        favored Italian music over that of Gluck and Berlioz,
        continually attacking their melodic style.

540.   Newman, Ernest. *Berlioz, Romantic and Classic: Writings by
        Ernest Newman*, edited by Peter Heyworth. London:
        Gollancz, 1972. 288 p. ISBN 0-575-01365-6 ML410 B5 N49
        OCLC 516762.

        Contains the title essay (originally published in *Musical
        Studies*, #175), as well as a selection of reviews and essays,
        mainly from the *Sunday Times*, which cover his entire critical
        career from 1905 to 1958. Subjects discussed include various
        aspects of Berlioz's style, personality, and writings, four
        essays on the *Symphonie fantastique*, and six on *Les Troyens*.

541.   _____. "The Tragedy of Berlioz." In *Berlioz, Romantic and
        Classic*, edited by Peter Heyworth, 73-78. London: Gollancz,
        1972. 288 p. ISBN 0-575-01365-6 ML410 B5 N49 OCLC
        516762.

        Suggests that Berlioz was perhaps too original to ever have
        succeeded, especially since he was without "predecessors,
        contemporaries or successors" in music.

542.   Pohl, Richard. "Hector Berlioz." *Die Zukunft* 18 (January 9
        1897): 75-78. OCLC 4572937.

        Describes Berlioz as a composer born before his time who
        died before his fame was secure, a true musician of the future.
        Claims that his most important work was done in the 1830s
        and 1840s. Uses *Benvenuto Cellini* as an example of Berlioz's
        modernism.

543. _____. *Hektor Berlioz. Studien und Erinnerungen.* Vol. 3 of *Gesammelte Schriften über Musik und Musiker.* Leipzig: B. Schlicke, 1884. OCLC 12321145. Facsimile. Wiesbaden: M. Sändig, 1974. xv, 275 p. ML410 B5 P7 1974 OCLC 1035987.

Collection of Pohl's writings on Berlioz from the 1850s through the 1880s. Describes his style as innovative with regard to its poetic idea and its orchestration, but not its form. Reports on the initially cool and confused public reception of Berlioz's works in Germany. Includes an analysis of the symphony since Beethoven with a defense of program music. Also compares Berlioz to Wagner, suggesting that although Berlioz was known as a composer of "music of the future," such was not the case, and that his music has little in common with Wagner's. Includes descriptive analyses of several works that were performed in Germany, most notably *Roméo et Juliette* and *Béatrice et Bénédict.*

544. Pontmartin, A. de. "Hector Berlioz." In *Nouveaux samedis.* Vol. 7, 49-61. Paris: Michel Lévy, 1870. PQ2383 P25 N6 OCLC 5131844.

Traces the "failed destiny" of Berlioz to musical circumstances in France during his career, an environment unsuited to the nurturing of a revolutionary spirit in music.

545. Prod'homme, J.-G. "Hector Berlioz jugé par Adolphe Adam." *Zeitschrift der Internationalen Musik-Gesellschaft* 5 (September 1904): 75-82. OCLC 1772499.

Includes excerpts from Adam's letters from 1836 to 1850 showing his total misunderstanding and dislike of Berlioz both as a composer and a person. See also #504.

546. Rannaud, Gérald. "Mensonge littéraire, vérité musicale." *Silex* no. 17 (September 1980): 13-22. ISSN 0151-2315 OCLC 3739044.

Suggests that through his reliance on a host of literary associations in his works, Berlioz was the first composer to raise music to the rank of a serious art.

547. Reckow, Fritz. *"Wirkung* und *Effekt.* Über einige Voraussetzungen, Tendenzen und Probleme der deutsche Berlioz-Kritik." *Die Musikforschung* 33 (no. 1 1980): 1-36. ISSN 0027-4801 OCLC 2669982.

Points out that in nineteenth-century Germany Berlioz was accused of writing music with "Effekt" (effects) but without "Wirkung" (innermost influence), until Hugo Wolf pointed out that Berlioz's "Effekt" had purely musical motivations.

548.   Richard, Jean-Vincent. "Un musicien qui nous intéresse beaucoup." *Silex* no. 17 (September 1980): 5-12. ISSN 0151-2315 OCLC 3739044.

Assesses the reasons for the continuing controversy over Berlioz's significance. Claims that to accept Berlioz is to reject conformity and embrace a music free of of limitations.

549.   Ritter, Hermann. "Berlioz' künstlerischer Bedeutung." In *Einiges zum Verständnis von Berlioz Haroldsinfonie und Berlioz Künstlerischer Bedeutung. Zwei Vorlesungen*, 35-54. Oppeln: Verlag von Georg Maske, 1899.

Finds that Berlioz's work is significant because he freed music from formal restraints whenever it was demanded by musical expression, and because he did not write music to give simple pleasure to the ear, but to express lofty ideals.

550.   Rosenfeld, Paul. "Berlioz." In *Musical Portraits*, 87-100. New York: Harcourt, Brace & Howe, 1920. OCLC 854294. Reprint. Freeport, N.Y.: Books for Libraries Press, 1968. 314 p. ML390 R78 1968 OCLC 449291. Also reprinted in *Musical Impressions: Selections from Paul Rosenfeld's Criticism*, edited by Herbert A. Leibowitz, 89-98. New York: Hill & Wang, 1969. xxxii, 302 p. ISBN 0-809-07172-X ML60 R79 M93 OCLC 17992.

Characterizes Berlioz as a rude, stupendous barbarian whose radical procedures look ahead to the twentieth-century styles of composers such as Stravinsky and Skryabin.

551.   Runciman, John F. "Berlioz." *The Saturday Review of Politics, Literature, Science and Art* 96 (November 21 1903): 638-39; (November 28): 667-68. OCLC 1765055.

A thorough condemnation of Berlioz's music by an ardent Wagnerite. Finds that Berlioz's style is nothing but a collection of empty effects without musical substance.

552.   Saint-Saëns, Camille. "Berlioz." *Le ménestrel* 83 (October 21 1921): 405-7. OCLC 6966764.

A sympathetic appraisal of Berlioz's contributions to music by one who knew and understood him well. Singles out his love of the gigantic and his orchestrational innovations for special mention. Admits that Berlioz's critical writings on music were marred by an insufficient knowledge of such past masters as Bach and Mozart.

553. Sand, Robert. "Berlioz et ses contemporains." *Le guide musical* 49 (November 29 1903 supplement): 23-24. OCLC 1509855.

Cites contrasting opinions of Berlioz by contemporaries such as Moscheles, Hauptmann, Mendelssohn, Marx, Cherubini, and Schumann, many of whom were shocked and mystified by the newness of Berlioz's musical style. Reproduces 1853 Baugniet lithograph.

554. Solenière, Eugène de. "Berlioz." In *1800-1900. Cent années de musique française.* Paris: Pugno, 1901. 110 p. ML270 S68 OCLC 14207561.

Analyzes Berlioz's place in the history of nineteenth-century French music and describes him as a man of extremes and contradictions. Concludes that French music became a serious art form at his hands.

555. Wolf, Hugo. [Essays on Berlioz]. In *Hugo Wolfs musikalische Kritiken, im Auftrage des Wiener akademischen Wagnervereins,* edited by Richard Batka and Heinrich Werner. Leipzig: Breitkopf & Härtel, 1911. OCLC 2901702. Reprint. Walluf-Nendeln: Sändig, 1976. vi, 378 p. ISBN 3-500-30250-5 ML60 W73 1976 OCLC 2891727.

Critical defences of the *Roi Lear* overture (32-34) and the *Symphonie fantastique* (169-73), but only reserved praise for *La damnation de Faust* (257-63; 266-67), which the author describes as a fragmentary mosaic that loses the Faustian ideal in an "idle show of arbitrary *fantastique.*"

556. Wotton, Tom S. "A Berlioz Conference." *The Musical Times* 70 (April 1 1929): 318-20. ISSN 0027-4666 OCLC 5472115.

Points out some of the adversities against which Berlioz's music has had to struggle over the years in order to make progress toward general acceptance. These include its unsuitability to piano transcription and the relative dearth of adequate performances. Written in response to #515.

557. Young, Filson. "Hector Berlioz." In *Mastersingers; Appreciation of Music and Musicians, With an Essay on Hector Berlioz*, 139-200. London: William Reeves, 1901. OCLC 2652918. New York: H. Holt and Co., 1911. 215 p. ML69 Y722 OCLC 1831498.

Depicts Berlioz as a wildly undisciplined composer who indiscriminately set down musical ideas both good and bad. Typical of the kind of negative evaluation of Berlioz that was common early in the twentieth century.

2. HISTORY

558. Barzun, Jacques. "Whirligig: Last Words on Berlioz." In *The Energies of Art; Studies of Authors, Classic and Modern*. 281-301. New York: Harper, 1956. OCLC 228155. Reprint. Westport: Greenwood Press, 1975. 355 p. ISBN 0-837-16856-2 PN511 B35 1975 OCLC 1217321.

Reviews the history of critical attitudes regarding Berlioz. Laments especially the lack of appreciation for his music in France, and suggests that much critical work remains to be done in order to clarify the many misunderstandings about him.

559. Bouyer, Raymond. "Petites notes sans portée: un portrait d'Hector Berlioz." *Le ménestrel* 69 (March 22 1903): 92-93; (March 29): 100; (April 5): 106-7; (April 12): 115-16. OCLC 6966764.

Provides an overview of critical opinion from 1869 to 1903. Repeats the commonly-held opinion that Berlioz's orchestration was brilliant but that he had no gift for melody. Maintains that a reassessment is necessary. Follows with a short biographical sketch which introduces the idea of three periods in Berlioz's career: 1825 to 1833--the tumultuous period of debuts; 1834 to 1848--the period of original masterpieces; 1849 to 1863--the classic period of pure and serene works.

560. Cairns, David. "Berlioz: a Centenary Retrospect." *The Musical Times* 110 (March 1969): 249-51. ISSN 0027-4666 OCLC 5472115.

Surveys changing attitudes toward Berlioz's music. Suggests
that they are the result of greater familiarity with his works
(through more performances and recordings) and a new
critical stance which does not judge the unfamiliar on the
basis of norms derived from more familiar styles.

561.   . "Berlioz and Criticism: Some Surviving Dodos."
The Musical Times 104 (August 1963): 548-51. ISSN 0027-
4666 OCLC 5472115.

Attacks past Berlioz criticism founded on misinformation and
outdated assumptions, some of which were derived from
Boschot's biography.

562.   D'Estrées, Paul. "L'art musical et ses interprètes depuis deux
siècles." *Le ménestrel* 68 (May 25 1902): 161-62. OCLC
6966764.

Summarizes both negative and positive critical opinions of
Berlioz by contemporary writers, musicians, and artists such
as Janin, Saint-Saëns, Gounod, Delacroix, Heine, and Liszt.

563.   Hince, Kenneth. "Hector Berlioz." *Canon, Australian
Journal of Music* 3 (April 1950): 542-47. OCLC 1553295.

Suggests that the errors that persistently appear in the
evaluation of Berlioz's music are the product of both the
degree to which his music diverges from the musical
mainstream of the nineteenth century and an ingrained
suspicion on the part of musical scholars of music that is
programmatic.

564.   Jullien, Adolphe. "La critique et Berlioz." *Revue d'art
dramatique* 31 (August 1893): 193-206. OCLC 5853914.
Reprinted in *Musique: mélanges d'histoire et de critique
musicale et dramatique*, 213-33. Paris: Librairie de l'Art,
1896. 462 p. ML270.1 J94 OCLC 5913288.

Reviews critical reactions to Berlioz throughout his career,
including opinions of Castil-Blaze and Fétis. Describes how
Berlioz alienated Fétis by criticizing his "corrections" of
Beethoven's symphonies.

565.   Laforet, Claude. "Hector Berlioz parmi les romantiques." *La
revue musicale* no. 233 (1956): 45-54. OCLC 1764223.

Compares critical opinions of Berlioz in his own day with
those of 1956 and finds that he is still a misunderstood
composer. Also comments on Berlioz's prose style,
concluding that it exhibits no unifying aesthetic.

566.   Newman, Ernest. "Berlioz and His Critics." In *Berlioz,
        Romantic and Classic*, edited by Peter Heyworth, 128-31.
        London: Gollancz, 1972. 288 p. ISBN 0-575-01365-6 ML410
        B9 N49 OCLC 516762.

        Suggests that Berlioz criticism over the years has made the
        error of adopting Germanic norms as the basis for judging his
        non-Germanic style.

567.   _____. "A Berlioz Revival?" In *Berlioz, Romantic and
        Classic*, edited by Peter Heyworth, 79-83. London: Gollancz,
        1972. 288 p. ISBN 0-575-01365-6 ML410 B5 N49 OCLC
        516762.

        Observes that Berlioz has long suffered from being judged by
        the "standards of classical German art," expecially the
        rhythmic squareness of German prosody.

568.   _____. "The Case for the Prosecution." In *Berlioz, Romantic
        and Classic*, edited by Peter Heyworth, 109-13. London:
        Gollancz, 1972. 288 p. ISBN 0-575-01365-6 ML410 B5 N49
        OCLC 516762.

        Cites years of anti-Berlioz criticism and concludes that even
        though some of it is accurate, Berlioz's reputation thrives in
        1935, although as that of a "flawed" genius.

569.   Roy, Jean. "Berlioz vivant." *La revue musicale* no. 233
        (1956): 7-14. OCLC 1764223.

        Quotes musicians from Rossini to Debussy and Varèse in
        order to portray the range of critical opinion on Berlioz.

570.   Wright, Michael G.H. "Berlioz and Anglo-American
        Criticism." *Adam International Review* nos. 331-333 (1969):
        93-101. ISSN 0001-8015 OCLC 1965286.

        Reviews English and American critical opinion of Berlioz
        from the mid-nineteenth century to 1969. Appendix includes
        Edward Holmes' *A First Impression of the Genius of Hector
        Berlioz*, reprinted from *Atlas*, February 12, 1848.

571.   _____. "A Berlioz XI." *Berlioz Society Bulletin* no. 58
(January 1968): 14-21; no. 59 (April 1968): 6-10; no. 60 (July
1968): 17-21; no. 61 (October 1968): 10-14. OCLC 2386332.

Demonstrates the changing attitudes toward Berlioz by
reviewing the work of eleven major Berlioz scholars
throughout the years. They are d'Ortigue, Fétis, Jullien,
Hippeau, Tiersot, Prod'homme, Boschot, Newman, Turner,
Wotton, and Barzun.

XI. Style Analysis

This chapter includes analytical studies of Berlioz's style and compositional process, some of a general nature, others devoted to specific musical parameters or other specialized topics.

1. GENERAL STUDIES

572.   Bockholdt, Rudolf. *Berlioz-Studien*. Tutzing: H. Schneider, 1979. ix, 255 p. ISBN 3-795-20272-8 ML410 B5 B63 1979 OCLC 5296738.

Analyzes *Roméo et Juliette* and *La damnation de Faust* with particular attention to their spatial and rhythmic elements. Follows with an analysis of aspects of Berlioz's vocal music, including the relationship between the French language and the musical setting of French texts. Revised dissertation from the University of Munich, 1970.

573.   Buenzod, Emmanuel. "L'accent de Berlioz." In *Musiciens*, 165-75. Lausanne: F. Rouge, 1945. 220 p. ML390 B93 OCLC 4903819.

Attempts to explain away some of the traditional misconceptions about Berlioz's music through a general style analysis.

574.   Collet, Robert. "Berlioz: Various Angles of Approach to His Work." *The Score and I.M.A. Magazine* no. 10 (December 1954): 6-19. OCLC 7984321.

Contains assessments of the following aspects of Berlioz's
style: the rhythmic structure of his melodies, the unusual
combinations of timbres in his orchestrations, the weakness of
his traditional fugal writing, and the lack of pianistic
influences on his harmony. Also analyzes Berlioz's
relationship to his predecessors and contemporaries, and
concludes that he was a composer who stood apart from the
major trends of his time.

575.   Cone, Edward T. "Inside the Saint's Head: the Music of
        Berlioz." *Musical Newsletter* 1 (no. 3 1971): 3-12; (no. 4):
        16-20; 2 (no. 1 1972): 19-22. ISSN 0047-8466 OCLC
        1758903. Reprinted in *Berlioz Society Bulletin* no. 86 (January
        1975): 8-14; no. 87 (April 1975): 8-16; no. 88 (July 1975): 7-
        15. OCLC 2386332.

        Beginning with Berlioz's description of the chief
        characteristics of his work as "*l'expression passionée,
        l'ardeur intérieure, l'entrainement rhythmique et l'imprévu,*"
        the author examines excerpts from his music to determine the
        exact nature of his musical style. Follows by discussing the
        creation of spatial effects and levels of multiple perspective in
        Berlioz's music.

576.   Dickinson, A.E.F. *The Music of Berlioz.* London: Faber,
        1972. OCLC 607012. New York: St. Martin's Press, 1973.
        280 p. bibliography, 259-73. ML410 B5 D5 1973 OCLC
        605047.

        Provides a history and mostly descriptive analysis with
        musical examples of all of Berlioz's major works, including
        the songs.

577.   Dömling, Wolfgang. "'En songeant au temps...à l'espace.'
        Über einige Aspekte der Musik Hector Berlioz." *Archiv für
        Musikwissenschaft* 33 (no. 4 1976): 241-60. ISSN 0003-9292
        OCLC 1481988.

        Identifies discontinuity as an important principle in modern art
        and in the music of Berlioz where it manifests itself in his
        orchestration (as a spatial element), in his polymetric
        combinations, and in his formal combination of disparate
        thematic materials. These devices are discussed in relation to
        the *Symphonie fantastique, Harold en Italie*, and *Lélio.*

578.   _____. "Romantik und Moderne I." In *Hector Berlioz und seine Zeit*, 150-77. Laaber: Laaber-Verlag, 1986. 360 p. bibliography, 347-53. ISBN 3-921-51890-3 ML410 B5 D63 1986 OCLC 15228157.

Finds in Berlioz's music three elements that mark the beginning of modernism: multi-dimensionality, musical structures that approximate the narrative techniques of prose, and the abandonment of beauty. In defining and illustrating these elements, the author extensively discusses Berlioz's "emancipation of rhythm," his use of musical contrast, and his adoption of a new "aesthetic of the unpleasant" through the use of the grotesque.

579.   _____. "Romantik und Moderne II." In *Hector Berlioz und seine Zeit,* 230-61. Laaber: Laaber-Verlag, 1986. 360 p. bibliography, 347-53. ISBN 3-921-51890-3 ML410 B5 D63 1986 OCLC 15228157.

Determines that the most modern characteristic of Berlioz's program music is the unification of a specific dramatic expression with a "poetic-imaginative freedom." Also discusses Berlioz's relationship to Wagner, calling him the intermediary between Beethoven and Wagner because of his invention of the "dramatic symphony."

580.   _____. "Uber den 'Effekt.'" In *Hector Berlioz und seine Zeit*, 129-49. Laaber: Laaber-Verlag, 1986. 360 p. bibliography, 347-53. ISBN 3-921-51890-3 ML410 B5 D63 1986 OCLC 15228157.

Claims that striving for effect was one of Berlioz's primary compositional goals, and that he achieved this through the creation of various kinds of contrast and discontinuity which thwart the listener's expectations. Uses examples from *Lélio* to illustrate the compositional techniques involved.

581.   Fleuret, Maurice. "La puissance d'une imagination prophétique." In *Berlioz*, 229-39. Paris: Réalités-Hachette, 1973. 269 p. ML410 B5 B33 OCLC 1011818.

Summarizes Berlioz as a true musical innovator who liberated musical thinking about color, rhythm, melody, and tonality, paving the way for many important twentieth-century composers.

582.   Gorer, Richard. "Berlioz Again." *Music and Letters* 27 (no. 2
        1946): 114-18. ISSN 0027-4224 OCLC 1758884.

        Introduces the idea that Berlioz the artist was part Romantic
        poet and part Classical composer. Also discusses French
        precedents for his orchestrational techniques, especially those
        found in the works of Gossec.

583.   Guiomar, Michel. *Le masque et le fantasme; l'imagination de
        la matière sonore dans la pensée musicale de Berlioz.* Paris:
        J. Corti, 1970. 447 p. bibliography, 433-35. ML410 B515 G83
        OCLC 310745.

        A phenomenological study which attempts to analyze the
        psycho-physiological aspects of Berlioz's musical thought (as
        distinct from his musical technique), quite apart from the
        usual literary-dramatic explanations of his work.

584.   Haggin, Bernard H. "Berlioz." *The Kenyon Review* 17 (no. 4
        1955): 525-42. ISSN 0163-075X OCLC 1782352.

        Contains descriptive analyses of *Les nuits d'été*, *Roméo et
        Juliette* and the *Requiem*--all intended to demonstrate
        Berlioz's artistic freedom from convention and his sensitivity
        to texts. Mentions his use of the compositional technique of
        repeating a musical figure "in the constantly changing context
        of the developing musical thought."

585.   Lewinski, Wolf-Eberhard von. "Der romantische
        Romantiker." *Schweizerische Musikzeitung* 109 (no. 3 1969):
        129-32. ISSN 0036-7710 OCLC 1916515.

        Claims that the Berlioz style is a mix of German and Latin
        spirits, and that Berlioz's experiments with instrumental color
        are only the first of his many compositional innovations to
        find expansion by twentieth-century composers.

586.   Macdonald, Hugh. *Berlioz Orchestral Music.* London:
        British Broadcasting Corporation, 1969. OCLC 63663.
        Seattle: University of Washington Press, 1969. 64 p. MT130
        B48 M3 1969b OCLC 80724.

        Offers good, non-technical discussions of the overtures
        (*Béatrice et Bénédict*, *Benvenuto Cellini*, *Le carnaval romain*,
        Le corsaire, *Les francs-juges*, *Le roi Lear*, *Rob Roy*,
        Waverley), all four symphonies, and miscellaneous marches.

Also included is a short discussion of Berlioz as an orchestrator.

587.   _____. "The Colossal Nightingale." *Music and Musicians* 17 (July 1969): 24-25. ISSN 0027-4232 OCLC 1758885.

Discusses Berlioz's penchant for the grandiose as seen in works such as the *Requiem*, the *Te Deum*, and the *Symphonie funèbre*. Mentions other compositions in a similar style that were projected but never completed.

588.   Mainzer, Joseph. *Chronique musicale de Paris: de M. Berlioz, de ses compositions et de ses critiques musicales.* Paris, Au bureau de Panorame de l'Allemagne, 1838. 95 p.

One of the earliest stylistic overviews, written early in Berlioz's career. Claims that his style is full of unpopular new ideas, but that it will moderate as he matures. Also discusses Berlioz's writing on music, finding in it contradictions, haphazard propositions, and unsupported maxims. Criticizes his prose writing as being too technical for average readers.

589.   Mellers, Wilfred H. "Berlioz." In *Man and His Music; the Story of Musical Experience in the West*, 759-81. New York: Oxford University Press, 1962. 1172 p. ML160 H284 OCLC 536798. New rev. ed. London: Barrie & Jenkins, 1988. xiv, 1245 p. ISBN 0-712-62201-X OCLC 17510397.

Analyzes all aspects of Berlioz's style in relation to his socio-political environment. Contrasts the French quality of his work with the Germanic spirit of Wagner. Contains many insightful observations about Berlioz's major works, concluding that his style is fundamentally Classical, melodic, and operatic.

590.   Ogdon, J.A.H. "Berlioz: the Earlier Phase." *Life and Letters* 6 (May 1931): 323-66. OCLC 5158596.

Applies to the analysis of Berlioz's music social-psychological concepts of instincts. Particularly relevant to Berlioz are those directed toward self-assertion and the macabre. Traces the influence of these instincts in such early works as the three symphonies, *Benvenuto Cellini*, and the *Requiem*.

Hector Berlioz

591.   Photiadès, Constantin. Hector Berlioz et Andromède. *La revue de Paris* 31 (February 15 1931): 897-916. OCLC 1775173.

Analyzes revolutionary aspects of the Berlioz style and traces the evolution of its acceptance from 1830 to 1930. Explains some of the stylistic irregularities of his concert music by relating them to their dramatic motivation. Also chronicles performances of *Les Troyens* from 1863 to 1930, listing cuts and alterations made in the work.

592.   Pizzetti, Ildebrando. "L'arte di Hector Berlioz." In *Musica e dramma*, 213-19. Rome: Edizioni della Bussola, 1945. 239 p. ML60 P73 OCLC 11385952.

States that Berlioz's writing and thinking about his life, career, and works were always marked by exaggeration. The author sees this as the explanation for the unpopularity of his music in Italy. Says that Berlioz's greatness lay in his creation of a new world of orchestral art based on unique rhythmic configurations, modulations, and timbres.

593.   Plantinga, Leon B. "Berlioz." In *Romantic Music: a History of Musical Style in Nineteenth-Century Europe*, 205-19. New York: W.W. Norton, 1984. xiii, 523 p. ISBN 0-393-95196-0 ML196 P6 1984 OCLC 10309380.

Excellent summary of the Berlioz style presented in a discussion of several of his most famous works.

594.   Pohl, Richard. "Hektor Berlioz." In *Hektor Berlioz. Studien und Erinnerungen*, 9-33. Leipzig: B. Schlicke, 1884. OCLC 12321145. Facsimile. Wiesbaden: M. Sändig, 1974. xv, 275 p. ML410 B5 P7 1974 OCLC 1035987.

Describes the poetic idea and orchestration of Berlioz's music as innovative, but finds that its formal organization is only slightly more ambitious and daring than that of Beethoven.

595.   Primmer, Brian. *The Berlioz Style*. London and New York: Oxford University Press, 1973. OCLC 637173. Reprint. New York: Da Capo Press, 1984. 202 p. ISBN 0-306-76223-4 ML410 B5 P865 1984 OCLC 9945329.

Review: Barzun, Jacques. "The Berlioz Style." In *Critical Questions*, edited by Bea Friedland. 136-41. Chicago:

University of Chicago Press, 1982. xvii, 269 p. ISBN 0-226-03863-7 ML60 B278 1982 OCLC 8032099.

Begins with a discussion of Berlioz's relationship to the French tradition. Follows with a thorough analysis of all aspects of his musical language, focusing on his prose-like melodies, his unorthodox juxtaposition of harmonies, and his treatment of key relationships. This book is discussed in #598.

596.   _____. "Some General Thoughts on Berlioz's Methods." *Berlioz Society Bulletin* no. 71 (April 1971): 3-4. OCLC 2386332.

Relates Berlioz's style to the French Romantic values of *contrastes et oppositions*, *combinaisons*, and *effets*.

597.   Rolland, Romain. "Berlioz." *La revue de Paris* 11 (March 1 1904): 65-88; (March 15): 331-52. OCLC 1775173. Reprinted in *Musiciens d'aujourd'hui*, 1-57. 3rd ed. Paris: Hachette, 1908. OCLC 387179. 13th ed. Paris: Hachette, 1949. 278 p. ML390 R65 1949 OCLC 7906197. Translated by Mary Blaiklock as *Musicians of Today*, 1-64. New York: H. Holt, 1915. OCLC 386985. Reprint. Freeport, N.Y.: Books for Libraries Press, 1969. xii, 324 p. ISBN 0-836-91188-1 ML390 R653 1969 OCLC 27347. Also reprinted in *Essays on Music*, 284-319. New York: Allen, Towne & Heath, 1948. xi, 371 p. ML60 R72 OCLC 573753.

Contains a short sketch of Berlioz's personality which finds the causes of his cynicism and bitterness in material hardships and a lack of public understanding. Follows with an analysis of his musical style, pointing to its Classical and characteristically French spirit.

598.   Rushton, Julian. "Berlioz Through the Looking Glass." *Soundings: a Music Journal* no. 6 (1977): 51-66. ISSN 0081-2080 OCLC 1948031.

Takes exception to the analytical method of Brian Primmer's *The Berlioz Style* (#595), particularly the author's disregard of the effects of harmony on melodic design and his analysis of formal structures as products of changing tonalities.

599.   _____. *The Musical Language of Berlioz*. Cambridge and New York: Cambridge University Press, 1983. xi, 303 p. bibliography, 293-96. ISBN 0-521-24279-7 ML410 B5 R87 1983 OCLC 8931226.

Along with Primmer (#595), this is the major style-analytic
study of Berlioz's works. Includes a consideration of the
influence of Berlioz's background and training on the
formation of his compositional style. Follows with detailed
essays on the role of counterpoint, rhythm, melody, formal
structures, and orchestration in his music. Includes detailed
analyses of the "Chanson de brigands" from *Lélio* (14-22), the
Benvenuto Cellini overture (202-27), and Faust's music from
La damnation de Faust (228-56).

600.   Sandford, Gordon Thomas. "The Overtures of Hector Berlioz:
         a Study in Musical Style." Ph.D. dissertation, University of
         Southern California, 1964. 336 p. bibliography, 326-36.
         OCLC 1579941.

         Analyzes the genre in terms of melody, harmony,
         orchestration, rhythm, and form. Also discusses the
         significance of the program in Berlioz's overtures and the
         conflicting elements of Classicism and Romanticism in his
         style [from abstract].

601.   Sollertinskii, I.I. "Hector Berlioz." In *Von Mozart bis
         Schostakowitsch*, 48-115. Leipzig: Philipp Reclam, 1979. 314
         p. ML60 S5815 OCLC 8188100.

         Opens with a biographical sketch concentrating on Berlioz's
         early years in Paris as a student which provides important
         information on his teacher Le Sueur. Continues with a
         discussion of the influence of Beethoven and the occasional
         music of the French Revolution on Berlioz's developing style.
         Concludes that his early music was a testament to his fierce
         devotion to both political and musical freedom. Follows with
         a discussion of Berlioz's orchestration which suggests that
         characteristics of timbre carry specific dramatic connotations
         and play an important role in the development of his program
         music. Formal analyses lead the author to the conclusion that
         Berlioz's sonata form movements are the most archaic aspect
         of his symphonic structure and that they do not adopt the
         formal innovations suggested by the work of Beethoven.

602.   Weingartner, Felix. "Hector Berlioz: ein Gedenkblatt,
         geschrieben zur Einführung in die Gesamtausgabe seiner
         Werke." In *Akkorde: gesammelte Aufsätze*, 154-63. Leipzig:
         Breikopf & Härtel, 1912. OCLC 2608838. Walluf-Nendeln:
         Sändig, 1977. iv, 304 p. ISBN 3-500-30490-7 ML60 W45
         1977 OCLC 4190155.

Speaks of Berlioz's stylistic originality, of his mastery of orchestral color, and of his reinterpretation of traditional musical forms. States that he had no imitators.

603.   Wotton, Tom S. "Berlioz the Blood-Curdler." *The Musical Mirror* 10 (November 1930): 319, 328. OCLC 10455631.

Attempts to show that Berlioz was not as preoccupied with the macabre as is usually thought.

604.   _____. "Einige Missverständnisse betreffs Berlioz." *Die Musik* 3 (December 1 1903): 358-65. OCLC 1696908.

Corrects three common misconceptions about Berlioz's music: that it is gigantic and over-orchestrated, that Berlioz hated fugues, and that he believed in the pictorially expressive potential of music.

605.   _____. *Hector Berlioz*. London: Oxford University Press, H. Milford, 1935. OCLC 1833505. Reprint. New York: Johnson Reprint Corporation, 1969. OCLC 811762. Reprint. Freeport, N.Y.: Books for Libraries Press, 1970. x, 224 p. ISBN 8-369-53061 ML410 B5 W62 1970 OCLC 73564.

Discusses Berlioz's compositional style as a reflection of his understanding of common harmonic "rules" and his use of the guitar to hear what he was writing. Analyzes many of his major works, as well as songs and student cantatas. Contains a critique of the Old Berlioz Edition. Begins with a character sketch emphasizing Berlioz's relationships with women and addressing common misconceptions about the composer.

606.   _____. "Hector Berlioz." *Proceedings of the Royal Musical Association* 30 (1903-1904): 15-36. ISSN 0080-4452 OCLC 1764602.

Discusses several aspects of Berlioz's musicianship, including the unevenness of his early training, his dislike of vocal ornamentation, his conflicting ideas about the value of fugues, the irregularity of his formal structures as the product of his Southern temperament, and his scoring practices for double basses and horns.

607.   _____. "Hector Berlioz, 1803-1869." In *The Heritage of Music*, edited by Hubert J. Foss. Vol. 2, 135-50. London:

Oxford University Press, 1927-34. 2 vols. ML390 F7 OCLC
1310330.

Claims that Berlioz's unique style resulted from his desire to
find a new system to replace what he perceived as tired old
constraints on creativity and that he did not lack understanding
of traditional compositional rules.

608.   _____. "Stray Notes on Berlioz." *Zeitschrift der
Internationalen Musik-Gesellschaft* 5 (July 1904): 395-99.
OCLC 1772499.

Contains the following observations: that Berlioz hated fast
fugues on *Amen* and *Kyrie Eleison*; that his program music is
not as specifically descriptive as is generally thought; and that
orchestrational effects that look poor on the page work when
played thanks to his instinctive "inner ear."

2. INFLUENCES ON BERLIOZ

a. General Studies

609.   Allix, G. "Sur les éléments dont s'est formée la personnalité
artistique de Berlioz." *Bulletin mensuel de l'Académie
delphinale* 4th series, tome 17 (1903): 8-75. OCLC 1961247.
Reprint. Grenoble: Imprimerie Allier frères, 1903. 72 p.

Explains the nature of the influences shaping Berlioz's
musical style, including composers of opera and dramatic
music (Gluck, Spontini, Weber, Beethoven, Le Sueur, Catel,
and Méhul), and major writers (Goethe, Shakespeare, and
Byron). Also discusses the influence of his stay in Italy on his
work and musical personality. Appendix consists of a list of
works performed at the *Opéra* between 1821 and 1831.

610.   Dent, Edward J. "The Romantic Spirit in Music."
Proceedings of the Royal Musical Association 59 (1932-33):
86-95. ISSN 0080-4452 OCLC 1764602.

Hypothesizes that Berlioz's harmonic irregularities resulted
from his greatly intensified melodic sense, and that this, in

turn, resulted from the influence of early-nineteenth-century Italian opera.

611.   Emmanuel, Maurice. "Berlioz." *Le correspondant* 92 (January 25 1920): 237-61. OCLC 5258641.

Analyzes Berlioz's relationship to his immediate predecessors (Weber, Gluck, and Beethoven) and concludes that as a student he followed their model more than that of his teachers at the *Conservatoire*, including Reicha.

612.   Lasserre, Pierre. "Berlioz." In *Faust en France et autres études*, 195-202. Paris: Calmann-Lévy, 1929. 234 p. PQ139 L35 1929 OCLC 5103657.

Claims that Berlioz's style derives its character from the influences of Virgil and Shakespeare and that Romanticism is its most superficial part. Also states that in his librettos Berlioz chose grand and noble subjects which he clothed with music that mixed beauty and deformity, because of his awkward (*fâcheuse*) technique.

613.   Liess, Andreas. "Hector Berlioz." In *L. van Beethoven und Richard Wagner im Pariser Musikleben*, 22-41. Hamburg: Hoffmann & Campe, 1939. 94 p. ML410 B41 L719 OCLC 12244166.

Examines the influence of German Romanticism on Berlioz, particularly in his introduction to the themes of "freedom" and "nature" through Gluck, Beethoven, and Goethe. Suggests that this influence was mixed in his music with traditional French rationalism and clarity.

614.   Lockspeiser, Edward. "Berlioz and John Martin." In *Music and Painting: a Study in Comparative Ideas From Turner to Schoenberg*, 20-29. London: Cassell, 1973. OCLC 708152. New York: Harper & Row, 1973. 197 p. ISBN 0-064-35325-7 ML3849 L62 1973 OCLC 749632.

Explains the influence of the nineteenth-century English painter, John Martin, on Berlioz's fascination with the grotesque and demonic. Appendix A contains a reprint of #491 (136-44).

b. French Tradition

615.   Bartenstein, Hans. "Die frühen Instrumentationslehren bis zu
        Berlioz." *Archiv für Musikwissenschaft* 28 (no. 2 1971): 97-
        118. OCLC 1481988.

        Discusses the role of early orchestration treatises by Francoeur
        (1772), Sundelin (1828), and Catrufo (1832) in the formation
        of a new sound-ideal in the nineteenth-century orchestra.
        Includes an analysis of the influence of Kastner's treatise
        (1837) on Berlioz's work.

616.   _____. *Hector Berlioz' Instrumentationkunst und ihre
        geschichtliche Grundlagen: ein Beitrag zür Geschichte des
        Orchesters.* Strassburg: Heitz, 1939. OCLC 1208955. 2nd
        rev. ed. Baden-Baden: Valentin Koerner, 1974. 247 p. ISBN
        3-873-20528-9 ML455 B37 OCLC 1148722.

        Surveys the history of French orchestration from Lully to
        Berlioz with particular attention to instrumentation treatises
        that predate the *Traité d'instrumentation*. The final chapter
        discusses orchestrational techniques used in the *Symphonie
        fantastique*. No musical examples.

617.   Deane, Basil. "The French Operatic Overture from Grétry to
        Berlioz." *Proceedings of the Royal Musical Association* 99
        (1972-73): 67-80. ISSN 0080-4452 OCLC 1764602.

        Draws attention to connections between the overtures of
        Berlioz and those of earlier French composers such as Méhul
        and Cherubini. Discusses parallels in form, harmony, and
        dramatic intent.

618.   Gräbner, Eric. "Berlioz and French Operatic Tradition."
        Ph.D. dissertation, University of York, 1967.

        Finds the source of what appear to be Berlioz's musical
        irregularities (from the nineteenth-century point of view) in
        the little-known tradition of eighteenth-century French opera
        [from abstract].

619.   Lockspeiser, Edward. "Berlioz and the French Romantics."
        Music and Letters 15 (no. 1 1934): 26-31. ISSN 0027-4224
        OCLC 1758884.

Describes Berlioz as primarily a composer of dramatic music for the concert hall and as a man whose frenetic, hysterical style was part of a French Romantic tradition that he shared with other early-nineteenth-century French artists.

620.   Masson, Paul-Marie. "Hector Berlioz et l'esthétique française du XVIIIe siècle." In *Mélanges d'esthétique et de science de l'art offerts à Etienne Souriau*, 179-88. Paris, Librairie Nizet, 1952. 277 p. N79 M44 OCLC 638509.

Claims that one of the primary characteristics of French music has always been its compliance with the "doctrine of imitation" in which instrumental music is said to express specific meanings and vocal music is closely linked to the sense of its texts. Sees Berlioz as continuing the use of these musical principles as handed down from Gluck and Méhul. Also suggests that the origin of the program symphony was in the French opera overture which attempted to depict dramatic moods in purely instrumental terms.

621.   Rushton, Julian. "Berlioz' Roots in 18th Century French Opera." *Berlioz Society Bulletin* no. 50 (April 1965): 3-10. OCLC 2386332.

Finds parallels between the musical aesthetics of eighteenth-century French opera composers such as Gluck, Piccinni, Sacchini, and Salieri, and those of Berlioz.

c. Ludwig van Beethoven

622.   Tiersot, Julien. "Berlioz symphoniste. *Musica* 7 (1908): 41-42. OCLC 1695501.

Calls attention to the connections between Berlioz's symphonies and those of Beethoven, particularly the Third, Fifth, Sixth, and Ninth. Emphasizes the regularity of form and other purely musical merits of Berlioz's works which are often obscured by the attention paid to his programs.

d. Jean-François Le Sueur

623.   Fouque, Octave. "J.-F. Le Sueur." In *Les révolutionnaires de la musique*, 136-83. Paris: Calmann-Lévy, 1882. 358 p. ML390 F7 F72 OCLC 5314173.

Finds similarities of musical style and technique between Berlioz and his teacher, especially regarding the use of the orchestra.

624.   Mongrédien, Jean. "Le Sueur et ses élèves: Berlioz." In *Jean-François Le Sueur: contribution à l'étude d'un demi-siècle de musique française (1780-1830)*. Vol. 2, 977-1022. Berne and Las Vegas: P. Lang, 1980. 2 vols. iv, 1204 p. bibliography, 1101-1153. ISBN 3-261-04694-5 ML410 L6 M6 OCLC 6982771.

Examines the paternal relationship of Le Sueur to the young Berlioz during 1823 and 1824 and concludes that, contrary to the statements of some biographers, Berlioz eagerly and wholeheartedly adopted his teacher's musical principles. Other references to Berlioz throughout the book attest to the influences of Le Sueur on some of his unusual orchestrational effects and on the dramatic shape and content of some scenes in *La damnation de Faust*.

625.   Schacher, Thomas. "Geistliche Musik als 'drame sacré.' Über den Einfluss Le Sueurs auf Berlioz' kirchenmusikalisches Werk." in *Hamburger Jahrbuch für Musikwissenschaft* 8 (1985): 203-21. OCLC 5791166.

Illustrates Le Sueur's theory of the extra-liturgical dramatic element of common sacred texts through an examination of his speculative essays and treatises on sacred music as well as some of his sacred music itself. Demonstrates that Berlioz knew, admired, and embraced this theory, and that he copied some of Le Sueur's compositional techniques in his own works.

e. Etienne Nicolas Méhul

626.   Bartlet, Mary Elizabeth Caroline. "Etienne Nicolas Méhul and Opera During the French Revolution, Consulate, and

Empire: a Source, Archival, and Stylistic Study." Ph.D. dissertation, University of Chicago, 1982. xviii, 2286 p. bibliography, 2244-86. OCLC 11315399.

Sets in historical perspective Méhul's contributions to the development of *opéra-comique* in the late eighteenth century, including his use of serious subjects and more sophisticated musical structures. Suggests that some of these developments were later exploited by Berlioz [from abstract].

f. Antoine Reicha

627.   Lazarus, Daniel. "Un maître de Berlioz: Anton Reicha." *La revue musicale* 3 (June 1 1922): 255-61. OCLC 1764223.

Demonstrates how Reicha's *Traité d' harmonie* (1814) might have influenced Berlioz's development of an unusual harmonic syntax and how the *Cours de haute composition musicale* (1826) might have introduced him to new ideas about orchestral size and balance.

g. William Shakespeare

628.   Barzun, Jacques. "Berlioz and the Band." In *Critical Questions...*, edited by Bea Friedland, 123-31. Chicago: University of Chicago Press, 1982. xvii, 269 p. ISBN 0-226-03863-7 ML60 B278 1982 OCLC 8032099.

Equates Shakespeare and Berlioz as "makers of flawed masterpieces." Shows how Shakespeare served as a model for the dramatic works of Berlioz, especially with regard to matters of "open form."

629.   Gury, Jacques. "Berlioz et Shakespeare jusqu'à *Roméo et Juliette*." *Romantisme* no. 12 (1976): 9-18. ISSN 0048-8593 OCLC 931119.

Claims that Berlioz, along with most of the other French Romantics, did not respond as much to the works of Shakespeare, which they knew only in imperfect translations,

as they did to the man as an artistic genius who understood
and expressed the "mysteries of man."

h. Gaspare Spontini

630.   Cairns, David. "Spontini's Influence on Berlioz." In *From
          Parnassus: Essays in Honor of Jacques Barzun*, edited by
          Dora B. Weiner and William R. Keylor, 25-41. New York:
          Harper & Row, 1976. xxii, 386 p. ISBN 0-060-14549-8 AC5
          F79 1975 OCLC 2609605.

          Demonstrates Berlioz's fondness for Spontini through
          quotations from his letters and the *Mémoires*. Includes specific
          musical examples to show how aspects of Berlioz's harmonic,
          rhythmic, and melodic style derive from Spontini.

3. BERLIOZ'S INFLUENCE ON OTHERS

631.   Abraham, Gerald. "The Influence of Berlioz on Richard
          Wagner." *Music and Letters* 5 (no. 3 1924): 239-46. ISSN
          0027-4224 OCLC 1758884.

          Explains that despite his condemnation of the programmatic
          quality of Berlioz's dramatic symphonies, Wagner was
          actually greatly influenced by his compositional methods,
          including the use of large orchestras, leitmotifs, and divisi
          string parts.

632.   Cresti, Renzo. "Berlioz e Liszt guidano Wagner." *Ricerche
          musicali* 5 (March 1981): 26-43. OCLC 6523233.

          States that Berlioz influenced Wagner in the areas of
          orchestral color, architectural scope, and the use of leitmotifs.
          Also differentiates the "dramatic symphonies" of Berlioz from
          the symphonic poems of Liszt on the basis of the
          psychological relationship between the music and the "poetic
          idea" in each.

633.   Floros, Constantin. *Gustav Mahler*. Vol. 2. *Mahler und die Symphonik des 19. Jahrhunderts in neuer Deutung*. Wiesbaden: Breitkopf & Härtel, 1977-85. 3 vols. ML410 M23 F55 OCLC 4189526.

Finds that many symphonic techniques employed by Berlioz (among others) influenced Mahler's symphonic style. These include exploded multi-movement forms, cyclic techniques, thematic transformation, "reunion" of different themes, development of the march and pastoral genre as character types, and exploitation of the unexpected.

634.   Freeman, John W. "Berlioz and Verdi." In *Atti del III Congresso internazionale di studi verdiani*, 148-65. Parma: Istituto di studi verdiani, 1974. xvi, 617 p. ML36 C769 1972 OCLC 2034247.

Traces possible (but not documented) influences of Berlioz's music on Verdi, particularly in the form of specific types of orchestral gestures. Quotes the *Mémoires* and various feuilletons to establish Berlioz's respect and admiration for Verdi, centering on his colorful orchestral writing and insistence on dramatic truthfulness in music.

635.   Niecks, Friedrich. "The Influence of Berlioz as an Orchestrator." *The Monthly Musical Record* 41 (May 1 1911): 111-13. OCLC 1605021.

Asserts that Berlioz's orchestration technique had no direct influence on Meyerbeer, Mendelssohn, Schumann, or Wagner, and only a slight influence on Liszt, who best knew his works.

636.   Runciman, John F. "After Berlioz." *The Saturday Review of Politics, Literature, Science and Art* 96 (December 12 1903): 729-31. OCLC 1765055.

Laments the influence of Berlioz on the work of later composers such as Strauss, who wrote elaborately detailed program music, and Mahler, whose music is full of "empty effects."

637.   Solenière, Eugène de. "L'influence de Berlioz." In *Le livre d'or du centenaire Hector Berlioz*, 181-85. Paris: G. Petit, 1907. vi, 224 p. ML410 B5 L59 OCLC 5781226.

Claims that Berlioz's influence was more general than specific since he had no students to carry on his innovations. Sees his

greatest influence in the work of later composers of
symphonic poems.

4. COMPARISONS

a. Ludwig van Beethoven

638.   Ambros, A.W. "Hector Berlioz." In *Bunte Blätter: Skizzen
         und Studien für Freunde der Musik und der bildenden Kunst.*
         Vol. 1, 93-106. 2nd ed. 62-71. Leipzig: F.E.C. Leuckart (C.
         Sander), 1872-74. 2 vols. OCLC 2583092. 2nd ed. Leipzig:
         F.E.C. Leuckart, 1896. xiv, 291 p. ML60 A492 OCLC
         15374270.

         An obituary that expresses in part the unusual view that
         Berlioz did not really understand Beethoven, despite his
         admiration and enthusiasm for the composer. Claims that his
         work is not an outgrowth of Beethoven's, because it lacks the
         powerful expression of the struggle and suffering of a great
         human heart that is characteristic of Beethoven's music.

639.   Bockholdt, Rudolf. "Eigenschaften des Rhythmus im
         instrumentalen Satz bei Beethoven und Berlioz." In *Bericht
         über den Internationalen Musikwissenschaftlichen Kongress:
         Bonn 1970,* edited by Carl Dahlhaus, 29-33. Kassel:
         Bárenreiter, 1971. xxii, 714 p. ISBN 3-761-80146-7 ML36
         I6277 OCLC 849785.

         Demonstrates that both Beethoven's and Berlioz's music is
         characterized by unexpected rhythmic irregularities, but that
         in Beethoven's music they can always be perceived against a
         clear *Taktordnung* (succession of beats), whereas in Berlioz's
         they cannot. Uses *Harold en Italie* to demonstrate this thesis.

b. Richard Wagner

640.   Panzacchi, Enrico. "Ettore Berlioz." In *Nel mondo della musica, impressioni e ricordi*, 257-66. Florence: G.C. Sansoni, 1895. 324 p. ML60 P17.

Claims that some of Berlioz's operatic ideas, particularly those concerning the relationship of words to music, presage those of Wagner. Nevertheless finds Berlioz to be closer to the Latin spirit than to the Teutonic spirit of Wagner.

641.   Passy, Jacques. "Berlioz et Wagner." *Le corréspondant* 151 (June 10 1888): 927-59. OCLC 5258641.

Examines the background, environment, musical philosophy, and compositional practices of both composers to prove that they were destined to oppose one another and that their temporary alliance contained the seeds of its eventual dissolution.

642.   Pohl, Richard. "Berlioz' künstlerische Stellung zur Gegenwart." In *Hektor Berlioz: Studien und Erinnerungen*, 111-30. Leipzig: B. Schlicke, 1884. OCLC 12321145. Reprint. Wiesbaden: M. Sändig, 1974. xv, 275 p. ML410 B5 P7 1974 OCLC 1035987.

Remarks that although in his own time Berlioz was known as a proponent of "music of the future," such was not really the case, since his music has little to do with Wagner's in either style or purpose.

5. COMPOSITIONAL PROCESS

643.   Holoman, D. Kern. "Autograph Musical Documents of Hector Berlioz, c. 1818-1840." Ph.D. dissertation. Princeton University, 1974. 495 p., bibliography, 482-93. OCLC 4781053. Revised as *The Creative Process in the Autograph Musical Documents of Hector Berlioz, c. 1818-1840*. Ann Arbor: UMI Research Press, 1980. xxii, 399 p. bibliography, 359-67. ISBN 0-835-70988-4 ML410 B5 H6 OCLC 4832169.

Contains a thematic catalog of works to 1840, general
analyses of Berlioz's handwriting, paper, sketches, drafts, and
revisions, and specific analyses of the compositional origins of
Les francs-juges, the *Requiem*, and the *Symphonie fantastique*.

644.   Macdonald, Hugh. "Berlioz's Self-Borrowings." *Proceedings
         of the Royal Musical Association* 92 (1965-66): 27-44. ISSN
         0080-4452 OCLC 1764602.

Lists themes borrowed by Berlioz from earlier works for reuse
in later ones. Attributes such borrowings to pressures from
lack of time and money, a desire not to see good music from
abandoned early works go to waste, and a general
programmatic similarity among many of his compositions.

6. COUNTERPOINT AND FUGUE

645.   Anon. "Berlioz, Student and Master." *The Saturday Review
         of Politics, Literature, Science and Art* 143 (January 29 1927):
         154-55. OCLC 8566200.

A critique of *La damnation de Faust* which calls attention to
the weakness of Berlioz's contrapuntal writing and the
awkwardness of some of his orchestrational effects, which the
author claims result from his unorthodox musical training.

646.   Favre, Georges. "Berlioz et la fugue." *La revue musicale* no.
         233 (1956): 38-44. OCLC 1764223.

Demonstrates that after Berlioz's failure in the 1826 *Prix de
Rome* competition, he quickly developed a "correct" fugal
technique while enrolled in Reicha's counterpoint class at the
Conservatoire. Although he frequently used fugal techniques
in his later works, Berlioz never wrote strict academic fugues
after those he did for the *Prix de Rome* competitions.

647.   Hirshberg, Jehoash. "Berlioz and the Fugue." *Journal of
         Music Theory* 18 (no. 1 1974): 152-88. ISSN 0022-2909
         OCLC 1783233.

Gathers remarks about fugal technique from Berlioz's writings. Shows that he did not hate fugue, as is often thought, but only its indiscriminate and unmotivated use in sacred vocal music. Includes analyses of the most important examples of fugal writing found in Berlioz's works.

648. Schenkman, Walter. "Fixed Ideas and Recurring Patterns in Berlioz's Melody." *The Music Review* 40 (no. 1 1979): 25-48. ISSN 0027-4445 OCLC 1758893.

Finds in the symphonies several recurring melodic shapes centering around the dominant or tonic scale degrees and involving the chromatic half steps just below each of them. Concludes that Berlioz's use of chromaticism is not "capricious" but is governed to some extent by these melodic formulae.

7. DRAMATIC TECHNIQUES

649. Boulez, Pierre. "L'imaginaire chez Berlioz." Translated by David Noakes as "Berlioz and the Realm of the Imaginary." *High Fidelity and Musical America* 19 (March 1969): 43-46. ISSN 0018-1463 OCLC 2336463. First published in French in *Points de repère*, edited by Jean-Jacques Nattiez, 239-47. Paris: C. Bourgeois, Seuil, 1981. 573 p. ISBN 0-267-00276-0 ML60 B796 P6 OCLC 8219840. Translated in *Orientations*, 212-19. Cambridge: Harvard University Press, 1986. 541 p. ISBN 0-674-64375-5 ML60 B796 P613 1986 OCLC 12971196. Reprinted in *Daedalus* 115 (no. 4 1986): 175-84. ISSN 0011-5266 OCLC 1565785.

Quotes Berlioz's comments on the "ideal orchestra" (from the *Traité d'instrumentation*), to show that the essence of his dramatic technique was the creation of an "imaginary" world between and beyond the boundaries of the traditions and genres of his own time.

650. Cone, Edward T. "A Lesson from Berlioz." In *The Composer's Voice*, 81-114. Berkeley: University of California Press, 1974, 1982. ix, 184 p. ISBN 0-520-04647-1 ML60 C773 C6 OCLC 9632269.

Describes the character of instrumental timbres as seen in the
Traité d'instrumentation and develops an elaborate and rather
abstract theory of instrumental personae and musical drama in
the *Symphonie fantastique* and *Harold en Italie*, as well as in
works not by Berlioz.

651.   Dömling, Wolfgang. "Szenerie im Imaginären." In *Hector
         Berlioz und seine Zeit*, 77-107. Laaber: Laaber-Verlag, 1986.
         360 p. bibliography, 347-53. ISBN 3-921-51890-3 ML410 B5
         D63 1986 OCLC 15228157.

         Explains how Berlioz creates a theater of the imagination in
         his music (i.e., a dramatic sense of time and space) through
         the use of specific techniques of harmony, instrumentation,
         rhythm, and counterpoint.

652.   _____. "Szenerie im Imaginaren. Über dramatisch-
         symphonische Werke von Hector Berlioz." *Melos/Neue
         Zeitschrift für Musikwissenschaft* 3 (no. 3 1977): 195-203.
         ISSN 0343-0138 OCLC 2327912.

         Demonstrates the correlations between the musical-dramatic
         intentions of Berlioz's symphonic works and the specific
         musical devices (such as the use of space and conflicting
         meters) that create this "imaginary" dramatic effect.

653.   Jahnke, Sabine. "Hector Berlioz--der Traum ins Masslose."
         Musik und Bildung 9 (July-August 1977): 396-99. ISSN 0027-
         4747 OCLC 2649663.

         Uses the *Symphonie fantastique* and the *Requiem* to illustrate
         Berlioz's musical technique of self-dramatization.

654.   Schacher, Thomas. *Idee und Erscheinungsformen des
         Dramatischen bei Hector Berlioz*. Hamburger Beiträge zur
         Musikwissenschaft. Vol. 33. Hamburg: Verlag der
         Musikalienhandlung K.D. Wagner, 1987. v, 202 p.
         bibliography, 184-92. ISBN 3-889-79020-8 ML410 B5 S28
         1987 OCLC 17353295.

         A detailed study of Berlioz's musical-dramatic technique as
         manifested in his non-operatic works, as well as of the
         aesthetic principles that lie behind it. The scope of the book is
         wide-ranging. Included are analyses of the overtures *Les
         francs-juges*, *Le roi Lear*, and *Le corsaire*, a discussion of
         Berlioz's views of the dramatic techniques of Gluck and
         Beethoven, his relationship to the dramatic works of writers

such as Chateaubriand, Shakespeare, Hugo, Stendhal, and de Vigny, his concept of the "grotesque" in literature and music, an analysis of the influence of Grétry's operatic aesthetics on the sacred music of Le Sueur and Berlioz (particularly the *Messe solennelle, Requiem,* and *Te Deum*), and a discussion of the unique blend of operatic and symphonic techniques in all of Berlioz's dramatic music. Originally presented as the author's thesis, University of Hamburg.

655.   Warrack, John. "Berlioz and the Theatre of the Mind." *The Listener and BBC Television Review* 72 (November 5 1964): 738. OCLC 5313690.

Proposes that Berlioz's dramatic music works against traditional operatic forms, processes, and limitations, and can only succeed and be understood as a kind of drama of the imagination. Uses *La damnation de Faust* to illustrate this hypothesis.

8. FORM

656.   Bourges, Maurice. "Examen de quelques compositions de M. Berlioz sous le rapport de plan." *Revue et gazette musicale de Paris* 9 (March 27 1842): 122-25. OCLC 10231154.

Uses the "Scène aux champs" from the *Symphonie fantastique* and the "Convoi funèbre de Juliette" from *Roméo et Juliette* to demonstrate the regularity and order of Berlioz's musical forms.

657.   Boutarel, Amédée. "Berlioz und seine Architecturale Musik." *Die Musik* 3 (December 1 1903): 323-31. OCLC 1696908.

Points out that most of the compositions that Berlioz called "architectural" are occasional pieces commemorating great men or important political events.

658.   Newman, Ernest. "The Mind of Berlioz." In *Berlioz, Romantic and Classic,* edited by Peter Heyworth, 84-88. London: Gollancz, 1972. 288 p. ISBN 0-575-01365-6 ML410 B5 N49 OCLC 516762.

Suggests that from an architectural point of view, Berlioz's
large-scale forms are often unsatisfying because they result
from the loose linking of unrelated pictorial vignettes, each of
which has its own multiple musical perspectives.

659.   Nowalis, Susan Marie. "Timbre as a Structural Device in
         Berlioz' Symphonies." Ph.D. dissertation, Case Western
         Reserve University, 1975. x, 192 p., bibliography, 182-87.
         OCLC 3796572.

         Demonstrates how Berlioz used timbre, both independently
         and in conjunction with other parameters of music, to create
         form and produce dramatic effects [from abstract].

9. HARMONY

660.   Ballif, Claude. "Berlioz aujourd'hui." *Cahiers de l' alpe* no.
         46 (1969): 106+. OCLC 12101098.

         Argues that Berlioz's harmonic style was influenced by the
         orchestral medium for which it was conceived. Uses an
         analogy with Delacroix to establish the relationship between
         design and color in painting and music.

661.   Biondi, Maurizio. "L'armonia di Berlioz: aspetti technici e
         stilistici." *Nuova rivista musicale italiana* 18 (no. 3 1984):
         406-19. ISSN 0029-6228 OCLC 1760926.

         Finds that Berlioz's freedom from functional harmony is
         based on three techniques: the substitution of third for fifth
         relationships, the connection between modality and
         pentatonicism, and a non-functional use of the diminished-
         seventh chord.

662.   Chailley, Jacques. "Berlioz harmoniste." *La revue musicale*
         no. 233 (1956): 15-30. OCLC 1764223.

         Finds influences of Berlioz's harmonic style in the music of
         later-nineteenth-century composers. Claims that, although he
         never understood the harmonic innovations of Wagner, he
         nevertheless revolutionized French harmonic practice by

throwing off the yoke of Rameau's *basse fondamentale* and laying the groundwork for the coloristic harmony of Debussy.

663.   Friedheim, Philip. "Radical Harmonic Procedures in Berlioz." *The Music Review* 21 (no. 4 1960): 282-96. ISSN 0027-4445 OCLC 1758893.

Claims that the unique flavor of Berlioz's harmony is the result of the systematic juxtaposition of common kinds of chords in uncommon relationships. Especially are root progressions moving up by thirds or down by seconds. Contains many examples drawn from Berlioz's works.

664.   George, Graham. "The Ambiguities of Berlioz." *Canadian Association of University Schools of Music Journal* 6 (Spring 1976): 1-10. ISSN 0315-3541 OCLC 2054039.

Regards harmonic ambiguity as an important stylistic element in Berlioz's music. Concludes that although he worked within a common harmonic vocabulary, he deliberately placed the harmonies of that vocabulary in unusual syntatical relationships.

665.   Koechlin, Charles. "Berlioz." In *Traité de l'harmonie*. Vol. 2, 175-79. Paris: M. Eschig, 1930. 3 vols. OCLC 2018471. Paris: M. Eschig, 1958. 3 vols. in 1. MT50 K75 T5 1958 OCLC 8438631.

Discusses Berlioz's rejuvenation of conventional early-nineteenth-century French harmony. Compares his harmonic innovations with those of Beethoven, claiming that Berlioz seemed to be a harmonic anarchist only in the eyes of those who did not know the music of Beethoven.

666.   Newman, Ernest. "An Answer to Ravel." In *Berlioz, Romantic and Classic*, edited by Peter Heyworth, 117-22. London: Gollancz, 1972. 288 p. ISBN 0-575-01365-6 ML410 B5 N49 OCLC 516762.

Responds to Ravel's criticism of Berlioz's "incorrect" harmony by suggesting that harmony is a matter of personal preference and that Berlioz was not technically incompetent but artistically different.

667.   Primmer, Brian. "Berlioz and Harmonic Intensification." *Berlioz Society Bulletin* no. 72 (July 1971): 3-6. OCLC 2386332.

Points to Berlioz's reharmonization of repeated notes or phrases as one of his most effective compositional techniques, one that he may have borrowed from Weber.

10. INSTRUMENTATION AND ORCHESTRATION

a. General Studies

668.   Bernoulli, Eduard. *Hector Berlioz als Aesthetiker der Klangfarben*. Zurich: Hug & Co., 1909. 28 p. ML410 B5 B37.

Attempts to establish the nature of Berlioz's orchestrational aesthetic as determined by an examination of musical examples that he selected from the works of other composers, such as Gluck, Beethoven, and Weber, for use in the *Traité d'instrumentation*. Concludes that Berlioz was the originator of the "enlarged instrumental complexes" characteristic of the Wagnerian orchestra.

669.   Carse, Adam. *The Orchestra from Beethoven to Berlioz; a History of the Orchestra in the First Half of the 19th Century, and of the Development of Orchestral Baton-Conducting*. Cambridge: W. Heffer, 1948. OCLC 3632206. Reprint. St. Claire Shores, Mich.: Scholarly Press, 1976. x, 514 p. bibliography, 495-99. ISBN 0-403-01521-9 ML469 C3 1976 OCLC 2780731.

A complete history of the orchestra including Berlioz's contributions to its growth in the first half of the nineteenth century. Also includes two chapters on the history of conducting.

670.   Duval-Wirth, Geneviève. "Berlioz et la voix." *Silex* no. 17 (September 1980): 87-94. ISSN 0151-2315 OCLC 3739044.

Discusses Berlioz's dislike of Italian fioriture and his insistence on a vocal style more appropriately molded to the sense of the words. Observes that he favored the lower female voices and the very high-tessitura tenor. From the latter,

however, he preferred to hear the chest voice in the upper
register rather than the sound of a falsetto.

671. Kindermann, Jürgen. "Der Klang als Mittel zu symphonischer
Gestaltung in Hector Berlioz' Festkompositionen." In *Über
Symphonien: Beiträge zu einer musikalischen Gattung*, edited
by Christoph-Hellmut Mahling, 117-27. Tutzing: Schneider,
1979. ix, 198 p. ISBN 3-795-20262-0 ML1255 U3 OCLC
6532476.

Uses the *Symphonie fantastique* and the *Requiem* to
demonstrate that Berlioz's monumental expansion of
orchestral sonority was a functional aspect of the music's
structure rather than mere coloristic decoration.

672. Lavoix, H. "La symphonie en France." In *Histoire de
l'instrumentation depuis le seizième siècle jusqu'à nos jours*,
429-43. Paris: Firmin-Didot, 1878. OCLC 751505. Reprint.
Bologna: Forni Editore, 1972. xi, 470 p. ML455 L39 1972
OCLC 2884225.

Discusses the role of the dramatic element in Berlioz's
orchestral music, the suppleness of his orchestration with
which he was able to capture any required mood, his use of
rhythmic counterpoint within single instrumental groups, his
creation of varied orchestral timbres through the use of
unusual instruments or combinations of instruments, his use of
valved brass instruments, and his gradual replacement of the
ophicleid with the tuba.

673. Le Roux, Maurice. "Jouer de l'orchestre." In *Berlioz*, 137-51.
Paris: Réalités-Hachette, 1973. 269 p. ML410 B5 B33 OCLC
1011818.

Explores some of the historical influences on Berlioz's
orchestration, including the *chants nationales* of the
Revolution, and points to some of his innovations such as the
exploration of musical space.

674. Macdonald, Hugh. "Berlioz's Orchestration: Human or
Divine?" *The Musical Times* 110 (March 1969): 255-58.
ISSN 0027-4666 OCLC 5472115.

Points out some of the weaknesses of Berlioz's orchestration,
including miscalculations of balance, harmony, and effects of
timbre, as well as simple inconsistencies in the marking of
performance directions.

675.   Marx, Adolph Bernhard. *Die Musik des neunzehnten
         Jahrhunderts und ihre Pflege*, 159-64. Leipzig: Breitkopf &
         Härtel, 1855. viii, 572 p. ML196 M2 1855 OCLC 6443998.
         Translated by August Heinrich Wehrhan as *The Music of the
         Nineteenth Century and Its Culture*, 69-70, 89-93. London: R.
         Cocks, 1855. 113 p. ML3795 M369 OCLC 3612354.

         Laments Berlioz's influence on the continued growth of the
         orchestra at the expense of the clarity of individual
         instrumental voices. Continues with an evaluation of the
         relationship of Berlioz to Beethoven, observing that Berlioz's
         music has an elevated seriousness similar to Beethoven's, but
         that his program symphonies lack Beethoven's formal purity.

676.   Puttmann, Max. "Hector Berlioz und sein Orchester." *Neue
         Musik-Zeitung* 25 (December 3 1903): 84-86. OCLC
         11930822.

         Credits Berlioz with being an important follower of Weber in
         raising instrumental color to a new level of musical
         importance, leading the way for all of the great "tone-painters"
         of the later nineteenth century.

677.   Rosell, Karen Joan. "Color: a Credible Link Between the
         Paintings of Eugène Delacroix and the Music of Hector
         Berlioz?" Ph.D. dissertation, Ohio University, 1986. 258 p.
         bibliography, 239-58. OCLC 15619435.

         Investigates the "color theories" of both artists and finds
         similarities in the way they apply color for the purpose of
         demarcating formal structures [from abstract].

678.   Strauss, Richard. "Vorwort." In *Instrumentationslehre*, i-iv.
         Leipzig, C.F. Peters, 1905, 1955. 2 vols. MT70 B484 1955
         OCLC 14008702. Translated by Ernest Closson as "Sur
         l'orchestration." *Bulletin S.I.M.* 5 (March 1909): 226-30.

         Suggests that despite his innovations in orchestration,
         Berlioz's major weakness was a lack of polyphony which
         made his work less effective than Wagner's.

679.   Weingartner, Felix. "Was können wir von Berlioz lernen?" In
         Akkorde: gesammelte Aufsätze, 164-70. Leipzig: Breitkopf &
         Härtel, 1912. OCLC 2608838. Walluf-Nendeln: Sändig, 1977.
         iv, 304 p. ISBN 3-500-30490-7 ML60 W45 1977 OCLC
         4190155.

Claims that Berlioz's orchestration is inseparable from the musical ideas to which it is attached. Compares Berlioz and Wagner and finds that Wagner's music is more socially and morally meaningful.

680. Weirauch, Robert F. "The Orchestrational Style of Hector Berlioz." D.M.A. dissertation, University of Cincinnati, 1968. iv, 99 p., bibliography, 96-99. OCLC 683851.

Studies Berlioz's orchestrational technique as it relates to other parameters of musical style, including form, melody, harmony, and rhythm. Suggests a relationship between his orchestrational style and specific devices of Renaissance counterpoint [from abstract].

b. Guitar

681. Dallman, Paul Jerald. "Influence and Use of the Guitar in the Music of Hector Berlioz." M.M. thesis, University of Maryland, 1972. v, 267 p. bibliography, 229-44. OCLC 2032972.

Finds in Berlioz's guitar music many of his most "unorthodox" stylistic characteristics, including unusual keys, chord inversions, harmonic progressions, and voice leading. Demonstrates that these characteristics clearly result from the physical idiosyncracies of the guitar. Concludes that Berlioz's style was shaped early in his career by using the guitar rather than the piano as a compositional tool. Includes a facsimile of the *Recueil de romances* (1819-22) for guitar and voice.

682. Zuth, Joseph. "Die Gitarre des Berlioz." *Zeitschrift für die Gitarre* 1 (April 1 1922): 8-11.

Briefly traces Berlioz's involvement with the guitar from his early experiences as a performer to his later use of the instrument in some of his dramatic works.

c. Organ

683.   McCaldin, Denis. "Berlioz and the Organ." *The Organ Yearbook* 4 (1973): 3-17. ISSN 0920-3192 OCLC 1785030.

Compares quotations regarding the organ from the *Traité d'instrumentation* with Berlioz's use of the instrument in *L'enfance du Christ* and the *Te Deum*. Concludes that he usually follows his own advice in not using the organ to double voice or orchestral lines, finding a more independent role for it to play.

684.   Verne, D. Batigan. "Berlioz *Versus* the Organ." *The Organ* 6 (January 1927): 171-78. ISSN 0030-4883 OCLC 1640101.

Claims that Berlioz's prejudices against the polyphonic music of J.S. Bach and Palestrina resulted from a musical mind lacking in an "inner intellectual element." Also notes the many technical misunderstandings of the organ that appear in the *Traité d'instrumentation*.

685.   Warrack, John. "Hector, Thou Sleep'st." *The Musical Times* 104 (December 1963): 896-97. ISSN 0027-4666 OCLC 5472115.

Demonstrates that the section of the *Traité d'instrumentation* devoted to the organ betrays an almost complete ignorance of the instrument, and the absurdities found therein are further compounded by Mary Cowden Clarke's English translation.

d. Percussion

686.   Tanner, Peter Hyde. "Timpani and Percussion Writing in the Works of Hector Berlioz." Ph.D. dissertation, Catholic University of America, 1967. xvi, 270 p., bibliography, 263-70. OCLC 9367917.

Discusses Berlioz's innovations in percussion writing, including the use of more than two timpani, different kinds of sticks, soft dynamics, solo effects, bass drum rolls, and the suspended cymbal.

e. Woodwinds and Brass

687. Collins, W.T. "Berlioz and the Trombone." D.M.A. thesis, University of Texas at Austin, 1985. vii, 143 p. bibliography, 141-43. OCLC 14372034.

 Traces Berlioz's contributions to the growing use of the trombone in the orchestra after 1830 by comparing his writing for this instrument with that of other composers before and after him [from abstract].

688. Sandor, E.P. "Development and Use of the Chromatic Trumpet in the Nineteenth-Century Orchestra." *NACWPI Journal* 33 (no. 4 1985): 4-12. OCLC 1793034.

 Briefly summarizes the emergence of the chromatic trumpet (and peripherally, the horn) writing in the late-nineteenth century. Compares this new style with Berlioz's more traditional use of valved instruments based on a continuation of older principles of natural (valveless) brass writing.

689. Whitwell, David. "Berlioz--His Music for Winds." *The Instrumentalist* 20 (January 1966): 71-75. ISSN 0020-4331 OCLC 1753312.

 Surveys Berlioz's interest in and use of wind instruments. Includes comments about their state of mechanical evolution between 1800 and 1850, and Berlioz's remarks on national differences in wind instruments and playing.

690. Wilson, Cecil Barley. "Berlioz' Use of Brass Instruments." Ph.D. dissertation, Case Western Reserve, 1971. xiv, 211 p., bibliography, 206-11. OCLC 1955197.

 Studies Berlioz's writing for brass in relation to what he prescribes for these instruments in the *Traité d'instrumentation*. Includes a discussion of factors affecting his choice of tunings and use of valved or valveless instruments.

11. MELODY

691.   Bass, Eddie Covington. "Thematic Procedures in the
        Symphonies of Berlioz." Ph.D. dissertation, University of
        North Carolina, 1964. 235 p. OCLC 6825893.

        Examines the structure of Berlioz's melodies in terms of their
        length, unpredictability, and asymmetry. Studies the nature of
        their development throughout the symphonies, comparing
        Berlioz's procedures with those of Liszt and Beethoven [from
        abstract].

692.   Marnold, Jean. "Hector Berlioz, musicien." *Mercure de
        France* 53 (January 15 1905): 205-20; (February 1 1905):
        362-78. OCLC 1681285.

        Contends that although he lived in an age when harmony was
        the most vital parameter of music, Berlioz remained
        exclusively monodic in his approach to composition, showing
        little sense of good harmonic effect or modulatory ability.
        Describes the essence of Berlioz's harmonic technique as
        "arbitrary enharmonics" and his forms as "antiquated or
        elementary" but admits that his melodic sense was original.

693.   Massougnes, Georges de. "Berlioz et les artistes
        d'aujourd'hui." In *Hector Berlioz: son oeuvre*, 107-43. Paris:
        Calmann-Lévy, 1919. 143 p.

        Contends that in 1903 there was still much disagreement over
        Berlioz's greatness, stating that the general public did not
        understand his melodic style due in part to its irregularity and
        unpredictability, and because they had adopted Wagner as a
        model of the ideal modern orchestral melodist. Originally
        appeared in *Monde musical*, November 30, 1903.

694.   Newman, Ernest. "Closing Phrases." In *Berlioz, Romantic
        and Classic*, edited by Peter Heyworth, 145-48. London:
        Gollancz, 1972. 288 p. ISBN 0-575-01365-6 ML410 B5 N49
        OCLC 516762.

        Claims that the final bars of many of Berlioz's melodies are
        weak and ineffective because of his inability to avoid the
        patterns of traditional cadential formulas.

695. Noufflard, Georges Frédéric. *Hector Berlioz et le mouvement de l'art contemporain.* Florence: Imprimerie coopérative, 1883. 170 p. 2nd ed. Paris: Fischbacher, 1885. 118 p. ML410 B51 N8 OCLC 12588788.

Discusses Berlioz's melodic style and the apparent conflict he felt between wanting vocal texts to assume primary importance and writing highly original, self-sufficient melodies. Contains some outdated ideas about the lack of unity in Berlioz's works.

696. Weirauch, Robert F. "The Neo-Renaissance Berlioz." *The Music Review* 36 (no. 4 1975): 245-52. ISSN 0027-4445 OCLC 1758893.

Adopts the view that Berlioz's orchestral style is thoroughly contrapuntal and often canonic in nature, and that this linear style extends to other parameters as well (i.e., color, rhythm, and dynamics). Suggests that these compositional techniques may have been borrowed from Renaissance music.

697. Wotton. Tom S. "Berlioz As Melodist." *The Musical Times* 70 (September 1 1929): 808-12. ISSN 0027-4666 OCLC 5472115.

Defends Berlioz's often criticized melodic style by calling attention to the vast variety of his melodies, including some in a popular folk style.

12. PERFORMANCE PRACTICE

698. Macdonald, Hugh. "Two Peculiarities of Berlioz's Notation." *Music and Letters* 50 (no. 1 1969): 25-36. ISSN 0027-4224 OCLC 1758884.

Discusses five possible meanings of the slur in Berlioz's music and suggests that present-day interpretations of this common notational sign may not be what the composer intended. Also determines that what look like very short diminuendo marks in Berlioz's manuscripts are in fact just that and not oversized accents. For a rebuttal of the author's views on the slur, see #700.

699.   Newman, Ernest. "The Eye and the Ear." In *Berlioz,*
         Romantic and Classic, edited by Peter Heyworth, 137-44.
         London: Gollancz, 1972. 288 p. ISBN 0-575-01365-6 ML410
         B5 N49 OCLC 516762.

         Shows how Berlioz's carefully irregular phrase markings are
         usually ignored and misheard by listeners and performers
         alike, resulting in serious distortions of the composer's
         intentions.

700.   Temperley, Nicholas. "Berlioz and the Slur." *Music and*
         Letters 50 (no. 3 1969): 388-92. ISSN 0027-4224 OCLC
         1758884.

         States that there is no historical evidence to suggest that the
         slur in Berlioz's music signifies a detachment of the last note
         of a group from the first note of the next. Includes musical
         examples. A rebuttal to Hugh Macdonald's "Two Peculiarities
         of Berlioz's Notation" (#698).

13. RHYTHM AND METER

701.   Friedheim, Philip. "Berlioz and Rhythm." *The Music Review*
         37 (no. 1 1976): 5-44. ISSN 0027-4445 OCLC 1758893.

         Quotes from Berlioz's theoretical and critical writings to
         establish his attitudes toward rhythm, following with a
         rhythmic analysis of his compositions in chronological order.
         Principal works analyzed are *Huit scènes de Faust,* the
         Symphonie fantastique, Harold en Italie, Benvenuto Cellini,
         La damnation de Faust, and *Les Troyens.* Extensive musical
         examples.

702.   Gräbner, Eric. "Some Aspects of Rhythm in Berlioz."
         Soundings: a Music Journal no. 2 (1971-72): 18-28. ISSN
         0081-2080 OCLC 1948031.

         Beginning with some of Berlioz's observations on rhythm, the
         author hypothesizes that he was able to create strikingly new
         rhythmic effects by divorcing this stylistic parameter from its
         traditional interdependence on harmony. The author further

demonstrates that the model for this procedure is found in the works of Gluck.

14. SPATIAL DIMENSION

703. Bockholdt, Rudolf. "Musikalischer Satz und Orchesterklang im Werk von Hector Berlioz." *Die Musikforschung* 32 (no. 2 1979): 122-35. ISSN 0027-4801 OCLC 2669982.

Analyzes the spatial element in works such as the *Symphonie funèbre*, the *Requiem*, *La damnation de Faust*, *Harold en Italie*, and the *Symphonie fantastique*. Finds that the traditional distinction between texture and orchestration does not apply to Berlioz's music.

704. Héron, Jean-François. "Jouer de l'espace." *Silex* no. 17 (September 1980): 81-86. ISSN 0151-2315 OCLC 3739044.

Investigates the use of space in Berlioz's music, not only in terms of the actual physical location of instrumental and vocal forces in a large performing space, but also in terms of the more limited arrangement of instruments within the orchestra and the organization of contrasts of timbre in the music.

705. Kunze, Stefan. "Raumvorstellungen in der Musik. Zur Geschichte des Kompositionsbegriffs." *Archiv für Musikwissenschaft* 31 (no. 1 1974): 1-21. ISSN 0003-9292 OCLC 1481988.

Describes Berlioz's role in the history of the development of the spatial dimension in music from the nineteenth century to Ligeti. Equates the growing importance of this spatial element with Berlioz's search for new timbres.

15. THEMATIC COMBINATION

706.   Schenkman, Walter. "Combination of Themes As a Hallmark
         of Romantic Style." *The Music Review* 37 (no. 3 1976): 171-
         92. ISSN 0027-4445 OCLC 1758893.

         Examines Berlioz's use of thematic combination in the
         Symphonie fantastique, Harold en Italie, and *Roméo et Juliette*
         in relation to similar usage by Beethoven and other Romantic
         composers. Suggests that this technique is just one of several
         manifestations of the Romantic fondness for the fusion of
         musical opposites.

707.   Silverman, Richard S. "Synthesis in the Music of Hector
         Berlioz." *The Music Review* 34 (no. 3-4 1973): 346-52. ISSN
         0027-4445 OCLC 1758893.

         Presents examples of thematic superimposition in Berlioz's
         music and concludes that, while dramatically effective, some
         of them are quite "artificial" and result in one theme
         dominating the other.

16. THEMATIC TRANSFORMATION

708.   Bass, Eddie Covington. "Musical Time and Space in Berlioz."
         The Music Review 30 (no. 3 1969): 211-24. ISSN 0027-4445
         OCLC 1758893.

         Hypothesizes that the works of Berlioz that involve the
         process of thematic transformation are those which imply a
         kind of literary "time," while those which do not are more
         concerned with creating musical "space."

709.   _____. "Thematic Unification of Scenes in Multimovement
         Works of Berlioz." *The Music Review* 28 (no. 1 1967): 45-51.
         ISSN 0027-4445 OCLC 1758893.

         Shows how Berlioz unified both his symphonies and dramatic
         works with the same "organic" procedures of thematic
         transformation.

XII. Groups of Works

This chapter contains studies devoted to the music of Berlioz considered by genre or other collective groupings.

1. ARRANGEMENTS

710.   Tiersot, Julien. "Berlioziana: oeuvres arrangées par Berlioz." *Le ménestrel* 72 (February 11 1906): 43-45. OCLC 6966764.

Discusses Berlioz's revisions of Gluck's *Orphée* (in which he restored the lead role to an alto) and *Alceste* (in which he made some transpositions of key and added sections from the original Italian version). Also discusses the French and Italian versions of scores used as sources for these revisions. Briefly mentions the arrangements of the *Hymne des Marseillais* (Rouget de Lisle), *Marche marocaine* (de Meyer), *Plaisir d'amour* (Martini), *Der Erlkönig* (Schubert, as *Le roi des aulnes),* and some of Bortnyansky's religious music (probably just retexting). Also mentions his never-realized plan to arrange Russian plainchant for sixteen-voice choir.

2. JUVENILIA

711.   Henke, M., and M. Stegemann. "Hector Berlioz: neue
        Aspekte zum Jugendwerk." *NZ/Neue Zeitschrift für Musik* no.
        3 (May-June 1980): 241-43. ISSN 0170-8791 OCLC
        4754773.

        Describes the contents of a guitar sketchbook located in the
        Berlioz Museum (La Côte-St-André) and provides
        information on some of the composers whose melodies
        Berlioz set to guitar accompaniments in the *Recueil de
        romances*. Both items date from his boyhood studies with
        Dorant.

712.   Hyatt, Raymond. *"Le cheval arabe, Beverley,* and *Estelle."*
        Berlioz Society Bulletin no. 60 (July 1968): 6-13. OCLC
        2386332.

        Reconstructs the proper chronology of these works and *Le
        passage de la mer rouge*, all of which Berlioz composed
        during his first years in Paris.

713.   _____. "The Earliest Compositions of Berlioz." *Berlioz
        Society Bulletin* no. 51 (July 1965): 1; no. 52 (October 1965):
        2-8. OCLC 2386332.

        Demonstrates the danger of accepting the dating of these
        works as given in the *Mémoires*. Establishes a new chronology
        for compositions written between 1816 and 1821.

714.   Tiersot, Julien. "Berlioziana: oeuvres semi-inédites." *Le
        ménestrel* 72 (February 18 1906): 51-52; (February 25): 59-
        60. OCLC 6966764.

        Establishes a chronology for some little-known early works
        and briefly describes each. They include *Le dépit de la
        bergère, Le maure jaloux,* and *Pleure pauvre Colette*, written
        before 1821, and *Le montagnard exilé, Toi qui l'aimas verse
        des pleurs, Amitié reprends ton empire,* and *Canon libre à la
        quinte*, all written during 1822 and 1823.

3. OPERAS

715.   Bailbé, Joseph-Marc. *Berlioz et l'art lyrique: essai d'interprétation à l'usage de notre temps.* Berne and Las Vegas: P. Lang, 1981. 239 p. ISBN 3-261-04916-2 ML410 B51 B155 OCLC 8877270.

Extracts Berlioz's theories concerning lyric-dramatic music from his critical writings. Presents these theories in relation to both his operatic procedures and the style of nineteenth-century French opera in general. Includes discussions of the following subjects: the relationship of poetry and music in French opera before Berlioz; the advent of a bourgeois operatic style circa 1830 and Berlioz's opposition to dilettante audiences and Italian music; his standards for good operatic singing and his dislike of vocal virtuosity; his opinions of contemporary writers, including Hugo, Balzac, Flaubert, Chateaubriand, and de Vigny; the correlation between and divergence of the operatic theories of Berlioz and Wagner; a structural and stylistic analysis of one of his typical feuilletons; and an analysis of the poetic style of *Les Troyens*. Includes a useful appendix that extracts from the *Traité d'instrumentation* all comments regarding opera or opera composers.

716.   Barraud, Henry. "Le musicien de théâtre." In *Berlioz*, 177-95. Paris: Réalités-Hachette, 1973. 269 p. ML410 B5 B33 OCLC 1011818.

Assigns the failure of some of Berlioz's operas to his inability to solve the problem of the conflicting needs of dramatic pacing and musical expansiveness.

717.   Dickinson, A.E.F. "Berlioz' Stage Works." *The Music Review* 31 (no. 2 1970): 136-57. ISSN 0027-4445 OCLC 1758893.

Introductory survey of Berlioz's operas, including those planned and/or left incomplete. Includes some valuable information amid the general descriptive analysis. Makes no attempt to explain the complex compositional history of *Benvenuto Cellini*. Intended primarily for readers with little familiarity with these works.

718.   Dömling, Wolfgang. "Oper." In *Hector Berlioz und seine
         Zeit*, 209-29. Laaber: Laaber-Verlag, 1986. 360 p.
         bibliography, 347-53. ISBN 3-921-51890-3 ML410 B5 D63
         1986 OCLC 15228157.

         Explains the compositional history and extra-musical
         symbolism of *Benvenuto Cellini* and discusses *Les Troyens* as
         a Classically motivated variation on the typical nineteenth-
         century grand opera subject matter.

719.   Ernst. Alfred. *L'oeuvre dramatique de H. Berlioz*. Paris:
         Calmann-Lévy, 1884. 372 p. ML410 B51 E71 OCLC
         12491465.

         Contains an evaluation of Berlioz's dramatic style, a
         discussion of Berlioz as writer and critic, and an analysis of
         similarities between Wagner and Berlioz, as well as critical
         analyses (of a non-technical type) of *Benvenuto Cellini,
         Roméo et Juliette, La damnation de Faust, L'enfance du
         Christ*, and *Les Troyens*, with contemporary reviews from
         Parisian papers.

720.   Klein, John W. "Berlioz As a Musical Dramatist." *The
         Chesterian* 35 (Autumn 1960): 35-43. OCLC 8182289.

         Characterizes Berlioz's operas as flawed masterpieces that
         have long been neglected. Claims that Berlioz too frequently
         sacrificed dramatic effectiveness to musical beauty, and in so
         doing demonstrated his lack of innate musical-dramatic
         genius. Notes Berlioz's influence on Bizet, Wagner,
         Mussorgsky, and even Britten.

721.   Langford, Jeffrey A. "Musical-Dramatic Parallels in the
         Operas of Hector Berlioz." In *Music and Drama*, 152-70.
         Studies in the History of Music. Vol. 2. New York: Broude
         Bros., 1988. 239 p. ISBN 0-845-07402-4 ML1700 M88
         OCLC 17782712.

         Demonstrates that in the operas of Berlioz (including *La
         damnation de Faust*) there are a remarkable number of
         dramatic scenes which are nearly identical in musical style or
         technique. Proposes that this results from Berlioz's proclivity
         toward specific kinds of dramatic situations and his belief
         (unstated) that for any particular situation there was only one
         best musical realization.

722.   _____. "The Operas of Hector Berlioz: Their Relationship to the French Operatic Tradition of the Early Nineteenth Century." Ph.D. dissertation, University of Pennsylvania, 1978. ix, 450 p. bibliography, 440-50. OCLC 6519949.

Surveys the history of opera in France from Gluck to Meyerbeer to demonstrate that many of the unusual and innovative techniques found in Berlioz's operas have their roots in the little-known works of his immediate predecessors.

723.   Massougnes, Georges de. "Le cycle Berlioz à Carlsruhe." *Revue politique et littéraire (Revue Bleue)* 30 (November 18 1893): 659-63. OCLC 8339424. Also in *Gazette des beaux-arts* 3rd period, tome 10 (1893): 500-506. ISSN 0016-5530 OCLC 1570479.

Reviews the performance cycle of Berlioz's operas at Carlsruhe in 1893 directed by Felix Mottl. Suggests that these works were not popular in France because of the seductive influence of Wagner on audiences after mid-century, and that their performance in Paris would not be possible until the improvement in quality of theatrical choristers.

724.   Meylan, Pierre. "Berlioz et la poesie." *Revue musicale de Suisse Romande* 31 (no. 3 1978): 120-26. ISSN 0035-3744 OCLC 9077868.

Draws on Berlioz's ideas as expressed in the *Mémoires* and *A travers chants* to define his "theory" of the relationship of words and music in opera. This theory was based on his conviction that music must be dramatically appropriate to the text without either dominating it or being subordinate to it. Similarities with Wagner's theories are pointed out.

4. OVERTURES

725.   Tiersot, Julien. "Berlioziana: ouvertures des *Francs-juges*, du *Roi Lear* et du *Carnival romain*." *Le ménestrel* 71 (September 24 1905): 308. OCLC 6966764.

Discusses piano four-hand transcriptions of the three works cited, the most attention being devoted to an unauthorized

German version of the overture to *Les francs-juges* ,
extensively quoting Berlioz's open letter complaining about
its poor quality (appearing in the *Revue et gazette musicale de
Paris*, May 8, 1836).

5. PROGRAM MUSIC

Since much of Berlioz's program music falls into the genres of
symphony and overture, the reader is referred to those sections of the
bibliography for additional citations.

726.   Barzun, Jacques. "The Meaning of Meaning in Music: Berlioz
        Once More." *The Musical Quarterly* 66 (no. 1 1980): 1-20.
        ISSN 0027-4631 OCLC 1642493. Reprinted in *Critical
        Questions...*, edited by Bea Friedland, 75-98. Chicago:
        University of Chicago Press, 1982. xvii, 269 p. ISBN 0-226-
        03863-7 ML60 B278 1982 OCLC 8032099.

        Maintains that all music is programmatic and that in the
        nineteenth century music critics viewed even absolute genres
        such as the symphony as "instrumental operas" with hidden
        stories.

727.   Condé, Gérard. "La forme et le prétext." *Silex* no. 17
        (September 1980): 23-28. ISSN 0151-2315 OCLC 3739044.

        Hypothesizes that the programmatic and literary associations
        in Berlioz's music resulted from his desire to create a unique
        identity for each composition. In refusing to accept any
        musical style *a priori*, he was forced to give each work the
        form that it alone demanded.

728.   Dömling, Wolfgang. "Die *Symphonie fantastique* und
        Berlioz' Auffassung von Programmusik." *Die
        Musikforschung* 28 (no. 3 1975): 260-83. ISSN 0027-4801
        OCLC 2669982.

        Demonstrates that Berlioz had no single concept of program
        music, and that the relationship between program and music
        was different for each of his dramatic instrumental works.

Compares his concept of the dramatic symphony with Liszt's idea of program music.

729. Elliot, J.H. "Berlioz in Our Time." *Hallé* (Manchester) no. 8 (January 1948): 1-4.

Contends that despite the programmatic associations in some of Berlioz's music and his own talk of musical revolution, the Berlioz style is primarily one of Classical purity and transparency in which the music stands complete in itself.

730. Klauwell, Otto. "Hektor Berlioz, Franz Liszt und seine Zeitgenossen." In *Geschichte der Programmusik von ihren Anfängen bis zur Gegenwart*, 99-122. Leipzig: Breitkopf & Härtel, 1910. OCLC 4175279. Reprint. Wiesbaden: M. Sändig, 1968. viii, 426 p. ML3000 K67 1968 OCLC 1060449.

Labels Berlioz the father of modern program music, and claims that his lack of pianistic training contributed to his natural interest in this mostly orchestral genre. Discusses the often conflicting requirements of drama and music in the formal process of Berlioz's symphonies.

731. Knepler, Georg. "Hector Berlioz zur 150. Wiederkehr seines Geburtstages." *Musik und Gesellschaft* 3 (December 1953): 13-15. ISSN 0027-4755 OCLC 1758911.

Discusses the relationship between the theme of isolation in Berlioz's works and his personal situation as an artist working in an emerging capitalist French society. Suggests that the significance of his program music lies in its frequent reliance on this underlying Romantic theme.

732. Orrey, Leslie. "Introduction"; "Tone Poem and Program Symphony." In *Programme Music: a Brief Survey From the Sixteenth Century to the Present Day*, 15-28; 68-74. London: Davis-Poynter, 1975. 223 p. ISBN 0-706-70171-2 ML3300 O77 OCLC 2215945.

The introduction traces the history of the programmatic meaning of instrumental timbre in musical writings before the *Traité d'instrumentation*. The later chapter describes the programs and historical background of the *Symphonie fantastique*, *Harold en Italie*, and *Roméo et Juliette*.

733.   Wotton, Tom S. "A Berlioz Caprice and Its "Programme."
        The Musical Times 68 (August 1 1927): 704-6. ISSN 0027-
        4666 OCLC 5472115.

        Contends that since Berlioz borrowed so many of his own
        themes for reuse in other musical contexts, his works cannot
        possibly be as graphically programmatic as is usually thought.
        Also notes that the detailed program printed in the published
        edition of *Réverie et caprice* was not written by Berlioz.

6. SONGS

734.   Charlton, David. "A Berlioz Footnote." *Music and Letters* 52
        (no. 2 1971): 157-58. ISSN 0027-4224 OCLC 1758884.

        Discusses the annual albums of songs and piano pieces
        published by Bernard Latte as supplements to *Le monde
        musical* in which *La belle Isabeau* and *Le chasseur danois*
        first appeared in 1844.

735.   Dickinson, A.E.F. "Berlioz's Songs." *The Musical Quarterly*
        55 (no. 3 1969): 329-43. ISSN 0027-4631 OCLC 1642493.

        Enumerates with brief descriptions the songs for voice and
        orchestra and those for voice and piano. Particular attention is
        paid to *La captive*, *Les nuits d'été*, and *Sara la baigneuse*.

736.   Grant, Kerry Scott. "The Orchestral Songs of Hector Berlioz."
        M.F.A. dissertation, University of California, Irvine, 1972.
        viii, 142 p. OCLC 11931931.

        Studies the songs in the context of the nineteenth-century
        history of the genre. Points out the influences of the guitar and
        the *Traité d'instrumentation* on Berlioz's orchestral
        accompaniments.

737.   Kemp, Ian. Foreword to *Songs for Solo Voice and Orchestra*,
        viii-xiv. Hector Berlioz. New Edition of the Complete Works.
        Vol. 13. Kassel: Bärenreiter, 1975. xxix, 137 p. M3 B52 vol.
        13 OCLC 8341074.

Provides detailed compositional and performance histories of all of Berlioz's songs for solo voice and orchestra. Describes alternate (sometimes now lost) settings for orchestra and/or piano. Included are *La belle voyageuse, La captive, Le jeune pâtre breton, Les nuits d'été, Le chasseur danois, Zaïde,* and *Aubade.*

738.   Noske, Frits Rudolf. *La mélodie française de Berlioz à Duparc,* 84-105. Amsterdam: North-Holland Pub. Co.; Paris: Presses universitaires de France, 1954. x, 356 p. ML2827 N6 1954 OCLC 9977140. 2nd ed. translated by Rita Benton as *French Song from Berlioz to Duparc,* 91-115. New York: Dover Publications, 1970, 1988. xiv, 454 p. ISBN 0-486-25554-9 ML2827 N613 1988 OCLC 16831562.

Presents a historical survey of Berlioz's songs, tracing his gradual evolution away from the simple *romance* and toward the Romantic *mélodie.* Hypothesizes that his relative lack of interest in the art song stemmed from his need for large performing forces to create the musical effects that characterized his style.

739.   Reuter, Evelyn. "Berlioz mélodiste." *La revue musicale* no. 233 (1956): 31-37. OCLC 1764233.

Asserts that Berlioz's early songs were little more than copies of the simple *romances* he heard as a boy, but that by 1830 the *Neuf mélodies* showed him abandoning the symmetrical phrases and monotonous couplets of his earlier style in order to embrace a more complex melodic style with which he raised the art of the *romance* to a new, more sophisticated level of sung poetry. Sees the culmination of this trend in *Les nuits d'été.*

740.   Tiersot, Julien. "Berlioziana: oeuvres diverses publiées du vivant de Berlioz." *Le ménestrel* 71 (November 19 1905): 371. OCLC 6966764.

Briefly discusses *Sara la baigneuse, La captive,* and *Fleurs des landes.* Also describes the title page of the autograph orchestral score of *La captive.*

741.   Walker, Ernest. "The Songs of Berlioz." *The Monthly Musical Record* 62 (June 1932): 103-4. OCLC 1605021.

Criticizes the songs, especially *Les nuits d' été* and *La captive*, for unevenness of quality. Cites Berlioz's "technical awkwardness in matters of harmony and counterpoint."

742.   Warrack, John. "Berlioz's *Mélodies*." *The Musical Times* 110 (March 1969): 252-54. ISSN 0027-4666 OCLC 5472115.

Describes the originality of the melodic style of Berlioz's little-known song repertoire as "founded on irregularity."

7. SYMPHONIES

743.   Cairns, David. "Hector Berlioz (1803-69)." In *The Symphony*, edited by Robert Simpson. Vol. 1, 201-31. Baltimore: Penguin Books, 1966-67. 2 vols. MT125 S54 OCLC 1526411.

Demonstrates that Berlioz's symphonic technique is based on extended melody and the process of "developing variation." Argues that his symphonies have a special musical logic of their own quite apart from their dramatic associations.

744.   Dömling, Wolfgang. *Hector Berlioz, die symphonisch-dramatischen Werke: mit 15 Notenbeispielen, sowie den Libretti und Programmen in Franzosisch und Deutsch.* Stuttgart: Philipp Reclam, 1979. 214 p. ISBN 3-150-10287-1 ML410 B5 D59 OCLC 6627661.

Adopts the view that Berlioz's development of a symphonic-dramatic genre was his primary contribution to nineteenth-century music. Presents analyses of the *Symphonie fantastique, Lélio, Harold en Italie, Roméo et Juliette*, and *La damnation de Faust*, each of which explores the historical background, dramatic program or text, and selected aspects of Berlioz's compositional style. A final chapter discusses the evolution of the symphonic ideal as developed by the Berlioz-Liszt-Wagner circle. Appendices include complete programs and texts for the works analyzed.

745.   _____. "Die Symphonie als Drama. Bemerkungen zu Berlioz' Beethoven-Verständnis." In *Festschrift Georg von Dadelsen zum 60. Geburtstag*, edited by Thomas Kohlhase

and Volker Scherliess, 59-72. Neuhasen: Hänssler, 1978. 384 p. ISBN 3-775-10405-4 ML55 D17 1978 OCLC 5683350.

Hypothesizes that Berlioz viewed Beethoven's symphonies as mirroring his own symphonic concerns. In his writings about Beethoven's music, he selected for comment only those rhythmic, harmonic, or coloristic effects for which he had already found use in his own works. Berlioz also saw in Beethoven's symphonies the legitimatization of his own approach to the symphony as a quasi-dramatic autobiographical projection of the artist-hero.

746.   Floros, Constantin. "Literarische Ideen in der Musik des 19. Jahrhunderts. Berlioz' Konzeption des instrumentalen Dramas." *Hamburger Jahrbuch für Musikwissenschaft* 2 (1977): 51-57. OCLC 5791166.

States that German critics since Wagner have misunderstood the nature of Berlioz's programmatic symphonies. Shows how these works are true instrumental music-dramas (i.e., operas without words).

747.   Langford, Jeffrey A. "The Dramatic Symphonies of Berlioz as an Outgrowth of the French Operatic Tradition." *The Musical Quarterly* 69 (no. 1 1983): 85-103. ISSN 0027-4631 OCLC 1642493.

Suggests that Berlioz's symphonies were the product of a sublimated desire to write opera, and that they contain a variety of truly operatic compositional techniques new to the symphonic genre of the 1830s.

748.   Lucas, Kay. "Hector Berlioz and the Dramatic Symphony. A Study of the Dramatic Structure of the Instrumental Works." MM dissertation, University of Melbourne, 1966. Abstract in *Miscellanea Musicologica* 6 (1972): 48-54. ISSN 0076-9355 OCLC 1758333.

Looks for the dramatic motivation and criteria necessary to explain unusual aspects of Berlioz's handling of melody, rhythm, form, and orchestration in his symphonic music. Introduces the theory that his adoption of the dramatic symphony was motivated by "aesthetic conviction" rather than "expediency or compromise" [from abstract].

749.   Massougnes, Georges de. "De la symphonie expressive." In
         Hector Berlioz: son oeuvre, 62-78. Paris: Calmann-Lévy,
         1919. 143 p.

         Attributes the poor reception of Berlioz's works in France to
         the inability of audiences there to grasp anything grand and
         serious in music, to their lack of familiarity with the genre of
         the "expressive symphony," and to the rarity and poor quality
         of symphonic performances by French orchestras.

750.   Scudo, P. "De la symphonie et de la musique imitative en
         France." *Revue des deux mondes* new series, tome 18 (April 1
         1847): 743-55. OCLC 8305048.

         Discusses the symphony in France in relation to the great
         German masters Haydn, Mozart, and Beethoven. Divides
         French symphonists into two groups: those who follow
         traditional formal patterns and those more "adventurous," who
         attempt to write "imitative" (i.e., program) music. Uses *La
         damnation de Faust* as an example of the latter and severely
         criticizes its excessive pictorial detail.

751.   Weingartner, Felix. "Berlioz und Brahms." In *Die Symphonie
         nach Beethoven*, 33-49. Leipzig: S. Fischer, 1901. OCLC
         6207800. 3rd ed. Leipzig: Breitkopf & Härtel, 1909. 113 p.
         ML1255 W43 OCLC 1312828. Translated from 2nd German
         ed. by Maude Barrows Dutton as "Berlioz." In *The Symphony
         Since Beethoven*, 51-71. Boston: Oliver Ditson Company,
         1904. 98 p. ML1255 W423 OCLC 907635. Translated from
         the 4th German ed. by H.M. Schott as "Berlioz and Brahms"
         in *Weingartner on Music and Conducting: Three Essays*, 262-
         78. New York: Dover Publications, 1969. vii, 304 p. SBN
         486-22106-7 ML60 W45 W45 OCLC 47792.

         Suggests that Berlioz's melodic style, bold, "abnormal"
         orchestrations, and unusual programs all contributed to the
         early lack of acceptance of his symphonies by the general
         public. Discusses his relationship to the history of program
         music and the appropriateness of his symphonic forms to the
         nature of his programs.

8. OTHER VOCAL MUSIC

This section includes the cantatas written for the *Prix de Rome* competitions and other choral works.

752. Alexander, Metche Franke. "The Choral-Orchestral Works of Hector Berlioz." Ph.D. dissertation, North Texas State University, 1978. 2 vols., xxiv, 556 p. bibliography, 544-56. OCLC 4127104.

Reviews the history of the late eighteenth- and early-nineteenth-century French choral music tradition from which Berlioz's choral-orchestral works grew. Also examines the formal patterns of his choral works, based mainly on strophic and rondeau forms, and his use of compositional techniques such as fugato, canon, and cantus firmus [from abstract].

753. Boschot, Adolphe. "La musique religieuse de Berlioz." *Le corréspondant* 41 (December 25 1909): 1172-94. OCLC 5258641.

Explains that Berlioz's religious music is the product of the combined influences of Le Sueur's large-scale Revolutionary music and Gluck's operas. Both the *Te Deum* and *L'enfance du Christ* are analyzed in detail and found to be concert pieces with theatrical tendencies.

754. Dickinson, A.E.F. "Berlioz' Rome Prize Works." *The Music Review* 25 (no. 3 1964): 163-85. ISSN 0027-4445 OCLC 1758893.

Describes the four Rome competition cantatas and examines similar works by other student competitors from 1819 to 1830. The author agrees with Wotton that the extant fragment of *Sardanapale* is only a sketch and not a finished product as Tiersot thought (see #932).

755. Dömling, Wolfgang. "Monumentalmusik." In *Hector Berlioz und seine Zeit*, 178-208. Laaber: Laaber-Verlag, 1986. 360 p. bibliography, 347-53. ISBN 3-921-51890-3 ML410 B5 D63 1986 OCLC 15228157.

Discusses Berlioz's large-scale occasional works, *Le cinq mai*, *L'impériale*, and the *Te Deum*, as well as the projected works, *Fête musicale funèbre à la mémoire des hommes illustres de la France* and *Le retour de l'armée d'Italie*, in the context of his imperialist political sympathies and in relation to Gossec's monumental choral-instrumental works of the Revolutionary era.

756.   _____. "Visionen vom Jüngsten Gericht." In *Hector Berlioz und seine Zeit*, 39-53. Laaber: Laaber-Verlag, 1986. 360 p. bibliography, 347-53. ISBN 3-921-51890-3 ML410 B5 D63 1986 OCLC 15228157.

Discusses Berlioz's preoccupation with the creation of a quasi-dramatic sacred music (especially in the *Requiem*) as an expression of his life-long concern with the theme of the contrast between the isolation of modern man and the communality of the religious experience.

757.   Puttmann, Max. "Hector Berlioz als Gesangkomponist." *Neue Zeitschrift für Musik* 70 (December 9 1903): 645-47. ISSN 0028-3509 OCLC 1776104.

Views Berlioz's vocal music as beginning a trend toward treating vocal works as yet another type of instrumental program music--one in which the program is articulated directly through the vocal part.

XIII. Individual Works

This chapter includes analytical and historical studies of individual compositions of Berlioz. Performance reviews have been omitted, except for those of premieres, those by noted critics, and those which offer some special perspective on a work. Additional information on individual works can be found in most of the general biographies in Chapter V.

1. *BEATRICE ET BENEDICT*

758.   Addison, A. *"Beatrice and Benedict*: the German Edition." *Berlioz Society Bulletin* no. 33 (September-October 1960): 1-3. OCLC 2386332.

Discusses some of the errors in the Old Berlioz Edition (vols 19 and 20) and describes the primary sources of the work.

759.   Dean, Winton. "Shakespeare and Opera." In *Shakespeare in Music*, edited by Phyllis Hartnoll, 89-175. London: Macmillan; New York, St. Martin's Press, 1964. ix, 333 p. ML80 S5 H37 OCLC 598395.

Within this survey of opera on Shakespearean subjects, the author discusses (133-35) the drastic excisions Berlioz made in *Much Ado About Nothing* to create *Béatrice et Bénédict* an the numerous scenes in it which have nothing to do with the original play. The author nevertheless admits that Berlioz successfully captured the ambiance of Shakespeare's play.

760.   Hanslick, Eduard. *"Beatrice and Benedict."* In *Studies in Music by Various Authors, Reprinted from "The Musician,"* edited by Robin Grey, 324-32. London: Simpkin, Marshall, Hamilton, Kent, 1901. OCLC 5182145. Reprint. New York: AMS Press, 1976. 339 p. ISBN 0-404-12937-4 ML55 G84 1976 OCLC 2491588.

        Complains that there is nothing new or revolutionary about the opera. States that it is just another example of the *opéra-comique* genre which Berlioz held in such low esteem. Suggests that he was not by nature a comic composer.

761.   Imbert, Hugues. *"Béatrice et Bénédict* d'Hector Berlioz." In *Symphonie; mélanges de critique littéraire & musicale, avec un portrait de Rameau,* 127-45. Paris: Fischbacher, 1891. 178 p. ML60 I53 OCLC 5518516.

        A compositional history and critique which suggests that Berlioz was not naturally disposed toward humor in his music despite the fact that his prose works are full of wit and humor.

762.   Macdonald, Hugh. Foreword to *Béatrice et Bénédict,* viii-xi. Hector Berlioz; New Edition of the Complete Works. Vol. 3. Kassel: Bärenreiter, 1980. xix, 312 p. M3 B52 vol. 3 OCLC 7138741.

        Traces the opera's compositional history and discusses Berlioz's adaptation of Laroche's French translation of *Much Ado About Nothing* for his libretto.

763.   Pohl, Richard. *"Beatrice und Benedikt."* In *Hektor Berlioz. Studien und Erinnerungen,* 176-200. Leipzig: B. Schlicke, 1884. OCLC 12321145. Reprint. Wiesbaden: M. Sändig, 1974. xv, 275 p. ML410 B5 P7 1974 OCLC 1035987.

        Written on the occasion of the opera's premiere in Baden-Baden on August 9, 1862, this review provides a mostly descriptive analysis. Observes that those who know *Benvenuto Cellini* will not find the new opera stylistically very different.

764.   Rushton, Julian. "Berlioz' Swan-song: Towards a Criticism of *Béatrice et Bénédict." Proceedings of the Royal Musical Association* 109 (1982-83): 105-18. ISSN 0080-4452 OCLC 1764602.

Analyzes the omissions and alterations of character that
Berlioz had to make in *Much Ado About Nothing* in order to
create his highly condensed two-act comic opera.

2. LA BELLE ISABEAU

765. Hopkinson, Cecil. "Berlioz: a Recent Discovery." *Brio* 7 (no.
2 1970): 32-33. ISSN 0007-0713 OCLC 1537097.

Announces the discovery of an early version of the song with
a dedication to Marie Recio published in 1844 by Bernard
Latte as part of a collection of songs by various composers.

3. BENVENUTO CELLINI

766. Barbier, Auguste. "*Benvenuto Cellini*. Avant-propos." In
Etudes dramatiques, 203-8. Paris: E. Dentu, 1874. 332 p.

Reports first-hand some of the circumstances surrounding
Berlioz's writing of the opera. Claims that it was intended to
be autobiographical and to satirize certain aspects of opera
that were in vogue at that time. Admits that one of the reasons
for its failure was that the subject of a rebellious artist
struggling against governmental authority held little interest
for Parisian audiences of the 1830s.

767. Brenet, Michel [Marie Bobillier]. "Le premier opéra de
Berlioz." *Courrier de l'art* 6 (September 3 1886): 400-401;
(September 10): 409-10; (September 17): 416-17; (September
24): 425-26; (October 8): 440-43. OCLC 13549352. Reprinted
in *Deux pages de la vie de Berlioz*, 45-72. Paris: L. Vanier,
1889. 72 p. ML410 B51 B66 OCLC 12737478.

Gives the history of the 1838 performances of *Benvenuto
Cellini* at the *Opéra*, quoting contemporary reviews by Liszt,
d'Ortigue, and others, drawn from Parisian journals.
Establishes that the music was found to be more objectionable

than the libretto, and that the musical politics involving the *Journal des débats*, for which Berlioz wrote, made an unbiased evaluation of the opera impossible.

768.   Bülow, Hans von. "Hector Berlioz: *Benvenuto Cellini*." *Neue Zeitschrift für Musik* 36 (April 2 1852): 156-59; (April 30): 204-8. ISSN 0028-3509 OCLC 1776104. Reprinted in *Briefe und Schriften*. Vol. 3, *Ausgewählte Schriften, 1850-1892*, 51-67. Leipzig: Breitkopf & Härtel, 1895-1908. 8 vols. OCLC 18354504.

A review of Liszt's 1852 production of the work in Weimar. Criticizes the dramatic subject as one with little appeal to modern audiences and the libretto as too disjunct and episodic.

769.   Cairns, David. "*Benvenuto Cellini*, an Introduction." *Berlioz Society Bulletin* no. 77 (October 1972): 5-12. OCLC 2386332.

Discusses the complex history of changes Berlioz made between the work's inception in 1834 and its Paris publication in 1863. Essay prepared for the 1973 Philips recording of the opera.

770.   Castil-Blaze [François Henri Joseph Blaze]. "De l'école fantastique et de M. Berlioz." *Revue des deux mondes* 4th series, tome 16 (October 1 1838): 97-121. OCLC 8305048.

A mostly negative review of the first performances of *Benvenuto Cellini* at the *Opéra*, in which the author describes Berlioz as a wild Romantic barbarian.

771.   Gautier, Théophile. "*Benvenuto Cellini*". In *Histoire de l'art dramatique en France depuis vingt-cinq ans*. Vol. 1, 171-74. Paris: Hetzel, 1858. 6 vols. OCLC 6974944. Reprint. Geneva: Slatkin, 1968. 6 vols. PN2634 G3 1968 OCLC 2519429. Reprinted in *La musique*, 143-46. Paris: Fasquelle, 1911. 310 p. PN2636 P2 G28m OCLC 10736748.

Criticizes the libretto for its "looseness" and the poor effect of its language. Equates Berlioz's melodic irregularity with Hugo's attempts to break the predictable regularity of Classical French poetic rhythms. Further links Berlioz's innovations in orchestration with similar uses of colorful language by the Romantic poets. Originally appeared in *La presse*, September 17, 1838.

772.   Guiomar, Michel. "Un rêve de carnaval tragique dans le
miroir d'un homme seul." *Association National Hector
Berlioz. Inter-Bulletin* no. 4 (1973): 16-21.

Analyzes the discontinuity of the opera as the result of the
conflicting demands of three distinctly different plot elements:
the love theme, the Carnival ballet, and the theme of artistic
creativity.

773.   Hammond, Arthur. *"Benvenuto Cellini." Opera* 8 (April
1957): 205-9. ISSN 0030-3526 OCLC 2574662.

Briefly sketches the history of the work. Also gives valuable
indications of how alterations made for the 1852 Weimar
production affected the opera's dramatic unity.

774.   Hyatt, Raymond. "Hoffmann's *Story of Salvator Rosa* and the
Libretto of *Benvenuto Cellini." Berlioz Society Bulletin* no.
119 (Winter 1983-84): 11-15. OCLC 2386332.

Suggests that the source for the role of Teresa may have been
supplied by one of E.T.A. Hoffmann's *Tales*. This character is
not found in Cellini's *Vita*, on which Berlioz modeled his
libretto.

775.   Labaste, Henri. "Alfred de Vigny collaborateur d'Hector
Berlioz." *Revue universitaire* 29 (December 1920): 369-74.
OCLC 1764259.

Presents proof of de Vigny's contribution of the words of the
"Chant de ciseleurs" to the *Benvenuto Cellini* libretto.

776.   La May, Thomasin K. "A New Look at the Weimar Versions
of Berlioz's *Benvenuto Cellini." The Musical Quarterly* 65
(no. 4 1979): 559-72. ISSN 0027-4631 OCLC 1642493.

Contains many significant observations about the early history
of the work, the most important of which are that revisions
were made during the opening Paris run and that the version
performed at Weimar in 1852 was the Paris version with a
large cut. Concludes that Berlioz's continual revision of the
opera suggests that he was never completely satisfied with it
and that it never existed in a definitive form.

777.   Macdonald, Hugh. *"Benvenuto Cellini." Revue de
musicologie* 63 (no. 1-2 1977): 107-14. ISSN 0035-1601
OCLC 1773306.

Traces the opera's heterogeneous mixture of styles to early
changes of intended genre (serious, comic and semi-serious)
and its failure to be understood in Paris to its musical
differences from any other contemporary French operatic
style.

778.   _____. "The Original *Benvenuto Cellini*." *The Musical
Times* 107 (December 1966): 1042-45. ISSN 0027-4666
OCLC 5472115.

Reconstructs the original shape of the 1838 Paris version of
the opera by unsewing collettes in the manuscript orchestra
parts.

779.   Ortigue, Joseph d'. "Benvenuto Cellini." In *Du théâtre
italien et de son influence sur le goût musical français*,
published in 1839 as *De l'école musicale italienne et de
l'administration de l'Académie royal de musique à l'occasion
de l'opéra de M. H. Berlioz*, 55-131. Paris: Au Dépot central
des meilleures productions de la presse, 1840. xxviii, 347 p.
ML1727 O7 OCLC 11395842.

Analyzes the influence of Gluck on Berlioz's use of melody,
rhythm, and orchestration in the work. Compares his style
with that of nineteenth-century Italian opera.

780.   Piatier, François. *Hector Berlioz, "Benvenuto Cellini": ou, le
mythe de l'artiste*. Paris: Aubier Montaigne, 1979. 137, [38]
p. ISBN 2-700-70160-7 ML410 B5 P44 OCLC 6330441.

Establishes sociological and artistic parallels between Berlioz
and Benvenuto Cellini the artist. Follows with a short
description of the different versions of the opera and a scene-
by-scene analysis of both music and drama. The final chapter
describes the failure of the work as the result of its unusual
mixture of genres, its "symphonic" style, and its unusual plot
based not on the theme of amorous intrigue but on that of
creativity struggling against officialdom. Includes a full
libretto (two acts, four tableaux) at the end.

781.   Prod'homme, J.-G. "Les deux *Benvenuto Cellini* de Berlioz."
Sammelbände der Internationalen Musik-Gesellschaft 14 (no.
3 1913): 449-60. OCLC 1772498.

Gives a complete synopsis of the original two-act version of
the opera. Then traces several stages of revision from the

printed libretto of 1838 through the Weimar productions of 1852 and the London production of 1853 to a "definitive" version of 1856. Suggests that a return to Berlioz's original two-act version, made possible by advances in staging techniques, would better serve the musical drama of the work.

782. Schmidgall, Gary. "Hector Berlioz--*Benvenuto Cellini*." In *Literature As Opera*, 151-77. Oxford and New York: Oxford University Press, 1977, 1980. xi, 431 p. ISBN 0-195-02213-0 ML3858 S37 1980 OCLC 5830517.

Discusses the work as an example of autobiographical opera and attributes its failure to its radically Romantic music and libretto which angered defenders of the French Classical style such as Castil-Blaze.

783. Searle, Humphrey. "Berlioz and *Benvenuto*." *Opera* 17 (December 1966): 932-38. ISSN 0030-3526 OCLC 2574662.

Uses the 1966 Covent Garden production of the opera as an opportunity to review its history from circa 1834, when Berlioz first offered it to the *Opéra-comique*, to 1853, when he conducted a performance of the revised version in London. Explains some of the alterations necessary in order to restore the spoken dialogue of the original two-act version in place of the normally-used recitative.

784. Switzer, Richard. "Cellini, Berlioz, Dumas and the Foundry." *Nineteenth-Century French Studies* 8 (1980): 252-57. ISSN 0146-7891 OCLC 1061280.

Discusses adaptations of Cellini's *Vita* in *Benvenuto Cellini* and *L'orfèvre du roi* (by Dumas *père*), noting especially alterations of the circumstances surrounding the casting of the statue of Perseus.

785. Tiersot, Julien. "Berlioziana: *Benvenuto Cellini*." *Le ménestrel* 71 (February 5 1905): 43-44; (February 19): 60-61; (February 26): 67-68; (March 5): 76-77; (March 12): 83-84; (March 19): 91-92; (March 26): 99-100; (April 2): 107-8; (April 9): 115-16; (June 4): 180-181; (June 25): 205-6; (July 2): 211-12. OCLC 6966764.

Chronicles the history of the work with quotes from the *Mémoires*, Barbier's preface to his poem in the *Etudes dramatiques* (#766), and various letters, mostly to Liszt. Describes the failure of the work, discussing the text as a

contributing factor. Traces the many stages of textual revision
between 1838 and 1852, with observations on Wagner's
reaction to the 1852 Weimar version. Concludes with a
detailed comparison of the 1838 and 1852 versions aimed at
reconstructing the original form of the opera.

786.   Würz, Anton. "Benvenuto Cellini." In *Franz Lachner als
         dramatischer Komponist*, 86-96. Munich: Druck von Knorr &
         Hirth, 1927. 124 p. ML410 L138 W95 OCLC 12748809.

         Describes parallels between the work and Lachner's 1849
         opera. Claims that despite many similar characters and
         situations, the theme of "tragic artistic destiny" treated by
         Berlioz is absent from Lachner's opera.

4. *CHANT DU NEUF THERMIDOR*

787.   Holoman, D. Kern. *"Chant du neuf Thermidor*--the
         Discovered Lost Manuscript." *Berlioz Society Bulletin* no.
         124 (Spring 1985): 24-29. OCLC 2386332.

         Provides a history of Berlioz's arrangement of Rouget de
         Lisle's *Hymne dithyrambique sur la conjuration de
         Robespierre et la revolution du 9 Thermidor*, and of its
         American premiere at the University of California at Davis.

788.   Tchamkerten, Jacques. "Un autographe inédite de Berlioz: *Le
         chant du neuf Thermidor." Revue musicale de Suisse
         Romande* 37 (no. 1 1984): 22-39. SSN 0035-3744 OCLC
         9077868.

         Gives a full history of this newly-discovered arrangement for
         chorus and orchestra of Rouget de Lisle's *Hymne
         dithyrambique sur la conjuration de Robespierre et la
         revolution du 9 Thermidor*. Includes a facsimile of the
         manuscript.

5. *CLEOPATRE*

789.   Tiersot, Julien. "Berlioziana: oeuvres de concours." *Le
        ménestrel* 72 (September 9 1906): 278-79. OCLC 6966764.

        Explains that because of his refusal to write the work in the
        academic style of his teachers, Berlioz was not awarded the
        Prix de Rome in 1829, despite the fact that he had won second
        prize the previous year. Describes later borrowings from the
        work in *Lélio*.

6. *LA DAMNATION DE FAUST*

790.   Ahouse, John B. "The 'Course à l'abîme': a Possible Source."
        Berlioz Society Bulletin no. 83 (April 1974): 13-17; no. 84
        (July 1974): 19-23. OCLC 2386332.

        Traces Berlioz's deviation from Goethe at the end of the work
        to his familiarity with *Lenore*, a German pre-Romantic poem
        by G.A. Bürger.

791.   Aycock, Roy E. *"Faust*: Literature and Opera." *The Opera
        Journal* 14 (no. 1 1981): 23-32. ISSN 0030-3585 OCLC
        1761319.

        Traces literary interpretations of the Faust legend and
        discusses Goethe's *Faust* as adapted by Berlioz, Gounod, and
        Boito.

792.   Bellaigue, Camille. *"La damnation de Faust."* *Revue des
        deux mondes* 5th period, tome 16 (July 1 1903): 220-29.
        OCLC 8305048.

        A negative review of Raoul Gunsbourg's 1903 staged version
        of the work in Monte Carlo, which clearly shows why it
        cannot be done as an opera.

793.   Boschot, Adolphe. *Le "Faust" de Berlioz; étude sur "La
        damnation de Faust" et sur l'âme romantique.* Paris:

Costallat, 1910. 3rd edition, Paris: Plon, 1945. viii, 179 p.,
bibliography, 160-62. ML410 B5 B73 1945 OCLC 2469966.

A complete compositional, source, and performance history of
Berlioz's Faust music beginning with the *Huit scènes de Faust*
(1828) and continuing with *La damnation de Faust*. Based on
"Le festival des 'Faust'--Le 'Faust' de Berlioz." *Le
correspondant* 233 (December 10 1908): 971-94.

794.   . "'L'invocation à la nature' et l'âme romantique." *La
revue musicale* no. 233 (1956): 79-86. OCLC 1764223.

Hypothesizes that the character of Faust, like Berlioz himself
on occasion, suffered from a typically Romantic "mal de
l'isolement." For Berlioz this was expressed in his fascination
with the vastness and absolute loneliness of nature.

795.   Carraud, Gaston. "Les marionettes du Docteur Faust." *Revue
des deux mondes* 5th period, tome 50 (March 1 1909): 85-115.
OCLC 8305048.

Claims that Berlioz's adaptation of *Faust* is superficial in
terms of its human drama, and that he is more successful in
presenting the elements of the demonic and nature.

796.   Colonne, Edouard. "Hector Berlioz et les concerts Colonne:
La damnation de Faust." *Musica* 7 (1908): 37. OCLC
1695501.

Recounts the history of the Colonne concerts which from 1875
to 1877 were responsible for bringing Berlioz's music before
the Parisian public. This series culminated with a complete
production of the work, which had not been heard in its
entirety since 1846.

797.   Debussy, Claude. "Berlioz et M. Gunsbourg." *Gil Blas* 25 no.
8674 (May 8 1903): [1]. Reprinted as "Berlioz." In *Monsieur
Croche, antidilettante*. Paris: Dorbon-Aîné, 1921, 127-32..
OCLC 1545339. Translated by B.N. Langdon Davies in *Three
Classics in the Aesthetics of Music*, 61-65. New York: Dover
Publications, 1962. iv, 188 p. ML90 T47 OCLC 598340.
Translated and edited by Richard Langham Smith in *Debussy
on Music*. Collected and introduced by François Lesure, 192-
95. London: Secker & Warburg; New York: Alfred A. Knopf,
1977. xxv, 353 p. ISBN 0-394-48120-8 ML410 D28 A333
OCLC 2317983.

Criticizes Raoul Gunsbourg's stage adaptation of *La damnation de Faust*. Also states that Berlioz had no influence on later French composers, and that he was not a naturally gifted stage composer.

798. Dickinson, A.E.F. "The Revisions for *The Damnation of Faust*." *The Monthly Musical Record* 89 (September-October 1959): 180-85. OCLC 1605021.

Lists the changes Berlioz made in each of the original numbers of the *Huit scènes de Faust* when he recast the work.

799. Dickson, Kay Reita. "Goethe and the Romantic Imagination: Delacroix's and Berlioz's Interpretations of 'Faust.'" Ph.D. dissertation, Emory University, 1982. xxx, 86 p. bibliography, 83-86. OCLC 9739871.

Explores the growth of Romanticism in Germany and France. Then considers correlations between the artistic languages of painting and music. Concludes with an analysis of parallels between Berlioz's and Delacroix's creative approaches to their *Faust* interpretations [from abstract].

800. Dutronc, Jean-Louis. "Faust: Goethe et les musiciens." *L'avant-scène opéra* no. 2 (March-April 1976): 62-71. OCLC 4254009.

Lists, without attempting explanations, the correlations between the various scenes of Goethe's *Faust* and the musical realizations by Gounod, Berlioz, Schumann, and Boïto. Mentions other settings of *Faust* in passing.

801. Ferchault, Guy. "Le Faust de Berlioz." In *Faust: une légende et ses musiciens*, 46-73. Paris: Larousse, 1948. 115 p. MT100 F3 OCLC 13506310.

Presents a history and analysis of Berlioz's *Faust* music. The author sees in this music a Romantic metaphor for the struggle between the ideal and real man.

802. Gut, Serge. "Atonalité et polytonalité dans *La damnation de Faust*." *L'avant-scene opéra* no. 22 (July-August 1979): 64-65. OCLC 4254009.

Points to Berlioz's melodic use of tritones in Mephistopheles's "Evocation" (Part 3) and to his harmonic superimposition of the keys of B-flat major and D minor in the

"Choeur de soldats, choeur d'étudiants" (Part 2) as instances
of special harmonic devices used to support particular
dramatic situations.

803.   _____. "La transformation du thème de Faust à travers
Goethe, Nerval et Berlioz." *Revue musicale de Suisse
Romande* 35 (no. 2 1982): 50-60. ISSN 0035-3744 OCLC
9077868.

Contends that Berlioz's adaptation of *Faust* produced
substantive changes in the psychology of the characters and
structural changes in the outline of the action. These changes
reflect Berlioz's own *fantastique* interpretation of the Faust
theme.

804.   Halm, August. "Typen aus der *Damnation de Faust* von
Berlioz." In *Von Grenzen und Ländern der Musik;
Gesammelte Aufsätze*, 81-95. 2nd edition, Munich: Georg
Müller, 1916. 255 p. ML60 H202 OCLC 9744781.

Claims that Berlioz's setting of "Amen" as a parody fugue in
the tavern scene is sacrilegious and that his music
misrepresents the character of Faust. Applauds, however, the
effectiveness of the "Choeur des soldats, choeur d'étudiants"
and the ballad of the "Roi de Thulé." Also comments on the
problems caused by the translation of the original German text
into French.

805.   Hanslick, Eduard. "*Faust's Verdammung*, dramatische
Legende von H. Berlioz." In *Aus dem Concertsaal. Kritiken
und Schilderungen aus den letzten 20 Jahren des Wiener
Musiklebens*, 411-16. Vienna: W. Braumüller, 1870.
ML246.8 V6 H2 OCLC 8829290.

Decries Berlioz's "butchery" of Goethe's drama. Complains
about the mixture of instrumental music and vocal music in a
single composition. Observes that the work is really an
imaginary opera which needs staging, and compares its
musical style unfavorably to that of Berlioz's earlier works, in
which the author finds "more beauty and expression."

806.   Haraszti, Emil. *Berlioz et la "Marche de Rákóczi";
conference faite en juin 1939 à la Société française de
musicologie.* Paris, 1939. Translated and excerpted as
"Berlioz, Liszt and Rákóczy." *The Musical Quarterly* 26 (no.
2 1940): 200-231. ISSN 0027-4631 OCLC 1642493.

The most complete study in English of the *Rákóczy March*. Describes the original Pest manuscript and compares it to Berlioz's printed revision which became part of *La damnation de Faust*. Reviews theories of the origin of the tune and suggests that Berlioz may first have heard it in 1839 at gypsy concerts he attended in Paris. Disproves Liszt's assertion that it was his piano transcription of the march that served as the basis for Berlioz's famous orchestration.

807.   _____. *Berlioz et la "Marche hongroise" d'après des documents inédits, avec six lettres de Berlioz*. Paris: Revue musicale, 1946. 127 p. ML410 B5 H27 OCLC 5365039.

Contains a complete history of the many versions of the "chanson de Rákóczi" in Hungary and France, its transformation into a march, and its appearance in works by composers other than Berlioz. Discusses his use of the melody as the "Marche hongroise" in *La damnation de Faust*.

808.   Hoechst, Coit Roscoe. *"La Damnation de Faust* by Hector Berlioz." In *"Faust" in Music*, 38-59. University of Pittsburgh dissertation. Gettysburg: Gettysburg Compiler Print, 1916. 118 p. ML2100 H6 OCLC 779225.

Contains a useful description of the stage directions associated with the production that Raoul Gunsbourg mounted for the Monte Carlo Opera in 1893 and 1903.

809.   Hofer, Hermann. "Faust einmal ganz anders *La damnation de Faust* von Hector Berlioz neu gelesen." *Lendemains* nos. 31-32 (1983): 30-42. OCLC 4525547.

Discusses Berlioz's part in writing the text for the work and his indecision about whether or not it was really an opera. Views the text not as a work of revolutionary socialism, but as an attempt by its author to define for himself the relationship of the artist-intellectual to mid-nineteenth-century French society.

810.   Isoz, Kálmán. "Berlioz 'Rákóczy'--jának eredeti kézirata. (Három szövegközti hasonmással)." *Magyar könyvszemle* 26 (January 1918): 1-13. OCLC 1756473. Translated as "Le manuscrit original du *Rákóczy* de Berlioz." *Revue des études hongroises et finno-ougriennes* 2 (1924): 5-17. OCLC 5210747.

Describes the manuscript of the *Rákóczy March* and compares
it with the version Berlioz later published in *La damnation de
Faust*. Agrees with Boschot that it must have been Liszt who
introduced Berlioz to the march tune and suggested that it be
orchestrated. See #806 for opposing view.

811.   Jahn, Otto. *"Die Verdammnis des Faust* von Hector Berlioz."
        In *Gesammelte Aufsätze über Musik*, 87-94. Leipzig:
        Breitkopf & Härtel, 1866. OCLC 1401710. Reprint.
        Farnborough: Gregg International, 1969. 337 p. ISBN 0-576-
        28160-3 ML60 J25 1969 OCLC 830167.

        Laments the manner in which Berlioz selected elements of
        Goethe's *Faust* to make his libretto. Claims that his work
        betrays a total misunderstanding of the original drama. Praises
        Berlioz's instrumental effects but complains about his
        undramatic use of fugue, his inclusion of the "Marche
        hongroise," his musical characterizations of Faust and
        Mephistopheles, and his use of musical humor. Originally
        published in *Grenzboten: Zeitschrift für Politik, Literatur und
        Kunst*, 1853.

812.   Jullien, Adolphe. *"La damnation de Faust* au théâtre." In
        Musiciens d'hier et d'aujourd'hui, 124-32. Paris:
        Fischbacher, 1910. 371 p. ML390 J95 OCLC 4795075.

        Justifies the 1903 Raoul Gunsbourg stage adaptation of the
        work on the basis of Berlioz's occasional references to *La
        damnation de Faust* as an opera. Also mentions some of the
        cuts and additions made to the score to facilitate the staging.

813.   Kreutzer, Léon. "Le *Faust* de Hector Berlioz." *Revue et
        gazette musicale de Paris* 21 (December 3 1854): 389-92; 22
        (January 14 1855): 10-12; (January 28); 27-29; (February 11):
        41-44; (March 25): 91-92; (April 1): 97-99. OCLC 10231154.

        Gives a detailed descriptive analysis of the work which
        mentions Berlioz's indebtedness to Le Sueur for the idea of
        polychoral performance forces and brushes aside objections
        that Berlioz was not faithful to Goethe's text. Interesting for
        being one of the earliest appreciations of *La damnation de
        Faust*.

814.   Macy, Carleton. "Musical Characterization in Selected Faust
        Works: a Study in Nineteenth-Century Musical Rhetoric."
        D.M.A. dissertation, University of Washington, 1978. 344 p.

Attempts to formulate a theory of nineteenth-century musical rhetoric based on an analysis of the *Faust* settings of Berlioz, Gounod, Schumann, Wagner, and Liszt. Concludes that areas of similar dramatic characterization conform to basic patterns of musical treatment regardless of the composer [from abstract].

815. Newman, Ernest. *"La Damnation de Faust."* In *Berlioz, Romantic and Classic,* edited by Peter Heyworth, 186-90. London: Gollancz, 1972. 288 p. ISBN 0-575-01365-6 ML410 B5 N49 OCLC 516762.

Discusses the relationship between the 1828 *Huit scènes de Faust* and the expanded 1846 version and suggests that staged productions of *La damnation de Faust* are acceptable and successful because the work "was never, as Berlioz made it and left it, a steadily planned organic unity in itself."

816. Prod'homme, J.-G. *Le cycle Berlioz. Essai historique et critique sur l' oeuvre de Berlioz: "La damnation de Faust."* Paris: Bibliothèque de l'Association, 1894. xii, 258 p. ML410 B51 P96D OCLC 12569671. 2nd ed. published as *La damnation de Faust.* Paris: Bibliothèque de l'Association, 1896. 253, xxx p. ML410 B5 P68y 1896 OCLC 1245713.

Uses extensive quotes from Berlioz's letters to trace the history of his interest in Goethe's *Faust* and his plans for various musical settings between 1828 and 1846. Lists Faust music by other nineteenth-century composers, some of whom are little-known today. A synopsis of the libretto includes a discussion of Berlioz's expansion of the nature motif and his decision to damn rather than save Faust (for reasons of better musical contrast and effect). Continues with a lengthy non-technical descriptive analysis of the music. Closes with a chapter on critical reaction to the work which reprints complete and excerpted reviews by important critics such as Scudo. Also presents a performance history from the work's premiere through 1896, documenting its better reception in Germany and its eventual acceptance in France. Five appendices contain additional material relating to *Huit scènes de Faust,* the relationship of Berlioz's fugal style to that of his teacher Le Sueur, and critical reviews from Russia and Germany (Hanslick and Jahn).

817. _____. "Wagner, Berlioz and Monsieur Scribe; Two Collaborations That Miscarried." Translated by Theodore

Baker. *The Musical Quarterly* 12 (no. 3 1926): 359-75. ISSN 0027-4631 OCLC 1642493.

An account of Berlioz's 1847 plan to get Scribe to recast the libretto of *Faust* to create an opera that was to be produced by Jullien in London. After Jullien's bankruptcy, the plan was abandoned.

818.   Reinisch, Frank. *"La damnation de Faust* in der Bühnenbearbeitung von Raoul Gunsbourg." *Die Musikforschung* 34 (no. 4 1981): 446-56. ISSN 0027-4801 OCLC 2669982.

A detailed account of the textual and musical changes made by Raoul Gunsbourg to create a viable stage version of the work for the Monte Carlo Opera in 1893 (first Paris production 1903). Draws on primary source materials including scores, librettos, and a production book.

819.   Rougier, Elzéard. *Hector Berlioz: "La Damnation de Faust" à Marseille, simples notes et impressions.* Paris: Auguste Ghio, 1884.

Beginning with the Neoclassical hypothesis that poetry is by its very nature meant to be sung, the author argues that opera is the most perfect musical genre, and that the work is a clear demonstration of Berlioz's ability to rejuvenate this dramatic medium by uniting elements of poetry and symphony in a single work.

820.   Rushton, Julian. Foreword to *La damnation de Faust,* 455-61. Hector Berlioz. New Edition of the Complete Works. Vol. 8b. Kassel: Bärenreiter, 1986. 2 vols. 556 p. M3 B52 vol. 8 OCLC 16712447.

Creates a detailed chronology of the composition of this work and of Berlioz's interest in the Faust legend from the time of his exposure in 1827 to Nerval's translation of Goethe's drama. Also suggests other sources for Berlioz's "libretto," including works by Spohr and Weber, French military retreats, and *Prix de Rome* cantata texts. Sketches performance and publication histories of the work and discusses Berlioz's instrumentation.

821.   _____. "The Genesis of Berlioz' *La damnation de Faust.*" *Music and Letters* 56 (no. 2 1975): 129-46. ISSN 0027-4224 OCLC 1758884.

Describes the autograph manuscript in detail, including its relationship to *Huit scènes de Faust*. Provides a complete chronology of the work's gestation, as well as a lengthy discussion of Berlioz's compositional process based primarily on two pages of sketches for the "Invocation à la nature."

822.   Schneider, Frank. *"Faust* bei H. Berlioz." *Musik und Gesellschaft* 19 (March 1969): 164-69. ISSN 0027-4755 OCLC 1758911.

Demonstrates that Berlioz's alteration of the ending of Goethe's *Faust*, resulting in the damnation rather than the salvation of Faust, was the product of an autobiographical projection onto the drama's hero of his own pessimistic attitude circa 1840.

823.   Sternfeld, Richard. "Hector Berlioz und seine Faustmusik." *Westermanns Illustrierte Deutsche Monatshefte* 95 (January 1904): 485-92. ISSN 0043-3438 OCLC 1769686.

Concludes that although Berlioz owed much to Weber and Mendelssohn for his successful development of the *fantastique* in music, *La damnation de Faust* nevertheless represents a new level of previously unheard effects of musical tone painting. Suggests that Berlioz borrowed elements of German Romanticism to use for his own French style.

824.   Tiersot, Julien. "Berlioziana. II: programmes, prologues et prefaces." *Le ménestrel* 70 (August 7 1904): 252-53; (August 14): 258-60. OCLC 6966764.

Discusses Berlioz's approach to publicity, via press releases, as a method of forming the taste of his audience, using examples relating to *La damnation de Faust*. Describes public reaction to the work in France and Germany. Reproduces portions of the preface to the first printed editions of the score in which Berlioz justifies his methods of adapting Goethe's work. Article begins by describing the title history of the *Symphonie funèbre et triomphale* and ends by reproducing the autograph press release relating to the *Te Deum* which subsequently appeared in *La France musicale* on April 22, 1855.

825.   _____. "Berlioziana. III: compositions inédites et
        autographes de Berlioz." *Le ménestrel* 70 (September 18
        1904): 299-300; (September 25): 307-8. OCLC 6966764.

        Describes the physical circumstances surrounding the
        composition of *La damnation de Faust* to account for the poor
        condition of the autograph full score. The title page is fully
        discussed, some wording being different from the later printed
        edition. Sections of the manuscript examined include the
        "Marche hongroise" (not autograph), "Chant de la fête de
        pâques," "Choeur de buveurs," "Chanson de Brander," and a
        portion of the "Ballet des sylphes." The second part of the
        article compares the printed score of *Huit scènes de Faust*
        with the autograph, noting changes and cuts.

826.   _____. "Etude sur *La damnation de Faust*." *Le guide
        musical* 44 (December 11 1898): 943-47; (December 18): 967-
        69; (December 25): 991-93. 45 (January 1 1899): 3-6;
        (January 8): 27-31; (January 15): 51-54; (January 22): 75-77;
        (January 29): 99-100; (February 5): 123-25; (February 12):
        147-49; (February 19): 171-76. OCLC 1509855. Revised as
        *"La damnation de Faust" de Berlioz; étude historique et
        critique, analyse musicale.* Paris: P. Mellottée, 1924. 176 p.
        ML410 B5 T52 OCLC 1701654.

        Begins with a biographical sketch highlighting Berlioz's main
        works. Follows with a detailed discussion of the
        compositional history, publication, and performance of the
        work (including *Huit scènes de Faust*), a comparison of
        Berlioz's libretto with Goethe's drama, and a descriptive
        analysis of the music. An excellent study.

827.   Vanderauwera, Eva. "Faust from Goethe to Nerval to
        Berlioz." *Adam International Review* nos. 425-427 (1980):
        57-63. ISSN 0001-8015 OCLC 1965286.

        Discusses Nerval's translation of *Faust* that Berlioz used as
        the source for both *Huit scènes de Faust* and *La damnation de
        Faust.* Suggests that Berlioz's sympathies lay with Faust's
        efforts to reconcile the "great oppostions of human nature,"
        and with the Byronic aspects of his character (i.e., tendencies
        toward self-destruction).

828.   Walsh, T.J. "Chapter 6: 1893"; "Chapter 13: 1903." In *Monte
        Carlo Opera, 1879-1909,* 72-73; 171-75. Dublin: Gill &
        Macmillan, 1975. xix, 321 p. ISBN 0-717-10725-6 ML1751
        M66 W3 OCLC 2591857.

.

Describes Raoul Gunsbourg's successful 1893 and 1903 productions of *La damnation de Faust* as a fully-staged opera in Monte Carlo.

829. Werth, Kent William. "Berlioz's *La damnation de Faust*: a Manuscript Study." Ph.D. dissertation, University of California at Berkeley, 1979. iii, 256 p. OCLC 8017826.

Examines the compositional genesis and various revisions of the work. Uses sketches for the "Invocation à la nature" to study Berlioz's compositional process [from abstract].

830. Wotton, Tom S. "Infernal Language: a Berlioz Hoax." *The Musical Times* 78 (March 1937): 209-10. ISSN 0027-4666 OCLC 5472115.

Establishes that the "unknown tongue" (synthetic language) used by Berlioz in *Lélio* and *La damnation de Faust* was not borrowed from the Swedish scientist and mystic Swedenborg. Further suggests that the footnote making this attribution in the 1855 full score of *Faust* was probably not written by Berlioz but by A. Gandonnière, who collaborated on the libretto.

7. *L'ENFANCE DU CHRIST*

831. Anon. "*L'enfance du Christ*." *Le guide musical* 57 (March 19 1911): 223-26; (April 2): 267-68. OCLC 1509855.

A review of the work that suggests that stagings of Berlioz's oratorios or cantata-like works usually fail because these compositions are purely musical realizations of vivid mental images. Nevertheless praise is given to Maurice Kufferath's staging of the work at the *Théâtre royal de la Monnaie*, March 28, 1911.

832. Angerer, Manfred. "Exotik und Historismus in *L'enfance du Christ* von Hector Berlioz." In *Festschrift Othmar Wessely zum 60. Geburtstag*, edited by Manfred Angerer, 1-10. Tutzing: Hans Schneider, 1982. xxxi, 585 p. ISBN 3-795-20346-5 ML55 W36 1982 OCLC 10021439.

Points out the stylistic conflict created by Berlioz's deliberate adoption in the "Adieu des bergers" of a mock-seventeenth-century tonal style within the larger context of his usual harmonic freedom.

833.   Barraud, Henry. "Analyse d'une oeuvre: *L'enfance du Christ.*" *Journal musical français musica-disques* no. 179 (April 1969): 25-27. OCLC 9888150.

Short descriptive analysis that points up stylistic differences among the work's three parts.

834.   Brunet, J. *"L'enfance du Christ." Le guide musical* 57 (April 2 1911): 265-67. OCLC 1509855.

Describes in detail the staging created by Maurice Kufferath for the work's March 28, 1911, theatrical production at the *Théâtre royale de la Monnaie.*

835.   Dukas, Paul. *"L'enfance du Christ* (Dec. 1892)." In *Les écrits de Paul Dukas sur la musique,* 77-83. Paris: Société d'éditions françaises et internationales, 1948. 691 p. ML60 D86 OCLC 1387305.

Discusses the techniques and styles of seventeeth-century music found in the work and calls the "antique" atmosphere created by the composer "more apparent than real."

836.   Gautier, Théophile. *"L'enfance du Christ."* In *La musique,* 153-65. Paris: Fasquelle, 1911. 310 p. PN2636 P2 G28m OCLC 10736748.

Descriptive analysis of the text and music. Defends Berlioz from the charge of having suddenly changed his style in the work by suggesting that his music suits the tender and simple nature of the subject. Originally appeared in *La presse,* December 28, 1854.

837.   Guichard, Léon. "Note sur Berlioz et Saboly." *La revue musicale* no. 233 (1956): 55-58. OCLC 1764223. Reprinted in *Cahiers de l'alpe* no. 46 (1969): 131-32. OCLC 12101098.

Claims that Berlioz quoted a seventeenth-century Provençal noël by Nicolas Saboly in the "Repos de la Sainte Famille."

838.   Hunwick, Andrew. "Berlioz and 'The Shepherds' Farewell'; a
        Misapprehension." *Studies in Music* no. 8 (1974): 32-37.
        ISSN 0081-8267 OCLC 1792275.

        Demonstrates that Berlioz's attribution of the "Adieu des
        bergers" to the imaginary Pierre Ducré was a musical joke
        aimed not just at professional Parisian critics, but at all
        presumptuous judges of modern music. Includes a translation
        of the section of *Les grotesques de la musique* in which
        Berlioz relates the circumstances surrounding the composition
        of this section of the work.

839.   Ortigue, Joseph d'. "*L'enfance du Christ.*" In *La musique à
        l'église*, 196-235. Paris: Didier et Cie., 1861. xviii, 478 p.
        ML3000 O71 OCLC 13485222.

        Contains three separate reviews of different performances of
        the work. The first, of the premiere, consists of a detailed plot
        summary with descriptive analysis and glowing praise of the
        music. Also praises Berlioz's use of the phrygian mode in Part
        II and mentions the relationship of his "antique" style to the
        noëls of Nicolas Saboly. The second review expands on the
        subject of the use of modal melodies and their compatibility
        with modern tonal harmony and metric rhythm. The third
        review comments on the physical inadequacies of Parisian
        operatic theaters for concert performances of works like this
        one.

840.   Prod'homme, J.-G. *Le cycle Berlioz, essai historique et
        critique sur l'oeuvre de Berlioz: "L'enfance du Christ."* Paris:
        Edition du Mercure de France, 1898. viii, 304 p. ML410 B53
        P7 OCLC 12094290.

        A detailed compositional and publication history that traces
        Berlioz's work on the three separate section of the
        composition from 1850 to 1855. Sketches the history of the
        oratorio, concentrating on French composers such as Le
        Sueur. Also discusses Berlioz's religious music in general,
        including several works abandoned, lost, or destroyed. Gives a
        synopsis of the libretto and a descriptive analysis of the music
        with examples of the main themes. Concludes with a history
        of performances and critical reaction to the work. Quotes
        extensively from reviews and feuilletons by critics such as
        d'Ortigue and Scudo. Five appendices include a reprint of
        Berlioz's article "Considerations sur la musique religieuse"
        from *Le correspondant* (April 11, 1829), a list of

performances of *La fuite en Egypte* from 1850 to 1897 and of the complete oratorio from 1854 to 1895.

841.   Tiersot, Julien. "Berlioziana. III: compositions inédites et autographes de Berlioz." *Le ménestrel* 70 (October 2 1904): 315. OCLC 6966764.

Comments on the location of the autograph in the *Bibliothèque Nationale*. Concentrates on describing the manuscript of *La fuite en Egypte* which is at the *Bibliothèque du Conservatoire*, reproducing the title page wording and instrumentation. Concludes with a personal reminiscence of buying at a second-hand book stand Berlioz's corrected proof copy of the printed score.

8. *FEUILLETS D'ALBUM*

842.   Tiersot, Julien. "Berlioziana: oeuvres diverses publiées du vivant de Berlioz." *Le ménestrel* 72 (January 14 1906): 11-12. OCLC 6966764.

Gives the compositional and publication history of the three works which form this 1850 collection (*Zaïde*, *Les champs*, and *Le chant des chemins de fer*). Also discusses Berlioz's planned addition to this opus of three other works (*La belle Isabeau*, *Prière du matin*, and *Le chasseur danois*).

9. *FLEURS DES LANDES*

843.   Macdonald, Hugh. "*Le trébuchet*: a Misattribution." *Berlioz Society Bulletin* no. 54 (April 1966): 4-7. OCLC 2386332.

Reports that the text of *Le trébuchet*, long thought to be solely by Deschamps, is actually a composite of one stanza from a poem by Bertin and two stanzas written by Deschamps at Berlioz's request.

10. *LES FRANCS-JUGES*

844.   Brenet, Michel [Marie Bobillier]. "Berlioz inédit: *Les francs-juges; La nonne sanglante.*" *Le guide musical* 42 (January 26 1896): 63-67; (February 2): 83-85. OCLC 1509855.

Reviews the compositional history of Berlioz's first opera (1826) and describes four musical fragments discovered in 1896 as well as the libretto for Berlioz's one-act condensation, *Le cri de guerre du Brisgaw* (1833). Second part of article compares parts of three fragments of *La nonne sanglante* with corresponding sections of the same work set by Gounod.

845.   Day, J. "*Goetz von Berlichingen* and *Les francs-juges.*" *Berlioz Society Bulletin* no. 66 (January 1970): 6-9. OCLC 2386332.

Suggests some possible connections between Goethe's early play *Götz von Berlichingen* and the opera, including an important role in each for the Fehmic Tribunal.

846.   Holoman, D. Kern. "Les fragments de l'opéra 'perdu' de Berlioz: *Les francs-juges.*" *Revue de musicologie* 63 (no. 1-2 1977): 78-88. ISSN 0035-1601 OCLC 1773306.

Establishes that the extant fragments of the opera represent different stages of work dating from 1826 to 1829 and suggests that the original version of the "Marche au supplice" from the *Symphonie fantastique* was intended for the opera's planned revision in 1829.

847.   Tiersot, Julien. "Berlioziana: oeuvres inédites; *Les francs-juges.*" *Le ménestrel* 72 (July 1 1906): 199-200; (July 8): 207-8; (July 15): 215-16; (August 12): 246-48. OCLC 6966764.

Presents a complete history of the work. Topics covered include: Berlioz's plan to recast it as a one-act drama entitled *Le cri de guerre du Brisga*w; synopses of both librettos; analyses of the overture and six extant fragments of music; evidence that the "Marche au supplice" in the *Symphonie fantastique* did not originate in *Les francs-juges* (later disproved); a transcription of the "Hymne des francs-juges" for three-part men's chorus, with a note of its similarity to the Revolutionary hymns of Gossec; and a note of a borrowing from the ensemble finale for later use in *Benvenuto Cellini*.

11. *GRANDE MESSE DES MORTS (REQUIEM)*

848.   Cone, Edward T. "Berlioz's *Divine Comedy:* the *Grande Messe des morts.*" *19th-Century Music* 4 (no. 1 1980): 3-16. ISSN 0148-2076 OCLC 3280195.

        Demonstrates how Berlioz made deliberate changes in the traditional Requiem text in order to create a "libretto" for a personal music-drama.

849.   Dukas, Paul. "Haydn et Berlioz (Jan. 1904)." In *Les écrits de Paul Dukas sur la musique*, 604-7. Paris: Société d'éditions françaises et internationales, 1948. 691 p. ML60 D86 OCLC 1387305.

        Finds parallels between the descriptive orchestrational techniques of Haydn's *Seasons* and the *Requiem*.

850.   _____. "Le *Requiem* de Berlioz." *La revue hebdomadaire* 3 (March 1894): 466-71. OCLC 1605845. Reprinted in *Les écrits de Paul Dukas sur la musique*, 168-73. Paris: Société d'éditions françaises et internationales, 1948. 691 p. ML60 D86 OCLC 1387305.

        Describes the work as an example of the juxtaposition of stylistic extremes--between banality and sublimity--that characterizes all of Berlioz's works and makes his music unique.

851.   Hallynck, Paul. "Comment fut exécuté pour le première fois le *Requiem* de Berlioz." *Annales politique et littéraires* 85 (November 22 1924): 537.

        Explores the circumstances surrounding the work's premiere. Supplies specific information regarding government expenditures, rehearsal time allotted, and personnel involved. Includes excerpts from a review in *Le moniteur universel*, December 6-7, 1837.

852.   Kindermann, Jürgen. Foreword to *Grande messe des morts*, viii-x. Translated by Ian Kemp. Hector Berlioz. New Edition of the Complete Works. Vol. 9. Kassel: Bärenreiter, 1978. xvii, 177 p. M3 B52 vol. 9 OCLC 5296915.

Describes the history of the work, which was commissioned, cancelled, and then recommissioned by the French government in 1837. Also mentions some of the work's sources in Berlioz's earlier *Resurrexit* and in his projected dramatic oratorio, *Le dernier jour du monde*.

853.   Lack, Leo. "A propos d'une lettre inédite de Berlioz." *La revue musicale* no. 233 (1956): 91-96. OCLC 1764223.

Presents a previously unpublished letter from Berlioz to the French Minister of War concerning the December 5, 1837, performance of the *Requiem* at *Les Invalides*. Also includes contemporary newspaper reviews of this performance.

854.   Saint-Saëns. Camille. "Le *Requiem* de Berlioz." In *Ecole buissonnière: notes et souvenirs*, 209-16. Paris: P. Lafitte & Cie., 1913. viii, 366 p. ML60 S14 OCLC 2567748. Translated by Edwin Gile Rich as "Berlioz's *Requiem*." In *Musical Memories*, 133-43. Boston: Small, Maynard, & Company, 1919. OCLC 385307. Reprint. New York: AMS Press, 1971. 282 p. ISBN 0-404-05502-8 ML60 S14 R4 1971 OCLC 203340.

Mentions Berlioz's stylistic indebtedness to Le Sueur and Reicha (particularly the latter's invention of timpani chords) and complains of the work's awkward vocal writing and overly noisy orchestration.

855.   Tiersot, Julien. "Berlioz compositeur de musique religieuse; le *Requiem* et le *Te Deum*." *Revue politique et littéraire (Revue Bleue)* 32 (April 20 1895): 500-503. OCLC 8339424.

Sets both the *Requiem* and the *Te Deum* apart from Berlioz's other music, characterizing them as "musical monuments of cathedral proportions" but lacking in a true sense of religious faith. Explains that the conception of the famous "Tuba mirum" dates back to the projected *Le dernier jour du monde* (1831) and that some of its musical ideas can be traced as far back as the *Resurrexit* (1824).

856.   _____. "Berlioziana: lettres et documents inédits sur le *Requiem* de Berlioz." *Le ménestrel* 70 (January 17 1904): 19-20; (January 24): 27-28; (January 31): 36-37; (February 7): 44-45. OCLC 6966764.

Documents the history of the commission, composition, first performance (December 5, 1837), and payment for the work

through previously unpublished letters of Berlioz to his
family, friends, and public officials. Verifies the accuracy of
passages in the *Mémoires* through references to these same
letters. Concludes with short extracts from several letters to
his family concerning the works's later performances and
public reception (1838, 1840, and 1846).

857.   _____. "Berlioziana. III: compositions inédites et
autographes de Berlioz." *Le ménestrel* 70 (August 28 1904):
275-76. OCLC 6966764.

Provides a detailed physical examination of the autograph full
score of the *Requiem*. First part of article lists locations of
autograph scores.

12. *GRANDE OUVERTURE DES FRANCS-JUGES*

858.   Casembroot, Jean-Louis de. *"L'ouverture des Francs-juges*:
opinions de Mendelssohn, Schumann et Moscheles." *Revue
internationale de musique* no. 21 (1899): 1329-33. OCLC
1644297.

Contrasts Schumann's favorable opinion with the critiques of
Mendelssohn ("orchestration so dirty one must wash one's
hands after handling the score") and Moscheles ("harmony
comprehensible only to cats in love").

859.   Lobe, J. C. "Sendschreiben an Herrn Hector Berlioz in Paris."
In *Consonanzen und Dissonanzen*, 313-18. Leipzig:
Baumgärtner's Buchhandlung, 1869. vi, 463 p. ML60 L79
OCLC 3351156.

An open letter written in appreciation of the work which the
author heard in Weimar in 1837. Calls Berlioz a genius of the
future whose music speaks directly to people of all levels of
musical sophistication.

13. *GRANDE OUVERTURE DU ROI LEAR*

860. Adelson, Deborah M. "Interpreting Berlioz's *Overture to King Lear*, Opus 4: Problems and Solutions." *Current Musicology* no. 35 (1983): 46-56. ISSN 0011-3735 OCLC 1565661.

Rebuts Tovey's view (#861) that the work is only casually related to the action of Shakespeare's play. Argues that both Lear and Cordelia are represented in specific sections and that this programmatic inspiration results in its irregular form.

861. Tovey, Donald Francis. "Berlioz: *Overture to King Lear*." In *Essays in Musical Analysis*. Vol 4. *Illustrative Music*, 82-86. London: Oxford University Press, H. Milford, 1939. 6 vols. OCLC 912417. Reprint. London: Oxford University Press, 1972. 6 vols. MT90 T6 E8 OCLC 930485.

Maintains that this and most of Berlioz's other program works show little specific relationship to their nominal subjects. Suggests that the work might just as well be titled *Othello*.

14. *GRANDE OUVERTURE DE WAVERLEY*

862. Tiersot, Julien. "Berlioziana: ouverture de *Waverley*." *Le ménestrel* 71 (September 17 1905): 301. OCLC 6966764.

Describes the autograph manuscript of the work, with particular attention paid to changes made in the title page and performing forces prior to its publication.

15. *GRANDE SYMPHONIE FUNEBRE ET TRIOMPHALE*

863. Cooper, Donald Andrew. "An Historical Account, Criticism, and Modern Performance Edition of the *Grand Symphony for*

Band by Hector Berlioz." Ed.D. dissertation, University of
Montana, 1967. vi, 68, 86 p. OCLC 6869453.

A critical edition of the work with five chapters of historical,
editorial, and pedagogic explication aimed primarily at high
school audiences [from abstract].

864.   Macdonald, Hugh. Foreword to *Grande symphonie funèbre et
        triomphale*, viii-xii. Hector Berlioz. New Edition of the
        Complete Works. Vol. 19. Kassel: Bärenreiter, 1967. xxii,
        110 p. M3 B52 vol. 19 OCLC 8341133.

Describes the various stages in the work's evolution from its
beginning as a piece for military band through the later
addition of string and choral parts. Also gives information
about the number and often unusual types of instruments
specified by Berlioz in the score.

865.   Tiersot, Julien. "Berlioziana: *Symphonie funèbre et
        triomphale, l'Apothéose.*" *Le ménestrel* 71 (September 3
        1905): 284; (September 19): 292-93. OCLC 6966764.

Discusses the popularity of the *Apothéose* movement during
the 1840s, and Tiersot's own setting of its principal theme for
the 1903 centenary. Then speaks of documents discovered by
Tiersot after 1903 relating to Berlioz's transcription of the
original choral part, with new words, for the 1844 *Festival de
l'Industrie* in Paris and his 1848 piano-vocal transcription of
the principal theme.

866.   Whitwell, David. "Concerning the Lost Version of the Berlioz
        Symphony for Band." *Journal of Band Research* 11 (no. 2
        1975): 5-11. ISSN 0021-9207 OCLC 1754464.

Suggests a new chronology for the work's evolutionary stages,
based on the hypothesis that there was an additional but now
lost version preceding the fair copy of 1843.

16. HAROLD EN ITALIE

867.   Carner, Mosco. "A Beethoven Movement and its Successors."
        Music and Letters 20 (no. 3 1939): 281-91. ISSN 0027-4224

OCLC 1758884. Reprinted in *Major and Minor*, 9-20.
London: Duckworth, 1980. OCLC 6431024. New York:
Holmes & Meier Publishers, 1980. 267 p. ISBN 0-841-90600-
9 ML60 C188 OCLC 5894037.

Traces parallels between the second movement of
Beethoven's Seventh Symphony and the "Marche de
pèlerins." Points of congruence include tempo, general march
style, repeated notes in the main theme, phrase structures, and
hymn-like second themes.

868.   Court, Glyn. "Berlioz and Byron and *Harold in Italy*." *The
Music Review* 17 (no. 3 1956): 229-36. ISSN 0027-4445
OCLC 1758893.

Describes Berlioz's life during the early 1830s. Studies the
background of the work's composition, autobiographical
elements, and program. Mentions Byron's enormous
popularity in France during the 1820s and Berlioz's first
reading of his works. Contends that the connections between
Harold en Italie and *Childe Harold* are minimal.

869.   Dahlhaus, Carl. "Allegro frenetico. Zum Problem des
Rhythmus bei Berlioz." *Melos/Neue Zeitschrift für Musik* 3
(no. 3 1977): 212-14. ISSN 0343-0138 OCLC 2327912.

Attributes the frenetic, orgiastic quality of the finale of *Harold
en Italie* to Berlioz's mixing of 3/2 and 2/2 meters within the
notated duple signature, and to his irregular placement of the
strong beats in these 3/2 patterns. Suggests that the
interpretation of this rhythmic technique depends upon
whether one accepts Riemann's "four-beat" theory of rhythm.

870.   _____. "Studien zu romantischen Symphonien. Form und
Thematik im ersten Satz der *Harold-Symphonie* von Berlioz."
Jahrbuch des Staatlichen Instituts für Musikforschung 1972
(1973): 116-19. ISSN 0572-6239 OCLC 1979029.

Analyzes the first movement of the symphony as a hybrid
rondo-sonata form related to the symphonic principles of Liszt
and motivated by the incompatability of the traditional sonata
form with elements of Berlioz's program.

871.   Danuser, Hermann. "Symphonisches Subjekt und Form in
Berlioz' *Harold en Italie*." *Melos/Neue Zeitschrift für Musik* 3
(no. 3 1977): 203-12. ISSN 0343-0138 OCLC 2327912.

Attempts to define and differentiate various aspects of the
concept of a "symphonic subject" (program) in Berlioz's
music. Discusses Berlioz's role in the development of
"abstract" and "concrete" symphonic subjects as well as the
differing and often contradictory demands of each type of
subject on musical form. Uses *Harold en Italie* to illustrate
this relationship.

872.   Iuzefovich, V. *Simfoniia "Garol'd v Italii" i ee avtor*.
        Moscow: Muzyka, 1972. 206 p. ML410 B5 I93 1972 OCLC
        9739449.*

873.   Levine, Alice. "Byron and the Romantic Composer." In *Lord
        Byron and His Contemporaries: Essays from the Sixth
        International Byron Seminar*, edited by Charles E. Robinson,
        178-203. Newark: University of Delaware Press; London:
        Associated University Presses, 1982. 251 p. ISBN 0-874-
        13180-4 PR4381 I5 1982 OCLC 7461475.

        Analyzes the relationship between the work and Byron's
        Childe Harold, admitting that it is more indirect than direct.
        Concludes that the relationship between Berlioz and his hero
        is less autobiographical than that found in the *Symphonie
        fantastique* and is similar to that found between Byron and the
        character of *Childe Harold*.

874.   Liszt, Franz. "Berlioz und seine Haroldsymphonie."
        Translated by Richard Pohl from the French original of Liszt
        and the Princess Wittgenstein. *Neue Zeitschrift für Musik* 43
        (July 13 1855): 25-32; (July 20): 37-46; (July 27): 49-55;
        (August 17): 77-84; (August 24): 89-97. ISSN 0028-3509
        OCLC 1776104. Reprinted in *Gesammelte Schriften*. Vol. 4,
        1-102. Leipzig: Breitkopf & Härtel, 1883. 6 vols. in 4.
        ML410 L7 A1 OCLC 10360373. Translated and abridged as
        "Berlioz and His *Harold Symphony*." In *Source Readings in
        Music History*, edited by Oliver Strunk, 846-73. New York:
        W.W. Norton, 1950. xxi, 919 p. ML160 S89 OCLC 385286.
        New York: W.W. Norton, 1965. 5 vols. ML160 S89 1965
        OCLC 177721.

        An overly long and frequently digressive article in which Liszt
        defends Berlioz's rule-breaking musical style and then
        launches into a vague philosophical discussion about program
        music. Discusses the connections between *Harold en Italie*
        and Byron's *Childe Harold*. Includes a detailed analysis of
        Berlioz's music.

875. Montaux, A. "Berlioz: son génie, sa technique, son caractère, à propos d'un manuscrit autographe d'*Harold en Italie* (Marche de pèlerins)." *Le ménestrel* 56 (July 27 1890): 235-36; (August 3): 243-44; (August 17): 259-61; (August 24): 269-70; (August 31): 276-77; (September 7): 284-85. OCLC 6966764.

Traces all the changes of musical detail made via collette, erasure, or overwriting by Berlioz in the autograph manuscript of the "Marche de pèlerins." Shows that Berlioz constantly improved and refined his orchestrational effects throughout the later stages of the compositional process.

876. Pinchard, Max. *"Harold en Italie* d'Hector Berlioz." *Musica* no. 88 (July 1961): 9-12. OCLC 9888150.

Traces the genesis of the work and suggests that Berlioz identified himself with Byron's poetic character.

877. Ritter, Hermann. "Berlioz' *Haroldsinfonie*." In *Einiges zum Verständnis von Berlioz "Haroldsinfonie" und Berlioz Künstlerischer Bedeutung. Zwei Vorlesungen*, 1-34. Oppeln: Verlag von Georg Maske, 1899.

Sketches the circumstances of Berlioz's life in the 1830s, calling him a "child of the literary mode." Cites the work's importance as being both the first purposeful use of the leitmotif technique and the foundation for all future developments in program music. Makes only passing reference to Byron.

878. Tiersot, Julien. "Berlioziana: *Harold en Italie*." *Le ménestrel* 71 (August 6 1905): 250-51; (August 20): 268. OCLC 6966764.

Provides a detailed physical description of the autograph manuscript belonging to Alexis Rostand. Part of this particular manuscript is discussed in depth in Montaux's article in *Le ménestrel* (#875), from which Tiersot quotes. Details borrowings from the *Rob Roy* overture and describes changes Berlioz made in orchestration when reusing the music. Particular attention is paid to the "convent clock" motif in the "Marche de pèlerins" which was criticized by Fétis after the work's Brussels premiere.

879. Tovey, Donald Francis. "Berlioz: *Harold in Italy*. In *Essays in Musical Analysis*. Vol. 4. *Illustrative Music*, 74-82. London:

Oxford University Press, H. Milford, 1939. 6 vols. OCLC
912417. Reprint. London: Oxford University Press, 1972. 6
vols. MT90 T6 E8 OCLC 930485.

Suggests that the work has nothing to do with Byron's *Childe
Harold* and that moreover there is nothing Byronic about the
viola's *idée fixe*. Attributes some of the work's formal
vagaries to Cherubini's influence on Berlioz.

17. *HERMINIE*

880.   Tiersot, Julien. "Berlioziana: oeuvres de concours." *Le
        ménestrel* 72 (September 2 1906): 270-71. OCLC 6966764.

        Discusses the work from which Berlioz borrowed the melody
        of the *idée fixe* in the *Symphonie fantastique*. Defends that
        borrowing by citing the parallel dramatic situations in each
        work. Also mentions a theme from *Herminie* that Berlioz later
        reused in the *Chant sacré* (*Neuf mélodies*).

18. *HUIT SCENES DE FAUST*

881.   Boutarel, Amédée. "Une lettre de Berlioz à Goethe." *Le
        ménestrel* 69 (February 15 1903): 52-53; (February 22): 59-
        60. OCLC 6966764.

        Explains that when Berlioz sent a copy of the work to Goethe
        for approval, Goethe (who couldn't read music) turned the
        score over to the German composer Zelter for evaluation.
        Zelter condemned the work.

882.   Polansky, Robert. "A Newly-Discovered Copy of the First
        Edition of Berlioz' *Huit scènes de Faust*." *Fontes artis
        musicae* 27 (no. 2 1980): 108-11. ISSN 0015-6191 OCLC
        1569603.

Describes a previously unnoticed copy of the score found in the Brandeis University library and compares it with other copies described by Julian Rushton in his edition of the work (NBE 5).

883. Rushton, Julian. Foreword to *Huit scènes de Faust*, viii-x. Hector Berlioz. New Edition of the Complete Works. Vol. 5. Kassel: Bärenreiter, 1970. xvi, 107 p. M3 B52 vol. 5 OCLC 8341093.

Presents the history of the work's composition, publication, and first, partial, performance. Discusses the lack of uniformity in the instrumentation of its individual sections, as well as some of Berlioz's more unusual orchestrational practices involving the use of the glass harmonica and the writing of impossibly low notes for the double basses.

884. _____. "Berlioz's *Huit scènes de Faust*. New Source Material." *The Musical Times* 115 (June 1974): 471-73. ISSN 0027-4666 OCLC 5472115.

Reports on new source material discovered since the work's publication in NBE 5, including some orchestral parts, an original piano-vocal manuscript of *Le roi de Thulé*, and a revision of the *Romance de Marguerite*.

885. Tiersot, Julien. "Berlioziana: *Les huit scènes de Faust* de Berlioz. Oeuvre première de Berlioz." *Le ménestrel* 76 (July 16 1910): 228-30; (July 23): 235-36; (July 30): 243-44. OCLC 6966764.

Examines the genesis of the work circa 1828. Provides a descriptive analysis of each section, concentrating especially on the *Concert de sylphes* and making note of compositional changes made by Berlioz when he expanded the work into *La damnation de Faust*.

886. _____. "Berlioziana: oeuvres semi-inédites. *Le ménestrel* 72 (March 4 1906): 67-68. OCLC 6966764.

Discusses the withdrawal of Berlioz's original opus 1, *Huit scènes de Faust*, and opus 2, *Le ballet des ombres*, and their replacement with the *Waverley* overture and the *Neuf mélodies* respectively.

19. *HYMNE DES MARSEILLAIS*

887.   Hopkinson, Cecil. "Berlioz and the *Marseillaise*." *Music and
        Letters* 51 (no. 4 1970): 435-39. ISSN 0027-4224 OCLC
        1758884.

        Discusses Berlioz's piano-vocal arrangement of the
        Marseillaise published in 1848 by the English music firm,
        Cramer-Beale & Co. Speculates about the existence of other
        Berlioz compositions published by the same company, with
        references to Berlioz's correspondence. Compares the piano-
        vocal with the orchestral arrangement, noting slight
        differences of text and vocal forces.

888.   Newman, Ernest. "Rouget de l'Isle, *La Marseillaise*, and
        Berlioz." *The Musical Times* 56 (August 1 1915): 461-63.
        ISSN 0027-4666 OCLC 5472115.

        Presents the history of the *Marseillaise*, which was composed
        by Rouget de Lisle in 1792 as the *Chant de guerre* and later
        retitled by soldiers from Marseilles during their march toward
        Paris. Describes Berlioz's setting for orchestra and chorus.
        Originally appeared in the *Birmingham Daily Post*, July 19,
        1915.

20. *HYMNE POUR LE CONSECRATION DU NOUVEAU TABERNACLE*

889.   Tiersot, Julien. "Berlioziana: oeuvres semi-inédites." *Le
        ménestrel* 72 (March 11 1906): 75-76; (March 18): 83-84.
        OCLC 6966764.

        Describes in detail the title page of three slightly different
        editions of the work. Then gives a biographical sketch of Dr.
        J.H. Vries, a mulatto charlatan who claimed to have developed
        a cure for cancer, and whom Berlioz visited for treatment of
        his intestinal neuralgia. Explains that Berlioz's hymn was
        written for a "Temple of Marble" that Vries planned to build
        in Paris. Also analyzes and describes the following little-
        known works: *Je crois en vous*, *Hymne pour six instruments à*

vent (a version of the *Chant sacré* from *Neuf mélodies*), and the *Ouverture de la tour de Nice* (later retitled *Ouverture du Corsaire*). Ends by briefly describing the three works that constitute *Le livre choral.*

21. *INTRATA DI ROB-ROY MACGREGOR*

890.   Tiersot, Julien. "Berlioziana: oeuvres inédites." *Le ménestrel* 72 (October 7 1906): 310-12. OCLC 6966764.

Notes that this was one of only two works written while Berlioz was in Italy in 1831-32 as a *Prix de Rome* winner. Describes the work's premiere at the *Société des Concerts* in April, 1833, and Berlioz's failed attempt to destroy all copies. Also discusses the dramatic scene *Erigone*, which is based on a mythological subject set to verses by Ballanche.

22. *L'INVITATION A LA VALSE*

891.   Tiersot, Julien. "Berlioziana: oeuvres arrangées par Berlioz." *Le ménestrel* 72 (February 4 1906): 35-36. OCLC 6966764.

Discusses the scenic-programmatic descriptions that Berlioz added to the score when he arranged it from Weber. Also discusses Berlioz's attempt to set the entire spoken dialogue of Weber's *Der Freischütz* when he wrote recitatives for the opera's 1841 Paris production.

23. *LELIO*

892.   Barzun, Jacques. "The Misbehavior of Lélio." In *Critical Questions...*, edited by Bea Friedland, 142-47. Chicago:

University of Chicago Press, 1982. xvii, 269 p. ISBN 0-226-03863-7 ML60 B278 1982 OCLC 8032099.

Contends that the *Symphonie fantastique* and *Lélio* were calculated by the composer to make a splash in Paris where music lovers were used to opera but not to symphonic concert music.

893.   Bennett, William K. "'Shakespeare Has Revolutionized My Inmost Being': Some Comments on Berlioz' *Lélio.*" *Selected Papers from the West Virginia Shakespeare and Renaissance Association* 4 (1979): 20-30. ISSN 0885-9574 OCLC 8620887.

Quotes the *Mémoires* on Berlioz's reactions to first seeing performances of Shakespeare's plays in Paris in 1827. Examines Shakespearean influences in *Lélio*--primarily "dramatic truth" and "organic unity"--and discusses both negative and positive critical opinions of the work.

894.   Bloom, Peter. "Une lecture de *Lélio ou le retour à la vie.*" *Revue de musicologie* 63 (no. 1-2 1977): 89-106. ISSN 0035-1601 OCLC 1773306.

A detailed and comprehensive study of the compositional sources and history of the work. Points out borrowings from Berlioz's letters in its spoken text.

895.   _____. "A Return to Berlioz's *Retour à la vie.*" *The Musical Quarterly* 64 (no. 3 1978): 354-85. ISSN 0027-4631 OCLC 1642493.

Analyzes the text as autobiographical drama and discusses the relationship between the *Symphonie fantastique* and its sequel. Also mentions the works of other writers (Hugo, Moore, Shakespeare, Hoffmann) who influenced Berlioz in the preparation of his text.

896.   Clavaud, Monique. "La première version du *Retour à la vie.*" *Bulletin de liaison* (Association nationale Hector Berlioz) no. 16 (1982): 26-28. OCLC 6952566.

Discusses references to Goethe's *Faust* and to Beethoven as well as the use of some verse by Hugo in the original text of the work. These were deleted by Berlioz from the 1855 version because they were no longer relevant to his life and musical career.

897. Day, David A. *"Le retour à la vie* e *Lélio*: il processo di revisione di Berlioz." Translated by Donatella Restani. *Rivista italiana di musicologia* 18 (no. 2 1983): 203-19. ISSN 0035-6867 OCLC 1764409. Originally appeared as part of "A Historical and Critical Study of Hector Berlioz's *Lélio: ou le retour à la vie.*" M.A. thesis, Brigham Young University, 1981. x, 409 p. bibliography, 391-408. OCLC 7964590.

A detailed listing of manuscript and printed sources relating to Berlioz's revision of *Le retour à la vie* as *Lélio* in 1855.

898. Dömling, Wolfgang. "Der einsame Held." In *Hector Berlioz und seine Zeit*, 108-28. Laaber: Laaber-Verlag, 1986. 360 p. bibliography, 347-53. ISBN 3-921-51890-3 ML410 B5 D63 1986 OCLC 15228157.

Discusses the character of Lélio as the prototypical Romantic artist in search of self-identity. Analyzes this character-type in relation to the Romantic protagonists of Sand's *Lélia* and Chateaubriand's *René*. Also discusses the phenomenon of "Byronism" in France circa 1830 and the influence of this movement on Berlioz.

899. Hopkinson, Cecil. "Two Important Berlioz Discoveries (copy with Berlioz's own performance directions)." *Fontes artis musicae* 15 (no. 1 1968): 14-16. ISSN 0015-6191 OCLC 1569603.

Reports the discoveries of a first edition piano-vocal score of *Lélio* with performance instructions by Berlioz and the autograph manuscript of *Le spectre de la rose* from *Les nuits d'été* with the eight-measure introduction that was used only in a revised version published in Germany in 1856. The manuscripts were later found to be forgeries ("Berlioz Discoveries." *Fontes artis musicae* 16 [no. 1-2 1969]: 28-29).

900. Newman, Ernest. *"Lélio."* In *Berlioz, Romantic and Classic*, edited by Peter Heyworth, 175-77. London: Gollancz, 1972. 288 p. ISBN 0-575-01365-6 ML410 B5 N49 OCLC 516762.

Sees the work as representative of the problematic nature of Berlioz's approach to creating large-scale musical structures by tacking together several unrelated short vignettes.

901. Sandring, Enid M. "The Lélios of Berlioz and George Sand." In *George Sand Papers: Conference Proceedings, 1976*, 174-

88. New York: AMS Press, 1980. xii, 213 p. ISBN 0-404-61651-8 PQ2417 G4 1976 OCLC 5410687.

Attempts to establish links between *Le retour à la vie* and Sand's short story *La Marquise*, both appearing in 1832. Concludes that Berlioz and George Sand had similar temperaments and that there was no direct influence in either direction. Included are summaries of the two works and a discussion of possible and documented connections between Berlioz and George Sand.

902.   Tiersot, Julien. "Berlioziana. III: compositions inédites et autographes de Berlioz." *Le ménestrel* 70 (October 16 1904): 331-32; (November 13): 363-64; (November 20): 371-72: (November 27): 378-80; (December 25): 411-12; 71 (January 1 1905): 4. OCLC 6966764.

Describes the background of the composition and revision of *Lélio*. Contends that it can be understood and valued only by taking into account the circumstances of Berlioz's personal life at the time. Speculates on his reasons for reviving and revising the work in 1855. Follows with a detailed comparison of the autograph of the six musical sections of the 1832 text and the 1855 full score, with its extensively revised text. Describes the 1832 printed text, with asides on the Parisian social and literary milieu of the early 1830s. Discusses the origins of each of the musical sections. Concludes that the original text is superior to the 1855 revision.

24. *MARCHE D'ISLY*

903.   Lott, R. Allen. "A Berlioz Premiere in America: Leopold de Meyer and the *Marche d'Isly*." *19th-Century Music* 8 (no. 3 1985): 226-30. ISSN 0148-2076 OCLC 3280195.

Examines the circumstances surrounding the orchestration of de Meyer's piano work by Berlioz, who intended for it to be a companion piece to his orchestration of the same composer's *Marche marocaine*. The orchestrated version of the *Marche d'Isly* was never performed by Berlioz himself; it had its premiere in the United States at several of de Meyer's concerts in 1846.

25. *LA MORT D'ORPHEE*

904. Bloom, Peter A.. "Orpheus' Lyre Resurrected: a *tableau musical* by Berlioz." *The Musical Quarterly* 61 (no. 2 1975): 189-211. ISSN 0027-4631 OCLC 1642493.

Discusses five slightly different versions of *La harpe éolienne*, from its first appearance in *La mort d'Orphée* (1827), to its last in *Lélio* (1855). Notes particularly some harmonic changes made when the work was reprinted in the second edition of the *Traité d'instrumentation*.

905. Boschot, Adolphe. "Berlioz: une cantate perdue pendant un siècle." In *Chez les musiciens (du XVIIIe siècle à nos jours); deuxième série*, 50-56. Paris: Plon-Nourrit, 1924. viii, 274 p. ML60 B785 OCLC 15309440.

Reports on the 1923 rediscovery of a copy of Berlioz's first *Prix de Rome* cantata which had been in the possession of Humbert Ferrand. Includes a description of the work and notes the manifestation of Berlioz's orchestrational genius at this early age.

906. Tiersot, Julien. "Berlioziana: *Choeur des mages*; oeuvres de concours." *Le ménestrel* 72 (August 26 1906): 263-64. OCLC 6966764.

Describes how Berlioz's first cantata for the *Prix de Rome* was disqualified for being "unplayable," and how he salvaged parts of the work for later reuse in *Lélio*. Traces the circumstances surrounding the disappearance of the work which had last been seen at auction in 1885 (see #905 for report on its rediscovery). Remainder of article discusses the nature of the *Prix de Rome* competition with its required fugues and short cantata. Mentions the weakness of all of Berlioz's competition fugues. Also discusses the *Choeur des mages*, a short work for chorus and orchestra dated Rome, 1832, which may be the same as the circa 1828 *Marche religieuse des mages*.

26. *NEUF MELODIES (IRLANDE)*

907.   Tiersot, Julien. "Berlioziana: oeuvres diverses publiées du
        vivant de Berlioz." *Le ménestrel* 71 (October 22 1905): 341.
        OCLC 6966764.

        Describes the first edition of the work published by
        Schlesinger in 1830. Quotes the *Mémoires* and
        correspondence relating to its composition and subsequent
        performances. Mentions revisions for the 1849 Richault
        edition.

27. *NOCTURNE A DEUX VOIX*

908.   Dallman, Paul Jerald. "Explanatory Notes for Hector Berlioz'
        Nocturne à deux voix." *The Guitar Review* no. 53 (Spring
        1983): 1-5. ISSN 0017-5471 OCLC 1751643.

        A manuscript facsimile and transcription of the work,
        accompanied by introductory notes on Berlioz's guitar music
        in general and this work in particular.

28. *LA NONNE SANGLANTE*

909.   Curtiss, Mina. "Gounod Before *Faust.*" *The Musical
        Quarterly* 38 (no. 1 1952): 48-67. ISSN 0027-4631 OCLC
        1642493.

        Contains a plot synopsis of the opera libretto by Scribe on
        which Berlioz worked for several years before giving it up to
        Gounod.

910.   Dickinson, A.E.F. "Berlioz's *Bleeding Nun.*" *The Musical
        Times* 107 (July 1966): 584-88. ISSN 0027-4666 OCLC
        5472115.

Describes in detail the extant music from the unfinished opera, consisting of two arias and most of a duet.

911. Tiersot, Julien. "Berlioziana: oeuvres inédites." *Le ménestrel* 72 (October 14 1906): 319-20; (October 21): 327-28. OCLC 6966764.

Presents the history of Berlioz's receipt of Scribe's libretto, along with a synopsis of the opera. Discusses the extant music of this incomplete opera and suggests that Berlioz gave up work on it because of his dislike of the completely conventional libretto. Provides a transcription for piano and voice of Agnès and Rodolphe's duet containing the "Légende de la nonne sanglante."

29. *LES NUITS D'ETE*

912. Pyle, Donald Alan. "The Mélodie of Hector Berlioz as Evidenced in *Les nuits d'été*." Ph.D. dissertation, Florida State University, 1972.*

913. Tiersot, Julien. "Berlioziana: oeuvres diverses publiées du vivant de Berlioz." *Le ménestrel* 71 (November 5 1905): 355-56. OCLC 6966764.

Briefly describes the printed scores *Le cinq mai*, *Les nuits d'été*, and *Réverie et caprice*, quoting from *A travers chants* regarding the circumstances surrounding the composition of *Le cinq mai*.

30. *OUVERTURE DU CORSAIRE*

914. Tiersot, Julien. "Berlioziana: ouverture du *Corsaire*." *Le ménestrel* 71 (October 8 1905): 324. OCLC 6966764.

Examines the autograph score and describes the work's
evolution from the *Tour de Nice* overture. Declares that the
composition's date is after 1844, not 1831 as has been
frequently stated.

31. *RECUEIL DE ROMANCES AVEC ACCOMPAGNEMENT DE GUITARE*

915.   Tiersot, Julien. "Berlioziana. I: au Musée Berlioz." *Le
        ménestrel* 70 (January 10 1904): 11-12; (February 14): 51-52;
        (February 21): 59-60; (February 28): 66-68. OCLC 6966764.

        Describes in detail the contents of the collection, extensively
        discussing the probability of Berlioz's authorship of the
        compositions or their guitar accompaniments, observing in
        them stylistic elements which appear in later works. Continues
        by describing individual songs in the collection. Concludes
        that certain stylistic peculiarities were developed in these early
        days due to the influence of the guitar.

32. *RESURREXIT*

916.   Tiersot, Julien. "Berlioziana: oeuvres inédites." *Le ménestrel*
        72 (April 8 1906): 107-8; (June 17): 184-85; (June 24): 190-
        92. OCLC 6966764.

        Supplies a history of the *Resurrexit* which was originally part
        of the *Messe solennelle*. This was the first large-scale
        composition Berlioz felt worthy of a public performance.
        Tiersot establishes its date as 1824. The work was rewritten in
        Rome and retitled *Le jugement dernier*. Sections were
        borrowed for later use in the *Requiem* and *Benvenuto Cellini*.

33. *ROMEO ET JULIETTE*

917. Barzun, Jacques. "*Romeo and Juliet* in Music." In *Critical Questions...*, edited by Bea Friedland, 148-55. Chicago: University of Chicago Press, 1982. xvii, 269 p. ISBN 0-226-03863-7 ML60 B278 1982 OCLC 8032099.

Shows how Berlioz transformed Shakespeare's play into a musical composition that was *sui generis*, neither symphony nor opera. States that its departure from the play in the finale results from the special needs of music in a dramatic genre.

918. Blaze de Bury, Ange Henri. "Shakespeare et ses musiciens." In *Tableaux romantiques de littérature et d'art*, 339-78. Paris: Didier et Cie., 1878. viii, 431 p. PN601 B6.

After surveying the history of French critical reaction to Shakespeare and some of the operatic adaptations of *Romeo and Juliet* (particularly Gounod's), the author concludes that Berlioz's symphony comes closer than those adaptations to capturing the spirit of the drama, because its more varied musical forms and modes of expression are not as limited as those of the old aria-based opera.

919. Chailley, Jacques. "*Roméo et Juliette*." *Revue de musicologie* 63 (no. 1-2 1977): 115-22. ISSN 0035-1601 OCLC 1773306.

Discusses the "Scène d'amour" as a piece of instrumental dramatic music which presages both the symphonic poem and the leitmotif technique of Wagner.

920. Dukas, Paul. "*Roméo et Juliette* d'Hector Berlioz." *La revue hebdomadaire* 3 (December 1894): 464-72. OCLC 1605845. Reprinted in *Les écrits de Paul Dukas sur la musique*, 234-40. Paris: Société d'éditions françaises et internationales, 1948. 691 p. ML60 D86 OCLC 1387305.

Compares Berlioz's symphonies with those of Beethoven, observing that the former are more specifically dramatic and make little sense apart from their textual associations. Concludes that *Roméo et Juliette* is not so much a unified symphony with chorus as it is a sharply deliniated juxtaposition of independent vocal and instrumental numbers based on a single dramatic inspiration.

921.   Friedheim, Philip. "Berlioz' *Romeo* Symphony and the
        Romantic Temperament." *Current Musicology* no. 36 (1983):
        101-11. ISSN 0011-3735 OCLC 1565661.

        Invokes the Romantic fondness for the irrational and sadness
        in isolation to account for some of Berlioz's divergences from
        the original plot of Shakespeare's play. Also theorizes that the
        purely instrumental sections of this symphony were based on
        Garrick's version of the play that Berlioz *saw*, while the vocal
        sections owe more to the French translation he had *read*.

922.   Gautier, Théophile. "*Roméo et Juliette.*" In *L'histoire de l'art
        dramatique en France depuis vingt-cinq ans.* Vol. 1, 338-41.
        Paris: J. Hetzel, 1858. 6 vols. OCLC 6974944. Reprint.
        Geneva: Slatkine Reprints, 1968. 6 vols. PN2634 G3 1968
        OCLC 2519429. Reprinted in *La musique*, 147-52. Paris:
        Fasquelle, 1911. 310 p. PN2636 P2 G28m OCLC 10736748.

        A sympathetic and understanding review of the work which
        applauds Berlioz's lack of rhythmic regularity and his refusal
        to pander to the mediocrity of Parisian audiences. Originally
        appeared in *La presse*, December 14, 1839.

923.   Jackson, Roland. "Leitmotif and Form in the *Tristan
        Prelude.*" *The Music Review* 36 (no. 1 1975): 42-53. ISSN
        0027-4445 OCLC 1758893.

        Makes passing reference to the similarity between the "Romeo
        seul" theme and the opening measures of Wagner's *Tristan
        Prelude*.

924.   Newman, Ernest. "*Romeo and Juliet.*" In *Berlioz, Romantic
        and Classic*, edited by Peter Heyworth, 181-85. London:
        Gollancz, 1972. 288 p. ISBN 0-575-01365-6 ML410 B5 N49
        OCLC 516762.

        Draws attention to the work's dramatic weaknesses that result
        from what the author calls a flawed formal structure.

925.   Pohl, Richard. "*Romeo und Julie.*" In *Hektor Berlioz: Studien
        und Erinnerungen*, 131-69. Leipzig, B. Schlicke, 1884.
        OCLC 12321145. Reprint. Wiesbaden: M. Sändig, 1974. xv,
        275 p. ML410 B5 P7 1974 OCLC 1035987.

        Provides a general introduction with comments on the work's
        overall form, followed by a detailed but mostly descriptive

analysis with musical examples up to and including the "Reine Mab" scherzo.

926.   Tiersot, Julien. "Berlioziana. II: programmes, prologues et prefaces." *Le ménestrel* 70 (July 17 1904): 227; (July 24): 238-39. OCLC 6966764.

Reconstructs the two original prologues for *Roméo et Juliette*, quoting portions of both prologues that were cut from the final, single, version. Reproduces Berlioz's preface to the work's piano reduction in order to clarify his compositional goals.

927.   _____. "Berlioziana: *Roméo et Juliette*." *Le ménestrel* 71 (August 27 1905): 276-77. OCLC 6966764.

Describes the autograph manuscript. Discusses revisions in the prologue made after early German performances, with musical examples and quotes from the *Mémoires*.

928.   _____. "Berlioz après 1830." In *La musique aux temps romantiques*, 164-180. Paris: F. Alcan, 1930. OCLC 2901557. Reprint. Paris: Presses universitaires de France, Editions d'aujourd'hui, 1983. 186 p. ISBN 2-730-70211-3 ML196 T4 1983 OCLC 12430578.

Discusses several of Berlioz's post-1830 works, concentrating on *Roméo et Juliette*. Emphasizes the function of the choral introduction, its relationship to the rest of the symphony, and the work's influence on Wagner's music dramas.

929.   Tovey, Donald Francis. "Berlioz: 'Scène d'amour' from *Roméo et Juliette*." In *Essays in Musical Analysis*. Vol. 4. *Illustrative Music*, 86-89. London: Oxford University Press, H. Milford, 1939. 6 vols. OCLC 912417. Reprint. London: Oxford University Press, 1972. 6 vols. MT90 T6 E8 OCLC 930485.

Claims that although Berlioz captured the *mood* of these particular lovers, there is no evidence that he tried to follow the exact sequence of events in this scene from Shakespeare's play.

930.   Wegrzyn-Klisowska, Walentyna. "Niezany autograf Hectora Berlioza we Wroclawiu." *Muzyka* 26 (no. 1 1981): 68-69. ISSN 0027-5344 OCLC 12139399.

Reports the discovery of the autograph libretto of *Roméo et Juliette* in the library of Wroclaw University. The manuscript was written after 1845 and dedicated to Johann Friedland. Also mentions Berlioz's 1845-46 tour which took him to Silesia, where parts of the work were performed.

32. *SARDANAPALE*

931.   Bloom, Peter. "Berlioz and the *Prix de Rome* of 1830." *Journal of the American Musicological Society* 34 (no. 2 1981): 279-304. ISSN 0003-0139 OCLC 1480473.

Discusses the *Prix de Rome* competition, Berlioz's prize-winning composition, *Sardanapale*, the Jean-François Gail text, and public reception of the composition (including newspaper reviews). Refers to contemporary sources, including *Académie des Beaux-Arts* archives. Appendices consist of the full Gail text and a reconstruction of Berlioz's setting.

932.   Tiersot, Julien. "Berlioziana: oeuvres de concours." *Le ménestrel* 72 (September 16 1906): 287; (September 23): 294-95; (September 30 1906): 302-3. OCLC 6966764.

Quotes Berlioz's comments on his music for this lost cantata. Analyzes the extant fragment from the end of the work (but see #933), and notes a similarity between the theme of the final aria and that of Dido's last aria in *Les Troyens*. Mentions themes from *Sardanapale* used later in *Roméo et Juliette* and *L'impériale*.

933.   Wotton, Tom S. "An Unknown Score of Berlioz." *The Music Review* 4 (no. 4 1943): 224-28. ISSN 0027-4445 OCLC 1758893.

Argues that the extant fragment of *Sardanapale* is not a finished copy, as Tiersot claimed (#932), but a sketch, and that it is not the section of the epilogue referred to by Berlioz in the *Mémoires* "where the explosion begins." Traces thematic connections with *Les Troyens*, *Roméo et Juliette*, and *L'impériale*.

35. *SCENE HEROIQUE (LA REVOLUTION GRECQUE)*

934. Tiersot, Julien. "Berlioziana: *Scène héroïque.*" *Le ménestrel*
72 (August 19 1906): 255-56. OCLC 6966764.

Presents the history of this early work, of which Berlioz
destroyed all but one copy. Analyzes both the poetic text by
Humbert Ferrand and the music, which Berlioz felt showed
Spontini's influence. Tiersot sees evidence in the work of the
"architectural proportions" that characterize much of Berlioz's
later music.

36. *SKETCHBOOK OF 1832-36*

935. Holoman, D. Kern. "The Berlioz Sketchbook Recovered."
19th-Century Music 7 (no. 3 1984): 282-317. ISSN 0148-2076
OCLC 3280195.

Describes a recently recovered sketchbook that Berlioz used
between 1832 and 1836 containing diary notes about his
return trip from Italy to France in 1832 and sketches for
several works, such as the projected Napoleonic military
symphony *(Le retour de l'armée d'Italie)*, *Harold en Italie*,
and *Benvenuto Cellini*. Holoman transcribes many of the
sketches and differs with Tiersot (#943) on the identification
of some of them. A facsimile of the sketchbook accompanies
the article (published separately by the University of
California Press, 1984. 79 p. OCLC 13991711).

936. Tiersot, Julien. "Berlioziana: pièces pour harmonium, album
de notes, feuilles éparses; oeuvres inédites." *Le ménestrel* 72
(November 10 1906): 351-52; (November 17): 361-62;
(November 24): 367-68; (December 1): 375-76. OCLC
6966764.

Describes a small note/sketchbook kept by Berlioz while in
Italy and shortly thereafter (1831 through 1835, but see #935),
containing preliminary ideas for such works as the projected
military symphony *(Le retour de l'armée d'Italie)*, *Benvenuto
Cellini*, *Harold en Italie*, and the romance *Je crois en vous*.

Also contains diary entries relating to Berlioz's trip home
from Rome in 1832. Part of the article is devoted to a short
description of three harmonium pieces: *Sérénade agreste à la
madone sur le thème des pifferari romains, Hymne pour
l'élévation,* and *Toccata.*

37. *SYMPHONIE FANTASTIQUE*

937.   Banks, Paul. "Coherence and Diversity in the *Symphonie
            fantastique.*" *19th-Century Music* 8 (no. 1 1984): 37-43. ISSN
            0148-2076 OCLC 3280195.

            Demonstrates how Berlioz's decision to reverse the original
            order of the second and third movements created a tension
            between coherence and diversity (based on how the *idée fixe*
            relates to the process of the developing musical foreground),
            which, in turn, influenced later compositional revisions aimed
            at maintaining the work's inter-movement continuity.

938.   Berger, Christian. *Phantastik als Konstruktion: Hector
            Berlioz' "Symphonie fantastique."* Kieler Schriften zur
            Musikwissenschaft. Vol. 27. Kassel: Bärenreiter, 1983. x, 202
            p. bibliography, 191-202. ISBN 3-761-80726-0 ML410 B5
            B32 1983 OCLC 10540606.

            Explores the history of the symphonic genre in France in
            relation to the development of the "poetic idea." Presents a
            detailed thematic-formal analysis of each movement of the
            Symphonie fantastique. Discusses the significance of Berlioz's
            conception of the *fantastique* for the dramatically motivated
            formal organization of his music.

939.   Bockholdt, Rudolf. "Die *idée fixe* der *Phantastischen
            Symphonie.*" *Archiv für Musikwissenschaft* 30 (no. 3 1973):
            190-207. ISSN 0003-9292 OCLC 1481988.

            Discusses the rhythmic, metric, and intervalic structures of the
            idée fixe and its transformations throughout the *Symphonie
            fantastique.*

940.	Boschot, Adolphe. "Curieuse variante d'un livret de Berlioz."
	Le mercure musical 2 (December 15 1906): 44-46. OCLC
	8603875.

	Argues that the libretto of *Les francs-juges,* which Tiersot had
	consulted in order to prove that the "Marche au supplice" of
	the *Symphonie fantastique* did not come from its "Marche des
	gardes," shows no evidence of such a "Marche," because it is a
	copy made after Berlioz extracted that section. Observes
	further that the libretto does mention a "recall" of a march
	theme.

941.	_____. "La 'Marche au supplice' vient des *Francs-juges*"
	and "La 'Marche au supplice' continue à venir des *Francs-
	juges.*" *Le ménestrel* 72 (May 27 1906): 160-61; (August 26):
	264. OCLC 6966764.

	Correspondence from Boschot rebutting Tiersot's contention
	that the "Marche au supplice" did not originate in the earlier
	opera, *Les francs-juges.*

942.	Bouyer, Raymond. "Petites notes sans portée: Berlioz et
	Schumann." *Le ménestrel* 69 (September 6 1903): 283-85.
	OCLC 6966764.

	Analyzes Schumann's critique of the *Symphonie fantastique* to
	show that it was not completely favorable, and that his
	objections to the work were determined by his Germanic
	training and background.

943.	Bozzetti, Elmar. "Die *Symphonie fantastique* von Hector
	Berlioz. Ein Dokument der Sozial-und Ideengeschichte der
	Romantik. *Musik und Bildung* 13 (October 1981): 616-26.
	ISSN 0027-4727 OCLC 2649663.

	Discusses the work as a manifestation of the common
	Romantic theme of the alienation of the artist from a
	materialistic society and of his escape into a utopian dream
	world, nature, and isolation.

944.	Brandstetter, Gabriele, and Norbert Brandstetter. "Phantastik
	in der Musik." In *Phantastik in Literatur und Kunst,* edited by
	Christian W. Thomsen and Jens Malte Fischer, 514-30.
	Darmstadt: Wissenschaftliche Buchgesellschaft, 1980. x, 563
	p. ISBN 3-534-08293-1 NX650 F3 P45 OCLC 6386057.

Establishes a definition of the *fantastique* in literature and art based on the principle of the confrontation of "reality" and the "unexplainable." Proceeds to explain how Berlioz's musical-dramatic technique in the *Symphonie fantastique* constitutes a musical equivalent of this same principle.

945.   Buck, David Allan. "Hector Berlioz from 1803-1830: the *Symphonie fantastique* in Perspective." D.M.A. dissertation, University of Washington, 1970. 79 p. bibliography, 72-76. OCLC 12093182.

Relates the work to events in Berlioz's life circa 1830 and to the music of his predecessors and contemporaries. Contains an analysis of all aspects of its music and invents the term "dramatic-psychological variation" to describe Berlioz's compositional technique [from abstract].

946.   Cairns, David. "Berlioz, the Cornet, and the *Symphonie fantastique*." *Berlioz Society Bulletin* no. 47 (July 1964): 2-6. OCLC 2386332.

Hypothesizes that Berlioz added the cornet part to the "Bal" movement of the work in 1844 under the combined influences of Sax's technically improved instrument and the virtuoso playing of the French cornetist Arban.

947.   _____. "Reflections on the *Symphonie fantastique* of 1830." In *Music in Paris in the Eighteen-Thirties*, edited by Peter Bloom, 81-96. Stuyvesant, N.Y.: Pendragon Press, 1987. ISBN 0-918-72871-1 ML270.8 P2 M76 1987 OCLC 15133545.

Summarizes the most recent scholarship relating to the old controversy about the provenance of the "Marche au supplice," the literary influence of Victor Hugo, the musical influence of Beethoven, and the performance practice problems involved in recreating the original sound of Berlioz's orchestration.

948.   Calvocoressi, M.-D. "An Old Berlioz Controversy Revived." *The Musical Times* 74 (December 1933): 1081-82. ISSN 0027-4666 OCLC 5472115.

Reviews the Tiersot-Boschot controversy over the origin of the "Marche au supplice" and suggests a simple solution to the debate: a re-examination of the manuscript score.

949. Clavaud, Monique. *Hector Berlioz: visages d' un masque: littérature et musique dans la "Symphonie fantastique" et "Lélio."* Lyon: Jardin de Dolly, 1980. 228 p. bibliography, 215-22. ISBN 2-903-57200-3 ML410 B5 C5 OCLC 7574691.

Describes Berlioz in relation to Parisian musical society of 1830. Follows with a history of the genesis of the programs of the *Symphonie fantastique* and *Lélio* with a discussion of the writers and musicians whose work influenced their composition, including Beethoven, Rousseau, Chateaubriand, Goethe, Hoffmann, and Thomas Moore.

950. Cone, Edward T. "The Composer and the Symphony." In *Fantastic Symphony*, 3-17. Norton Critical Scores. New York: W.W. Norton, 1971. viii, 305 p. ISBN 0-393-02160-2 M1001 B53 op. 14 1971 OCLC 273785.

Explains the relationship between the work's composition and events in Berlioz's life at that time.

951. _____. "The Symphony and the Program." In *Fantastic Symphony*, 18-35. Norton Critical Scores. New York: W.W. Norton, 1971. viii, 305 p. ISBN 0-393-02160-2 M1001 B53 op. 14 1971 OCLC 273785.

Explains the genesis and various stages of revision of the work's program. Interprets Berlioz's "theory" of program music as "not to duplicate the music, but to fill in what the music has left unsaid."

952. Dömling, Wolfgang. *Hector Berlioz: "Symphonie fantastique."* Munich: W. Fink, 1985. 98 p. bibliography, 95-96. ISBN 3-770-51608-7 MT130 B48 D6 1985 OCLC 14376990.

Begins with a sketch of the work's historical background, following with detailed formal analyses of each of the five movements. Another chapter discusses the work's relationship to traditional symphonic structure and the development of its program, three principal versions of which are reprinted. Concludes with quotes from contemporary reviews from *La revue musicale* and the *Neue Zeitschrift für Musik*.

953. Fétis, François-Joseph. "Analyse critique: *Episode de la vie d' un artiste.*" *Revue musicale* 9 (February 1 1835): 33-35. OCLC 6631697. Translated and edited by Edward T. Cone in

Fantastic Symphony, 215-20. Norton Critical Scores. New York: W.W. Norton, 1971. 305 p. ISBN 0-393-02160-2 M1001 B53 op. 14 1971 OCLC 273785.

A completely unfavorable critique of the work based on Liszt's piano transcription. Offers many of the common criticisms such as "monstrous harmony" and "lack of melodic sense." It was this essay that sparked Schumann's analysis of the work in rebuttal (#962).

954.   Garlington, Aubrey S. "Le Sueur, *Ossian* and Berlioz." *Journal of the American Musicological Society* 17 (no. 2 1964): 206-8. ISSN 0003-0139 OCLC 1480473.

Cites the dream sequence in Le Sueur's *Ossian*, part of which is labelled *simphonie* [sic] *fantastique*, as the possible source for the work's title and program.

955.   Holoman, D. Kern. "Reconstructing a Berlioz Sketch." *Journal of the American Musicological Society* 28 (no. 1 1975): 125-30. ISSN 0003-0139 OCLC 1480473.

Explains Berlioz's technique of using the blank side of sketch pages to make collettes for the purpose of pasting corrections into scores and parts. Specifically discusses the recovery of a set of performance parts for the *Symphonie fantastique* in which the versos of several collettes contain a sketch for a revision of part of the second movement.

956.   Le Roux, Maurice. "Invention de Berlioz; l'exemple de la *Symphonie fantastique. Domaine musicale* no. 1 (1er semestre 1954): 81-93. ISSN 0416-2374 OCLC 5592480.

Claims that Berlioz marked the beginning of a French revolution in music by writing in a style absolutely independent from all traditional modes of musical organization. Uses the *Symphonie fantastique* to demonstrate specific rhythmic-metric techniques which foreshadow the work of such twentieth-century masters as Stravinsky and Messiaen.

957.   Magnette, Paul. *Les grandes étapes dans l'oeuvre de Hector Berlioz, i: "La Symphonie fantastique."* Liége, Vve. L. Muraille, 1908. 54 p.

Depicts the musical environment in France in the 1820s and Berlioz's response to it. Gives a detailed compositional and performance history of the work along with the several different versions of the program. Concludes with a descriptive analysis of the music.

958. Newman, Ernest. "Schumann on the *Symphonie fantastique*." In *Berlioz, Romantic and Classic*, edited by Peter Heyworth, 165-68. London: Gollancz, 1972. 288 p. ISBN 0-575-01365-6 ML410 B5 N49 OCLC 516762.

Reflects on the astuteness of Schumann's criticism despite the fact that he was working only from Liszt's piano transcription.

959. _____. "The *Symphonie fantastique*." In *Berlioz, Romantic and Classic*, edited by Peter Heyworth, 155-59. London: Gollancz, 1972. 288 p. ISBN 0-575-01365-6 ML410 B5 N49 OCLC 516762.

Repeats the by-now-discredited theory that the symphony was almost entirely patched together from bits and pieces of other works.

960. Prod'homme, J.-G. "Musset et Berlioz." *Le ménestrel* 92 (October 17 1930): 434-36; (October 31): 461-62. OCLC 6966764. Revised in *Mercure de France* 296 (January 1940): 90-100. OCLC 1681285. Translated by Abram Loft as "Berlioz, Musset, and Thomas de Quincey." *The Musical Quarterly* 32 (no. 1 1946): 98-106. ISSN 0027-4631 OCLC 1642493.

Examines the influence of de Musset's fanciful translation of de Quincey's *Confessions of an English Opium Eater* on Berlioz's program for the *Symphonie fantastique*. This translation embroidered the original version of the book with additional scenes, one of which Berlioz later incorporated into the program as "Un bal."

961. Roman, Zoltan. "The Limits of Romantic Eschatology in Music and Literature: from Byron and Berlioz to Mahler and Kafka." *Studia Musicologica Academiae Scientiarum Hungarica* 22 (no. 1 1980): 273-98. ISSN 0039-3266 OCLC 1589216.

Hypothesizes that under the combined influence of Byron's Satanic poetry and the English Gothic novel, Berlioz developed a disposition toward the belief in the inevitability of damnation. This is manifested in his parodistic treatment of the "Dies Irae" chant in the fifth movement of the *Symphonie fantastique.*

962.   Schumann, Robert. *"Aus dem Leben eines Künstlers: Phantastischen Symphonie in 5 Abteilungen* von Hector Berlioz.*" Neue Zeitschrift für Musik* 3 (July 3 1835): 1-2; (July 31): 33-35; (August 4): 37-38; (August 7): 41-44; (August 11): 45-48; (August 14): 54-57. ISSN 0028-3509 OCLC 1776104. Also appeared as *"Phantastische Symphonie* für Orchester." In *Gesammelte Schriften über Musik und Musiker.* Vol. 1, 118-51. Leipzig: G. Wigan, 1854. 2 vols. in 1. OCLC 11239675. Translated and excerpted by Fred Goldbeck in *La revue musicale* no. 297 (1977): 12-24. OCLC 1764223. Translated and edited by Edward T. Cone as "A Symphony by Berlioz" in *Fantastic Symphony*, 220-48. Norton Critical Scores. New York: W.W. Norton, 1971. viii, 305 p. ISBN 0-393-02160-2 M1001 B53 op. 14 1971 OCLC 273785. Translated by Paul Rosenfeld as "Berlioz." In *On Music and Musicians*, edited by Konrad Wolff, 164-92. New York: Pantheon, 1946. OCLC 603113. Berkeley: University of California Press, 1983. 274 p. ISBN 0-520-04685-4 ML410 S4 A124 1983 OCLC 9693928.

A detailed and objective analysis of the work written in response to Fétis's attack (#953). Working only from Liszt's piano transcription, Schumann analyzes the unusual form of each movement, notes the originality of Berlioz's rhythms, his novel successions of simple harmonies, and the absence of traditional thematic development. Also defends the quality of Berlioz's melodies.

963.   Temperley, Nicholas. Foreword to *Symphonie fantastique*, viii-xvi. Hector Berlioz. New Edition of the Complete Works. Vol. 16. Kassel: Bärenreiter, 1972. xxv, 221 p. M3 B52 vol. 16 OCLC 8159618.

Traces the rather complex evolution of the work and its program in historical perspective by tracing Berlioz's revisions of both music and text over a twenty-five year period. Also discusses the autobiographical nature of the program. Concludes with a publication and performance history of the work and a description of some of the unusual instruments called for in the score.

964.   _____. "The *Symphonie fantastique* and Its Program.*" The Musical Quarterly* 57 (no. 4 1971): 593-608. ISSN 0027-4631 OCLC 1642493.

Notes that the one major change Berlioz made in the program (making all five movements part of the opium dream), dates from 1855 when he resurrected *Lélio* for performances of the entire *Episode de la vie d'un artiste* at Weimar. The author also sees evidence, in some of the detailed changes in the program over a twenty-year period, of Berlioz's intention not to relate actual events in music but to supply keys to the emotions and atmospheres expressed.

965.   Tiersot, Julien. "The Berlioz of the *Fantastic Symphony*." Translated by Theodore Baker. *The Musical Quarterly* 19 (no. 3 1933): 303-13. ISSN 0027-4631 OCLC 1642493.

Describes the Romantic ambiance of Paris in the 1830s and its influence on the young Berlioz. Explains the compositional background of the work and its relation to the symphonies of Beethoven which Berlioz had recently discovered. Reiterates the argument with Boschot about the provenance of the "Marche au supplice." Tiersot firmly maintains that it was not extracted from *Les francs-juges*.

966.   _____. "Berlioziana. II: programmes, prologues et prefaces." *Le ménestrel* 70 (June 26 1904): 203-5; (July 3): 210-11; (July 10): 219-20. OCLC 6966764.

Relates the circumstances surrounding the work's composition. Compares and contrasts the different versions of the program according to contemporary documents, from which excerpts are reproduced.

967.   _____. "Berlioziana: sur la 'Marche au supplice'; la 'Marche au supplice' ne vient pas des *Francs-juges*; *Francs-juges* et *Symphonie fantastique*." *Le ménestrel* 72 (May 20 1906): 153; (June 3): 169-70; (August 5): 240-42. OCLC 6966764.

Tiersot's rebuttal to Boschot concerning the origin of the "Marche au supplice." Boschot claimed it was definitely drawn from the "Marche des gardes" in *Les francs-juges*, because the manuscript score of the *Symphonie fantastique* shows that the *idée fixe* was added at a later date via a collette. Tiersot claims that the manuscript of the work shows no evidence of such an alteration via collette in order to add the *idée fixe* to what was originally the "Marche des gardes," and further that there was no place in *Les francs-juges* for any "Marche des gardes" of the type Boschot claimed was the source for the "Marche au supplice."

"Marche des gardes" of the type Boschot claimed was the
source for the "Marche au supplice."

968.   _____. "Berlioziana: *La Symphonie fantastique*." *Le
            ménestrel* 71 (July 16 1905): 228-29; (July 23): 237-38.
            OCLC 6966764.

            Presents a detailed physical description of the autograph
            manuscript. Includes a discussion of modifications made by
            the composer between the work's initial performance in May,
            1830, and the its premiere on December 5, 1830, including
            cuts, erasures, and kinds of paper used. States that there is
            nothing in the manuscript to confirm the assertion that the
            "Marche au supplice" was borrowed from *Les francs-juges*.

969.   Wotton, Tom S. *Berlioz: Four Works*. London: Oxford
            University Press, H. Milford, 1929. 52 p. MT130 B48 W7
            OCLC 1978676.

            Provides a general historical background, discussion of
            programs, and non-technical musical analysis (with examples)
            of the *Symphonie fantastique* (5-31), *Benvenuto Cellini*
            overture (32-39), *La captive* (40-44), and *Le corsaire* (44-52).
            For the general reader.

38. TE DEUM

970.   Bourges, Maurice. "*Te Deum*, composée par Hector Berlioz."
            Revue et gazette musicale de Paris 22 (May 6 1855): 137-39.
            OCLC 10231154.

            A review of the work's premiere on April 30, 1855, significant
            for its mention of both Berlioz's nervously powerful
            conducting and his use of ophicleides as well as tubas in the
            orchestra.

971.   McCaldin, Denis. Foreword to *Te Deum*, viii-xi. Hector
            Berlioz. New Edition of the Complete Works. Vol. 10. xx, 195
            p. Kassel: Bärenreiter, 1973. M3 B52 vol. 10 OCLC
            8341114.

l'armée d'Italie, and in the projected dramatic work, *Fête musicale funèbre à la mémoire des hommes illustres de la France*. Includes a discussion of some specific problems relating to Berlioz's instrumentation.

972.   Ortigue, Joseph d'. "Le *Te Deum* de M. H. Berlioz." In *La musique à l'église*, 238-53. Paris: Didier et Cie., 1861. xviii, 478 p. ML3000 O71 OCLC 13485222.

A descriptive review-analysis which mentions the acoustic problems associated with the large performing spaces necessary for such works.

973.   Tiersot, Julien. "Berlioziana: le *Te Deum*." *Le ménestrel* 71 (January 15 1905): 19-20. OCLC 6966764.

Relates the circumstances of Berlioz's gift via Stasov of the autograph score to the Russian Imperial Library at St. Petersburg (now the Saltykov-Shchedrin Public Library), with quotes from Fouque's *Les révolutionnaires de la musique*. Examines and describes the "Prelude" as printed in the 1901 Breitkopf & Härtel score and discusses Berlioz's reasons for dropping it before the work's first performance and not including it in the French printed score.

39. LE TEMPLE UNIVERSEL

974.   Tiersot, Julien. "Berlioziana: oeuvres diverses publiées du vivant de Berlioz." *Le ménestrel* 72 (January 28 1906): 27-28. OCLC 6966764.

Gives the compositional and performance history of the work which was written in 1860 for an English men's choral society. It exists in two versions: one for double chorus and organ, the other for four-voice men's chorus.

40. *TRISTIA*

975.   Tiersot, Julien. "Berlioziana: oeuvres diverses publiées du
        vivant de Berlioz." *Le ménestrel* 71 (November 26 1905):
        379-80. OCLC 6966764.

        Describes the background, compositional history, and
        different settings of the three separately dated parts of the
        work: *Méditation religieuse, La mort d' Ophélie*, and *Marche
        funèbre pour la dernière scène d' Hamlet*.

41. *LES TROYENS*

976.   Bertrand, Jean Edouard Gustave. "La crise musicale; à propos
        des *Troyens* de M. Hector Berlioz. *Revue germanique et
        française* 27 (December 1 1863): 755-73. OCLC 13999312.
        Reprint. Saint-Germain: L. Toinon et Cie., 1863. 19 p. ML550
        B47.

        Examines the first performances of the opera at the *Théâtre-
        lyrique* within the context of the opposing trends of innovation
        and tradition in nineteenth-century French music. Most
        interesting in that it gives a much more favorable impression
        of the opera's staging than does Berlioz in the *Mémoires*.

977.   Boschot, Adolphe. La première de *La prise de Troie*." In *Le
        livre d' or du centenaire Hector Berlioz*, 85-93. Paris: G. Petit,
        1907. vi, 224 p. ML410 B5 L59 OCLC 5781226.

        Discusses the background and influences bearing on the
        creation of the work, including Virgil, Homer, Shakespeare,
        Gluck, Italy, and Berlioz's love of nature.

978.   Bouyer, Raymond. *"Les Troyens* de Berlioz à l'Opéra."
        Revue politique et littéraire (Revue Bleue) 57 (November 15
        1919): 700-703. OCLC 8339424.

        Reviews the performance history of *Les Troyens* between
        1863 and 1919 with indications of the kinds of cuts and

shortened versions that were usually made in order to make the work producable.

979. Burger, Vanessa. "Berlioz and *Les Troyens*." Ph.D. dissertation, University of the Witwatersrand (South Africa), 1979.

First sketches the development of French opera to Berlioz. Then analyzes the work's libretto and its relationship to the *Aeneid*. Includes a complete musical analysis emphasizing the dramatic significance of tonal relationships and "characteristic rhythmic patterns" [from abstract].

980. Busch, Gudrun. "Die Unwetterszene in der romantischen Oper." In *Die couleur locale in der Oper des 19. Jahrhunderts*, edited by Heinz Becker, 161-212. Regensburg: Bosse, 1976. 408 p. ISBN 3-764-92101-3 ML1704 C68 OCLC 2577241.

Examines the history of musical storm scenes from the eighteenth century to their culmination in nineteenth-century opera. Contrasts Berlioz's view of nature in the "Chasse royale et orage" with that of Wagner in the *Ring* cycle.

981. Cairns, David. "Berlioz and Virgil; a Consideration of *Les Troyens* as a Virgilian Opera." *Proceedings of the Royal Musical Association* 95 (1968-69): 97-110. ISSN 0080-4452 OCLC 1764602. Revised as "*Les Troyens* and the *Aeneid*." In *Responses; Musical Essays and Reviews*, 88-110. London: Secker & Warburg; New York: Knopf, 1973. xiv, 266 p. ISBN 0-394-48520-3 ML60 C14 A3 1973 OCLC 495125. Translated and excerpted as "*Les Troyens et l'Enéide*." *Romantisme* no. 12 (1976): 43-50. ISSN 0048-8593 OCLC 931119.

Presents a detailed account of the relationship between the *Aeneid* and *Les Troyens*. Demonstrates how Berlioz frequently created new dramatic situations by expanding that which was only implied by Virgil, and how he reordered events where necessary to suit the needs of music drama.

982. Clark, Robert S. "Berlioz and His Trojans." *The Hudson Review* 26 (no. 4 1974): 677-84. ISSN 0018-702X OCLC 1639704.

Presents a concise review of early productions of the opera and of the vicissitudes which Berlioz's reputation has undergone since the mid-nineteenth century. Explains the essential differences between the operatic style of Berlioz and that of his rival, Wagner.

983.   Dickinson, A.E.F. "Berlioz and *The Trojans*." *The Durham University Journal* new series, vol. 20 (1958): 24-31. ISSN 0012-7280 OCLC 1707754.

Demonstrates, with a brief resumé of Berlioz's works, that the "musico-dramatic experience" of the opera was anticipated in many of his earlier compositions.

984.   _____. "Music for the *Aeneid*." *Greece and Rome* 2nd series, vol. 6 (no. 2 1959): 129-47. ISSN 0533-2451 OCLC 1751571.

Compares *Les Troyens* with Baroque and Classical operas on the same subject in an attempt to show its greater scope and dramatic truthfulness.

985.   Dukas, Paul. "Les Troyens (July, 1892)." In *Les écrits de Paul Dukas sur la musique*, 40-50. Paris: Société d'éditions françaises et internationales, 1948. 691 p. ML60 D86 OCLC 1387305.

Recounts the history of the opera to 1892, mentioning some of the cuts "approved" by Berlioz for its first production. Also discusses the work's Gluckian style which so confused contemporary audiences.

986.   Fouque, Octave. *"La prise de Troie."* In *Les révolutionnaires de la musique*, 257-67. Paris: Calmann-Lévy, 1882. 358 p. ML390 F7 F72 OCLC 5314173.

A compositional history and general descriptive analysis of Part I of *Les Troyens*. Mentions the opposition of Classical and Romantic traits in the music.

987.   Fraenkel, G.S. "Berlioz, the Princess and *Les Troyens*." *Music and Letters* 44 (no. 3 1963): 249-56. ISSN 0027-4224 OCLC 1758884.

Describes the author's discovery of a previously unknown copy of the earliest edition of the piano-vocal score of the complete, five-act opera with its dedication to the Princess Carolyne Sayn-Wittgenstein. Hugh Macdonald's response appears in *Music and Letters* 45 (no. 1 1964): 102-3.

988. Goldberg, Louise. *"Les Troyens* of Hector Berlioz: a Century of Productions and Critical Reviews." Ph.D. dissertation, University of Rochester, 1973. 2 vols. xiv, 464 p., bibliography, 441-52. OCLC 5283856.

Analyzes the dramatic structure and melodic unity of the work and supplies a list of performances, including dates, casts, and cuts, from 1863 to circa 1969. Also surveys the history of critical opinion of the opera.

989. Halm, August. "Hector Berlioz' *Trojaners in Karthago*." In *Von Grenzen und Ländern der Musik; Gesammelte Aufsätze*, 95-100. 2nd ed. Munich: Georg Müller, 1916. 255 p. ML60 H202 OCLC 9744781.

Suggests that the opera's subject matter, scenic structure in static tableaux, and musical style all combine to produce an immense set of theatrical variations on a basically pastoral theme.

990. Heuze, Philippe. "Berlioz lecteur de Virgile, d'après les deux premiers actes des *Troyens*." In *Influence de la Grèce et de Rome sur l'"occident moderne*, 365-73. Paris: Les Belles Lettres, 1977. 396 p. CB203 I44 OCLC 3450280.

Analyzes the libretto of the first two acts of Berlioz's adaptation of the *Aeneid*. Finds hints in Virgil for those scenes which had previously been thought to have been freely invented by the composer.

991. Jullien, Adolphe. "Les Troyens de Berlioz à Carlsruhe." *Revue d'art dramatique* 21 (January 15 1891): 65-74. OCLC 5853914. Reprinted (except for 68-top of 70) in *Musiciens d'aujourd'hui*. Vol. 1, 10-21. Paris: Librairie de l'Art, 1892. 2 vols. ML390 J94 OCLC 2530156.

Written upon the occasion of the first complete performance of *Les Troyens* in Germany in December, 1890. Suggests that Berlioz was close in spirit, if not style, to Wagner, both having been dedicated to fighting routine, bad taste, and banality in music.

992. Klein, John W. *"Les Troyens." The Monthly Musical Record* 87 (May-June 1957): 83-91. OCLC 1605021.

Presents a critique with historical background of the work
upon the occasion of the 1957 Covent Garden production.
Points out that the limitations of the stage seem to have
frustrated Berlioz's dramatic vision, and that the work is
uneven in its overall effect. Views the work as "Gluck
modernized."

993.   Kühn, Hellmut. "Antiken Massen. Zu einigen Motiven in Les
Troyens von Hector Berlioz." In *Anna Amalie Abert zum 65.
Geburtstag: Opernstudien*, edited by Klaus Hortschansky,
141-52. Tutzing: Schneider, 1975. 243 p. ISBN 3-795-20155-
1 ML55 A15 1975 OCLC 1638718.

Characterizes the work as a "choral opera" typical of the mid-
nineteenth-century grand opera tradition. Demonstrates its
connections with the large-scale musical *fêtes* of the
Revolutionary period and points to Berlioz's use of both a
"public" and a "private" style within the same work.

994.   Langford, Jeffrey A. "Berlioz, Cassandra, and the French
Operatic Tradition." *Music and Letters* 62 (nos. 3-4 1981):
310-17. ISSN 0027-4224 OCLC 1758884.

Demonstrates that one of Berlioz's most daring departures
from the *Aeneid* was his creation of the role of Cassandra, and
that the need for such a character was dictated by conventional
operatic demands. Also suggests that her death scene (not
found in the *Aeneid*) was borrowed directly from Rossini's *Le
siège de Corinthe*.

995.   Lasalle, Albert de. *Mémorial du Théâtre Lyrique; catalogue
raisonné des cent quatre-vingt-deux opéras qui y ont été
représentés depuis sa fondation jusqu'à l'incendie de sa salle
de la place du Châtelet, avec des notes biographiques et
bibliographiques*, 69-70. Paris: J. Lecuir et Cie., 1877. 103 p.
ML1727.8 P2 L2.

Provides production information for the first performance of
Les Troyens; lists lead singers, mentions the "magnificent"
costumes, and lists some of the periodicals in which reviews
appeared.

996.   Lee, M.O. "The Exasperated Eagle and the Stoic Saint." *The
Opera Quarterly* 2 (no. 4 1984-85): 76-84. ISSN 0736-0053
OCLC 9068655.

States that despite Berlioz's claim that he was a kindred spirit to Virgil, *Les Troyens* shows little understanding of the themes of the *Aeneid*. Nevertheless, the author finds numerous subtle allusions in the opera to scenes, dramatic techniques, and symbols from the *Aeneid* which demonstrate a more intricate relationship between the two works than has previously been noticed.

997.   Macdonald, Hugh. "A Critical Edition of Berlioz's *Les Troyens*." Ph.D. dissertation, Cambridge University, 1968. 4 vols.

Supplies a compositional, performance, and publication history of the opera. Follows with edited full orchestra score. Includes alternate and rejected versions of parts of the work [from abstract].

998.   _____. Foreword to *Les Troyens*. Hector Berlioz, 755-59. New Edition of the Complete Works. Vol. 2c. Kassel: Bärenreiter, 1970. 3 vols. M3 B52 vol. 2 OCLC 18260063.

Lists in detail the compositional sources of and various changes in the libretto and music as the opera evolved between 1856 and 1858. Also supplies a publication and performance history of the work and discusses Berlioz's use in the score of now-obsolete wind and brass instruments.

999.   Macnutt, Richard P. "A Storm Over the Royal Hunt." *Berlioz Society Bulletin* no. 31 (January 1960): 4-6. OCLC 2386332. Reprinted in *Opera* 11 (May 1960): 332-34. ISSN 0030-3526 OCLC 2574662.

Discusses possible reasons for the common misplacement of the "Chasse royale et orage" scene after rather than before the "garden" scene in Act 4. These include possible misinterpretations of the order of events in the *Aeneid* by the editorial staff at the Choudens publishing house, or, more likely, simple carelessness on the publisher's part.

1000.   Newman, Ernest. *"Les Troyens."* In *Opera Nights*, 283-324. London: Putnam, 1943. OCLC 7840346. Reprint. London: Putnam, 1956. 629 p. MT95 N49 1956 OCLC 10720267.

Along with a musical and dramatic précis, the author supplies an interesting historical sketch that draws attention to some of the work's performance impracticalities, all of which Berlioz seems to have been aware of.

1001.   Robinson, Paul A. "The Idea of History: Hector Berlioz'
         The Trojans." In *Opera & Ideas: from Mozart to Strauss*,
         103-54. New York: Harper & Row, 1985. OCLC 11370867.
         Ithaca: Cornell University Press, 1986. 279 p. ISBN 0-060-
         15450-0 ML1720 R6 1986 OCLC 14272546.

         Contains some significant new ideas about the work from
         the point of view of an intellectual historian. Hypothesizes
         that it reflects the Hegelian concept of history as "the
         working out of a universal drama with a logic entirely its
         own."

1002.   Rushton, Julian. "The Overture to *Les Troyens.*" *Music
         Analysis* 4 (nos. 1-2 1985): 119-33. ISSN 0263-5245
         OCLC 8889408.

         Contends that the opening chorus functions as an overture
         by introducing important melodic, rhythmic, and tonal
         relationships which accumulate dramatic meaning
         throughout the rest of the opera.

1003.   Schlösser, Louis. "Gedenkblätter an Hektor Berlioz."
         Allgemeine Deutsche Musik-Zeitung 9 (April 28 1882): 145-
         46. OCLC 1641284.

         Describes a gathering of Berlioz's friends for the purpose of
         hearing and discussing the libretto of his projected opera.
         The primary reservations voiced by this group concerned the
         work's extraordinary length and the fear that the libretto
         contained enough material for two complete operas.

1004.   Servières, Georges. "Pièces inédites relatives aux *Troyens.*"
         La revue musicale 5 (August 1 1924): 147-51. OCLC
         1764223.

         Finds no clear reason why Berlioz dedicated the manuscript
         libretto of *Les Troyens* to the singer Rosine Stolz since all
         available evidence indicates that she had nothing to do with
         performances of the opera.

1005.   Tiersot, Julien. "Berlioziana. II: programmes, prologues et
         prefaces." *Le ménestrel* 70 (August 21 1904): 267-68.
         OCLC 6966764.

         Mentions the prologue to *Les Troyens à Carthage* which
         makes use of material from *La prise de Troie.* Reproduces

the *Avis* from the last page of the first edition of *Les Troyens à Carthage*, which did not appear in subsequent editions. The rest of the article describes Berlioz's dedications, including two that never appeared in printed editions: *Benvenuto Cellini* to Ernest Legouvé and *Les Troyens* to the Princess Carolyne Sayn-Wittgenstein (see also #987).

1006. _____. "Berlioziana. III: compositions inédites et autographes de Berlioz." *Le ménestrel* 70 (September 11 1904): 290-92. OCLC 6966764.

Notes that the autograph of *La prise de Troie* is a fair copy--no changes, erasures, etc. Details those portions of the score of *Les Troyens à Carthage* that are not autograph. Reproduces notes from the ends of the prologue and Acts I through IV authorizing optional cuts, most of them in Berlioz's writing. Quotes that portion of Berlioz's will restricting the publication of works left to the *Bibliothèque du Conservatoire* to those willing to publish them in unaltered form. Explains that this led to litigation by Berlioz's executors against Choudens in 1874 and 1876 for their publication of a full score of *Les Troyens à Carthage* with unauthorized cuts. Also briefly describes the original autograph of *Béatrice et Bénédict*, part of Berlioz's legacy to the *Conservatoire*.

1007. _____. "Berlioziana: notes additionelles sur *Les Troyens* et *Lélio ou le retour à la vie*." *Le ménestrel* 71 (July 9 1905): 220-21. OCLC 6966764.

Quotes letters written by Berlioz during the composition of *Les Troyens*. Discusses the circumstances surrounding Berlioz's piano reduction and describes its printed edition. Briefly mentions Liszt's composition of a fantasy for piano and orchestra on themes from *Le pêcheur* and the *Chanson de brigands* from *Lélio*.

1008. _____. "Berlioziana: appendice sur *Les Troyens* et *Béatrice et Bénédict*." *Le ménestrel* 72 (October 27 1906): 335-36. OCLC 6966764.

Describes the discovery of a manuscript containing an alternate ending for *Les Troyens*, which Berlioz worked out in full score before rejecting it. Also discusses the recovery of the spoken dialogue for *Béatrice et Bénédict* which had been lost after the work's premiere in Germany.

1009.   _____. *"Les Troyens* en Allemagne." *Revue internationale de musique* no. 8 (June 15 1898): 471-84. OCLC 1644297.

Traces the long history of the cuts made in both performances and printed scores previous to the German production which prompted this essay.

1010.   *Les Troyens. Opera News* 38 (March 16 1974): entire issue. ISSN 0030-3507 OCLC 1590631.

Contains several informal articles related to the Metropolitan Opera premiere in October 1973, and radio broadcast in March 1974. Includes an interview with Rafael Kubelik, who discusses staging, casting, musical style, and form in the opera (8-11); Jon Vickers's comments about the role of Aeneas from a singer's point of view (12-14); a synopsis and historical background (17-19); and a musical analysis (22-23).

42. VOX POPULI

1011.   Tiersot, Julien. "Berlioziana: oeuvres diverses publiées du vivant de Berlioz." *Le ménestrel* 72 (January 21 1906): 20-21. OCLC 6966764.

Discusses the *Hyme à la France*, which exists in two versions (one with orchestral, the other with piano accompaniment) and was composed for the 1844 *Festival de l'Industrie*. Also gives a brief description of the cantata, *L'impériale*, for two choruses and orchestra.

APPENDIX

Complete Issues of Periodicals Devoted to Berlioz

Adam International Review nos. 331-333, 1969. ISSN 0001-8015 OCLC 1965286.

Cahiers de l'alpe no. 46, 1969. OCLC 12101098.

Le guide musical vol. 49, November 29 1903 supplement. OCLC 1509853.

Journal musical français musica disques no. 179, April 1969. OCLC 9888150.

Die Musik vol. 3, December 1903 OCLC 1696908.

Neue Musik-Zeitung vol. 25, December 3 1903. OCLC 11930822.

Neue Zeitschrift für Musik vol. 70, December 9 1903. OCLC 1776104.

Revue de musicologie vol. 63, nos. 1-2 1977. ISSN 0035-1601 OCLC 1773306.

La revue musicale no. 233, 1956. OCLC 1764223.

Romantisme no. 12, 1976 ISSN 0048-8593 OCLC 931119.

Silex no. 17, September 1980. ISSN 0151-2315 OCLC 3739044.

Author Index

Abraham, Gerald, 631
Adam, Adolphe, 509
Addison, A., 758
Adelson, Deborah M., 860
Ahouse, John B., 147, 189, 790
Aldrich, Richard, 510
Alexander, Metche Franke, 752
Allix, G., 609
Ambros, August Wilhelm, 638
Amy, Gilbert, 511
Angerer, Manfred, 832
Appert, Donald L., 311
Apthorp, William Foster, 236
Aycock, Roy E., 791

Bailbé, Joseph-Marc, 387, 416, 455, 493, 512, 715
Ballif, Claude, 208, 660
Banks, Paul, 937
Barbier, Henri-Auguste, 237, 766
Barraud, Henry, 209, 716, 833
Barsham, Eve, 415
Bartenstein, Hans, 615, 616
Bartlet, Mary Elizabeth Caroline, 626
Barzun, Jacques, 126, 190, 210, 211, 238, 513, 558, 628, 726, 892, 917
Baser-Heidelberg, Friedrich, 378

Bass, Eddie Covington, 691, 708, 709
Bate, A. Jonathan, 494
Batka, Richard, 438, 514
Baud-Bovy, Samuel, 403
Beale, William, 368
Beaunier, André, 239
Bellaigue, Camille, 792
Bellasis, Edward, 404
Bennett, William K., 893
Berger, Christian, 938
Bernard, Daniel, 240
Bernoulli, Eduard, 668
Bertrand, Jean Edouard Gustave, 516, 976
Besnier, Patrick, 424
Biondi, Maurizio, 661
Bird, Alan, 330
Bischoff, Friedrich A., 334
Blaze de Bury, Ange Henri, 918
Blondel, Raoul, 301
Bloom, Peter Anthony, 150, 192, 314, 317, 379, 411, 412, 894, 895, 904, 931
Bockholdt, Rudolf, 572, 639, 703, 939
Bondeville, Emmanuel, 241, 242
Bone, Philip James, 343
Bonnefon, Paul, 432

Proper Name and Subject Index